POLARITY™

VOLUME ONE

BOOM! ™ ROSS RICHIE CEO & Founder • MATT GAGNON Editor-in-Chief • FILIP SABLIK VP-Publishing & Marketing • LANCE KREITER VP-Licensing & Merchandising • PHIL BARBARO Director of Finance • BRYCE CARLSON Managing Editor
STUDIOS   DAFNA PLEBAN Editor • SHANNON WATTERS Editor • ERIC HARBURN Editor • CHRIS ROSA Assistant Editor • ALEX GALER Assistant Editor • WHITNEY LEOPARD Assistant Editor • JASMINE AMIRI Assistant Editor
STEPHANIE GONZAGA Graphic Designer • MIKE LOPEZ Production Designer • DEVIN FUNCHES E-Commerce & Inventory Coordinator • BRIANNA HART Executive Assistant • AARON FERRARA Operations Assistant

POLARITY Volume One — December 2013. Published by BOOM! Studios, a division of Boom Entertainment, Inc. Polarity is Copyright © 2013 Boom Entertainment, Inc. Originally published in single magazine form as POLARITY 1-4. Copyright © 2013 Boom Entertainment, Inc. All rights reserved. BOOM! Studios™ and the BOOM! Studios logo are trademarks of Boom Entertainment, Inc., registered in various countries and categories. All characters, events, and institutions depicted herein are fictional. Any similarity between any of the names, characters, persons, events, and/or institutions in this publication to actual names, characters, and persons, whether living or dead, events, and/or institutions is unintended and purely coincidental. BOOM! Studios does not read or accept unsolicited submissions of ideas, stories, or artwork.

A catalog record of this book is available from OCLC and from the BOOM! Studios website, www.boom-studios.com, on the Librarians Page.

BOOM! Studios, 5670 Wilshire Boulevard, Suite 450, Los Angeles, CA 90036-5679. Printed in China. First Printing. ISBN: 978-1-60886-346-4

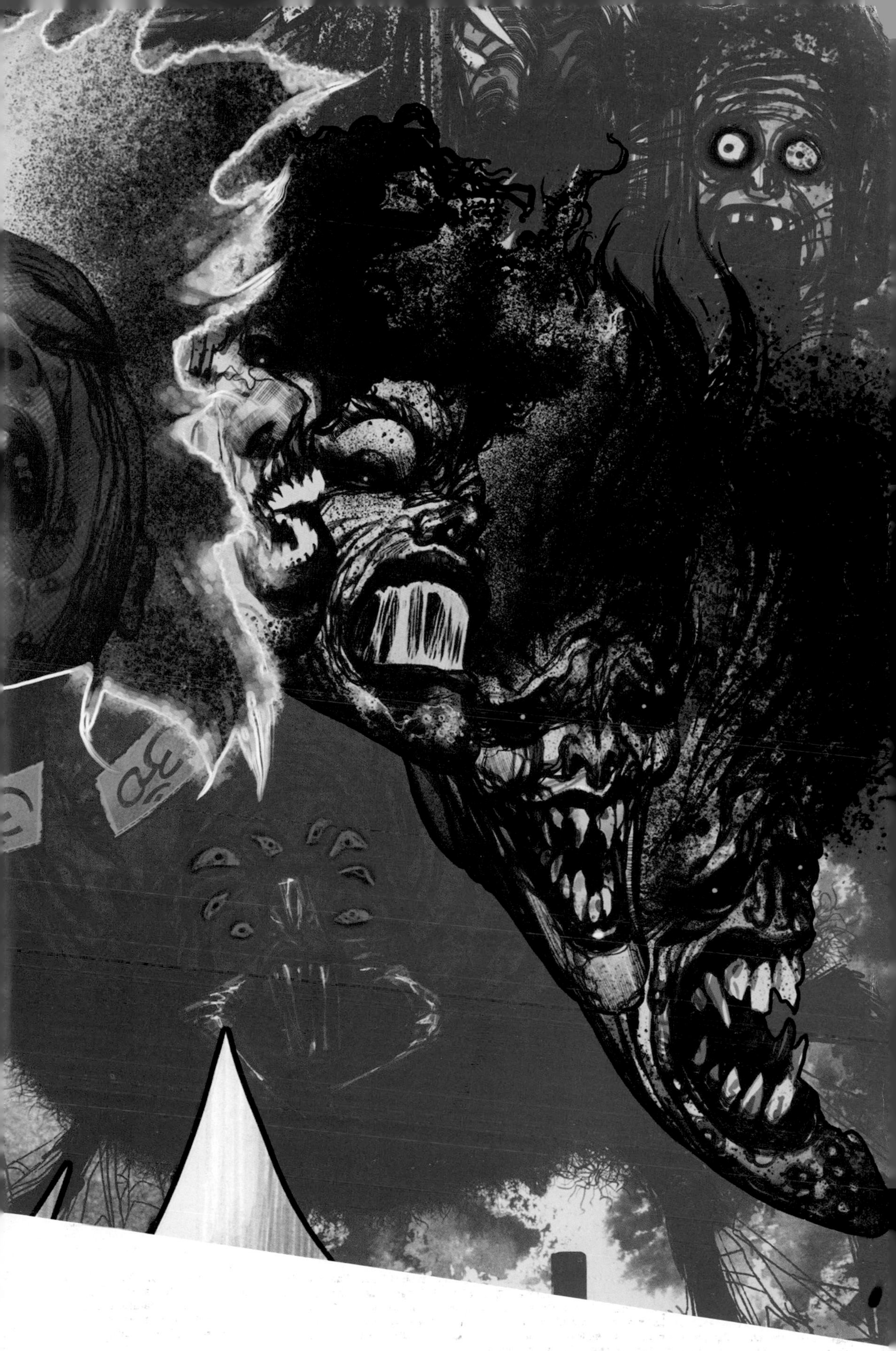

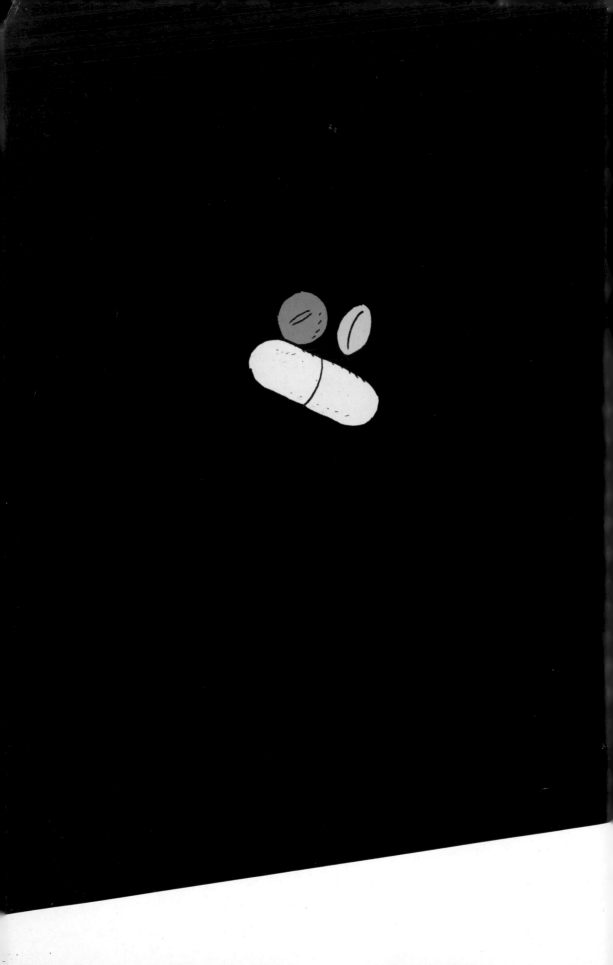

WRITTEN AND CREATED BY
MAX BEMIS

ART BY
JORGE COELHO

COLORS BY
FELIPE SOBREIRO

LETTERS BY
STEVE WANDS

COVER BY
FRAZER IRVING

ASSISTANT EDITOR
JASMINE AMIRI

EDITOR
BRYCE CARLSON

DESIGNER
MIKE LOPEZ

POLARITY™

"THEY SAY NOT TO LET YOUR ILLNESS DEFINE YOU."

CHAPTER

1

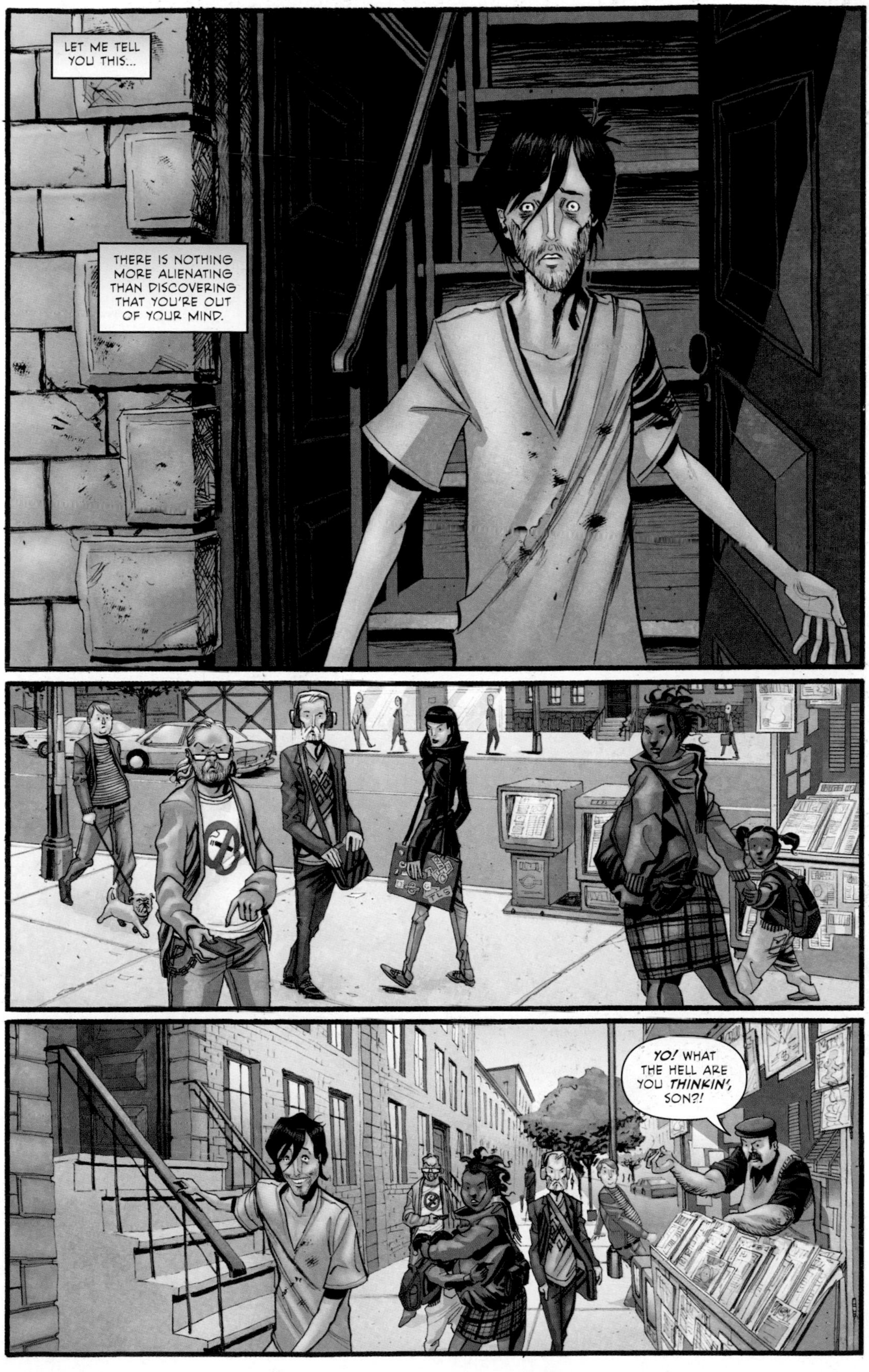
LET ME TELL YOU THIS...
THERE IS NOTHING MORE ALIENATING THAN DISCOVERING THAT YOU'RE OUT OF YOUR MIND.
YO! WHAT THE HELL ARE YOU THINKIN', SON?!

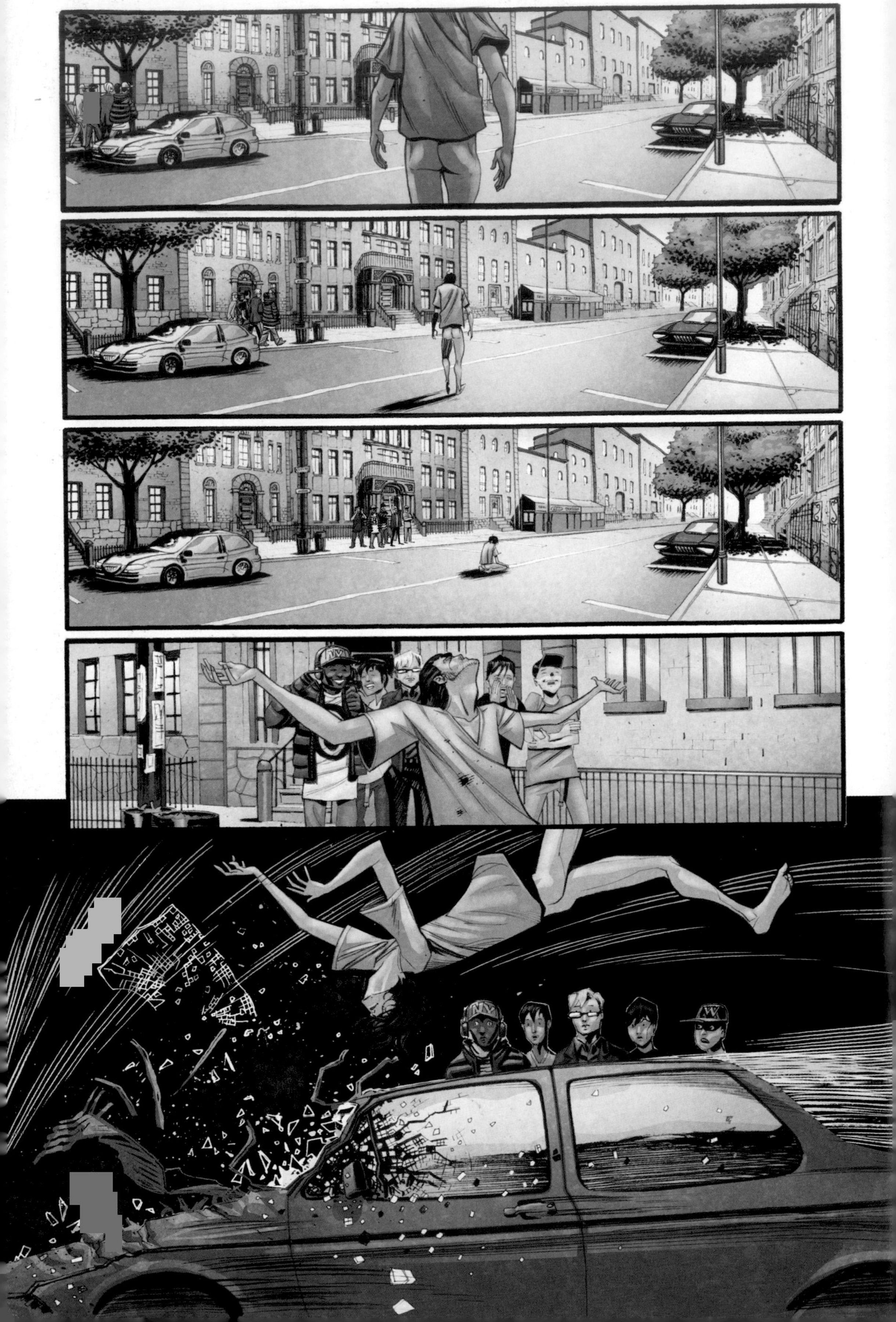

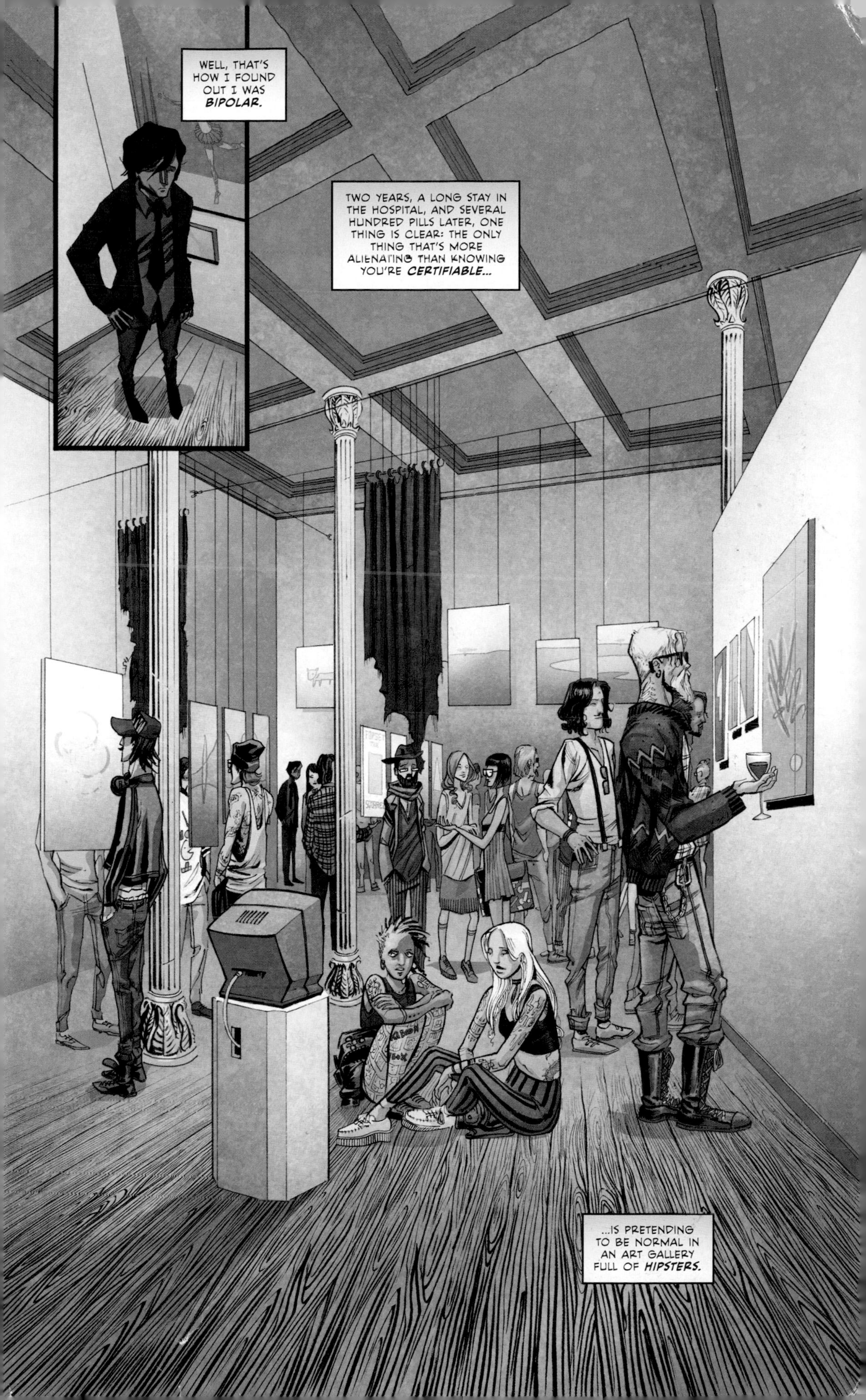
WELL, THAT'S HOW I FOUND OUT I WAS BIPOLAR.
TWO YEARS, A LONG STAY IN THE HOSPITAL, AND SEVERAL HUNDRED PILLS LATER, ONE THING IS CLEAR: THE ONLY THING THAT'S MORE ALIENATING THAN KNOWING YOU'RE CERTIFIABLE...
...IS PRETENDING TO BE NORMAL IN AN ART GALLERY FULL OF HIPSTERS.

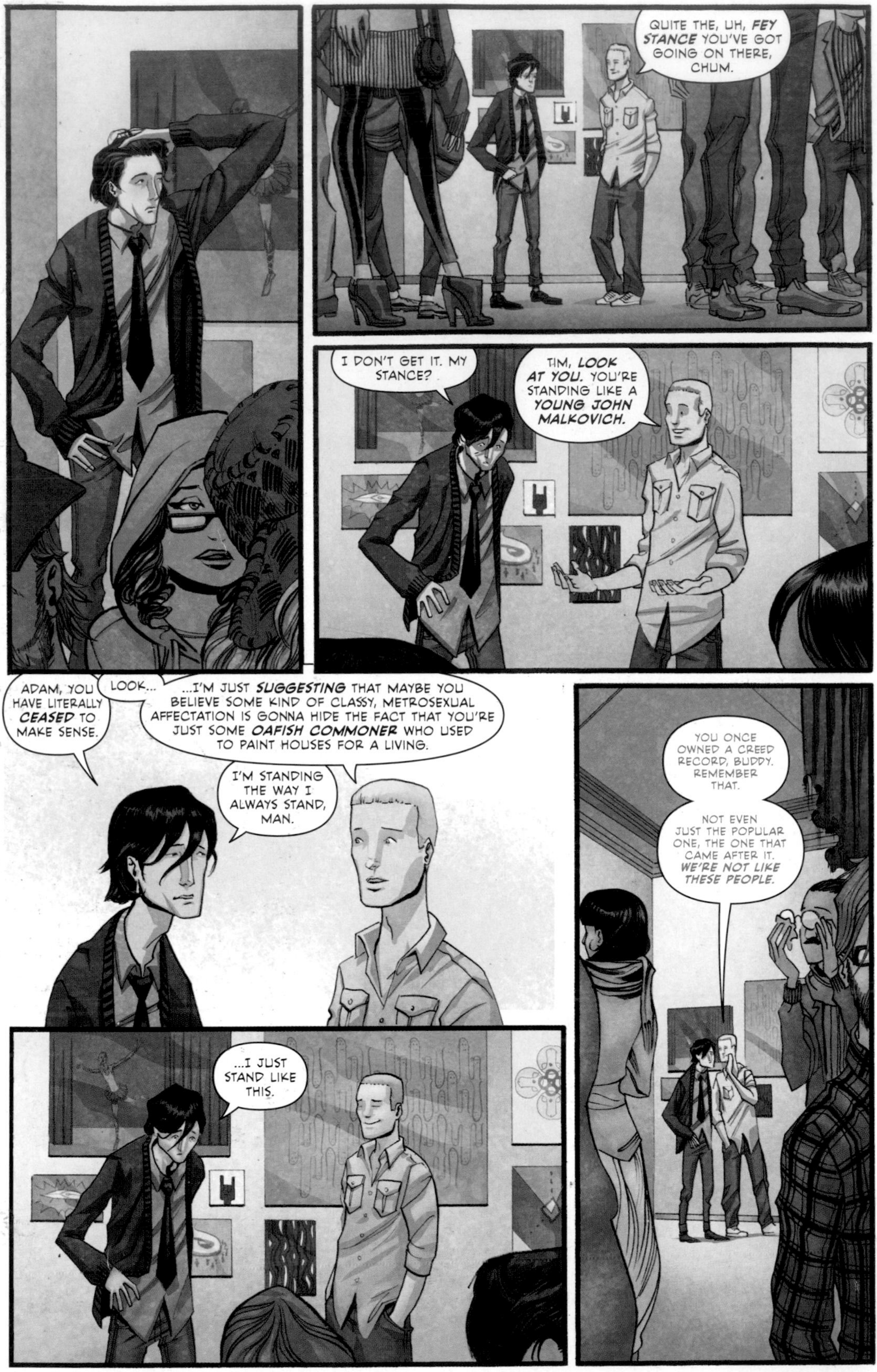
QUITE THE, UH, FEY STANCE YOU'VE GOT GOING ON THERE, CHUM.
I DON'T GET IT. MY STANCE?
TIM, LOOK AT YOU. YOU'RE STANDING LIKE A YOUNG JOHN MALKOVICH.
ADAM, YOU HAVE LITERALLY CEASED TO MAKE SENSE.
LOOK...
...I'M JUST SUGGESTING THAT MAYBE YOU BELIEVE SOME KIND OF CLASSY, METROSEXUAL AFFECTATION IS GONNA HIDE THE FACT THAT YOU'RE JUST SOME OAFISH COMMONER WHO USED TO PAINT HOUSES FOR A LIVING.
I'M STANDING THE WAY I ALWAYS STAND, MAN.
...I JUST STAND LIKE THIS.
YOU ONCE OWNED A CREED RECORD, BUDDY. REMEMBER THAT.
NOT EVEN JUST THE POPULAR ONE, THE ONE THAT CAME AFTER IT. WE'RE NOT LIKE THESE PEOPLE.

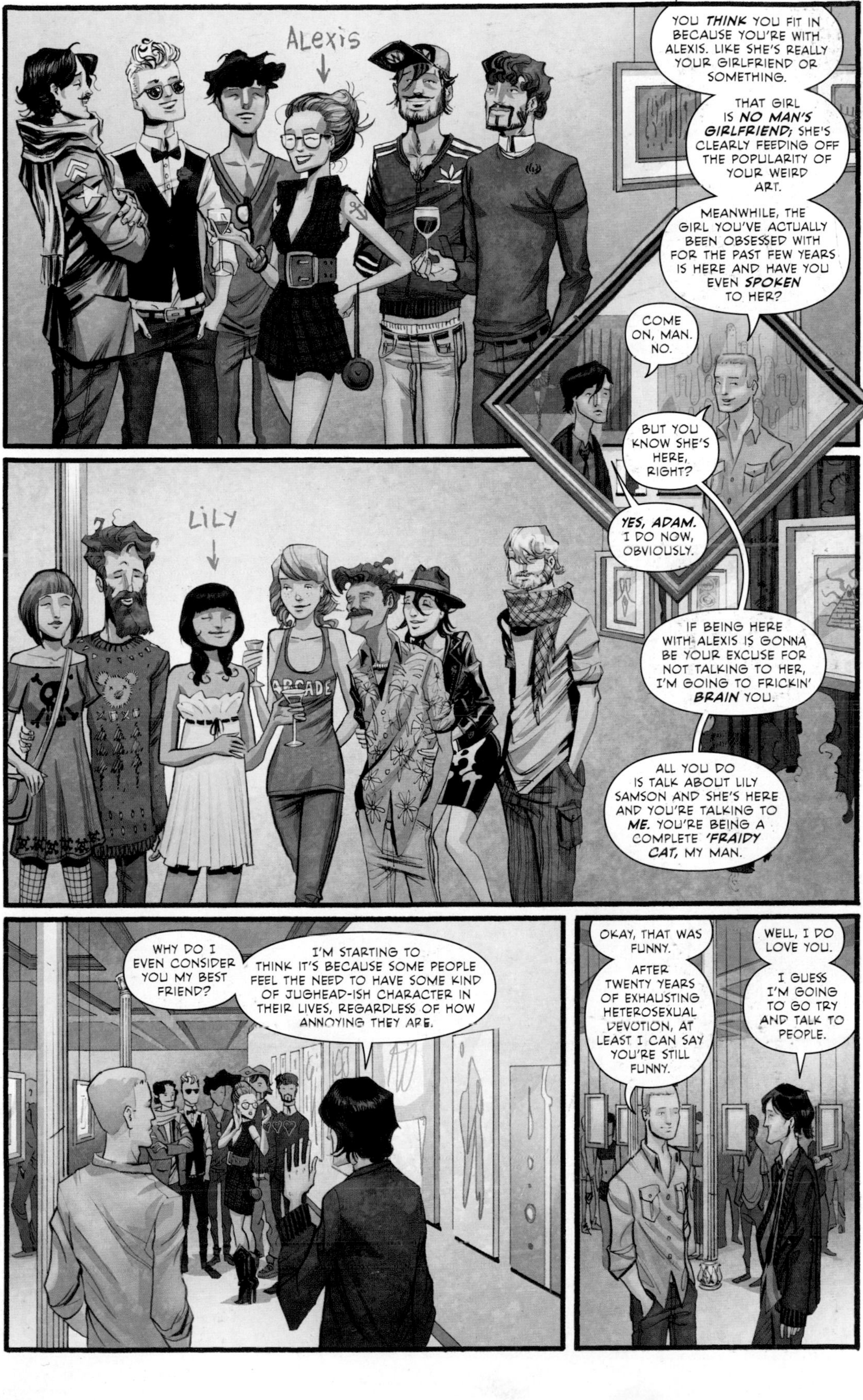
ALEXIS
YOU THINK YOU FIT IN BECAUSE YOU'RE WITH ALEXIS. LIKE SHE'S REALLY YOUR GIRLFRIEND OR SOMETHING.
THAT GIRL IS NO MAN'S GIRLFRIEND; SHE'S CLEARLY FEEDING OFF THE POPULARITY OF YOUR WEIRD ART.
MEANWHILE, THE GIRL YOU'VE ACTUALLY BEEN OBSESSED WITH FOR THE PAST FEW YEARS IS HERE AND HAVE YOU EVEN SPOKEN TO HER?
COME ON, MAN. NO.
BUT YOU KNOW SHE'S HERE, RIGHT?
YES, ADAM. I DO NOW, OBVIOUSLY.
LILY
IF BEING HERE WITH ALEXIS IS GONNA BE YOUR EXCUSE FOR NOT TALKING TO HER, I'M GOING TO FRICKIN' BRAIN YOU.
ALL YOU DO IS TALK ABOUT LILY SAMSON AND SHE'S HERE AND YOU'RE TALKING TO ME. YOU'RE BEING A COMPLETE 'FRAIDY CAT, MY MAN.
ARCADE
WHY DO I EVEN CONSIDER YOU MY BEST FRIEND?
I'M STARTING TO THINK IT'S BECAUSE SOME PEOPLE FEEL THE NEED TO HAVE SOME KIND OF JUGHEAD-ISH CHARACTER IN THEIR LIVES, REGARDLESS OF HOW ANNOYING THEY ARE.
OKAY, THAT WAS FUNNY.
AFTER TWENTY YEARS OF EXHAUSTING HETEROSEXUAL DEVOTION, AT LEAST I CAN SAY YOU'RE STILL FUNNY.
WELL, I DO LOVE YOU.
I GUESS I'M GOING TO GO TRY AND TALK TO PEOPLE.

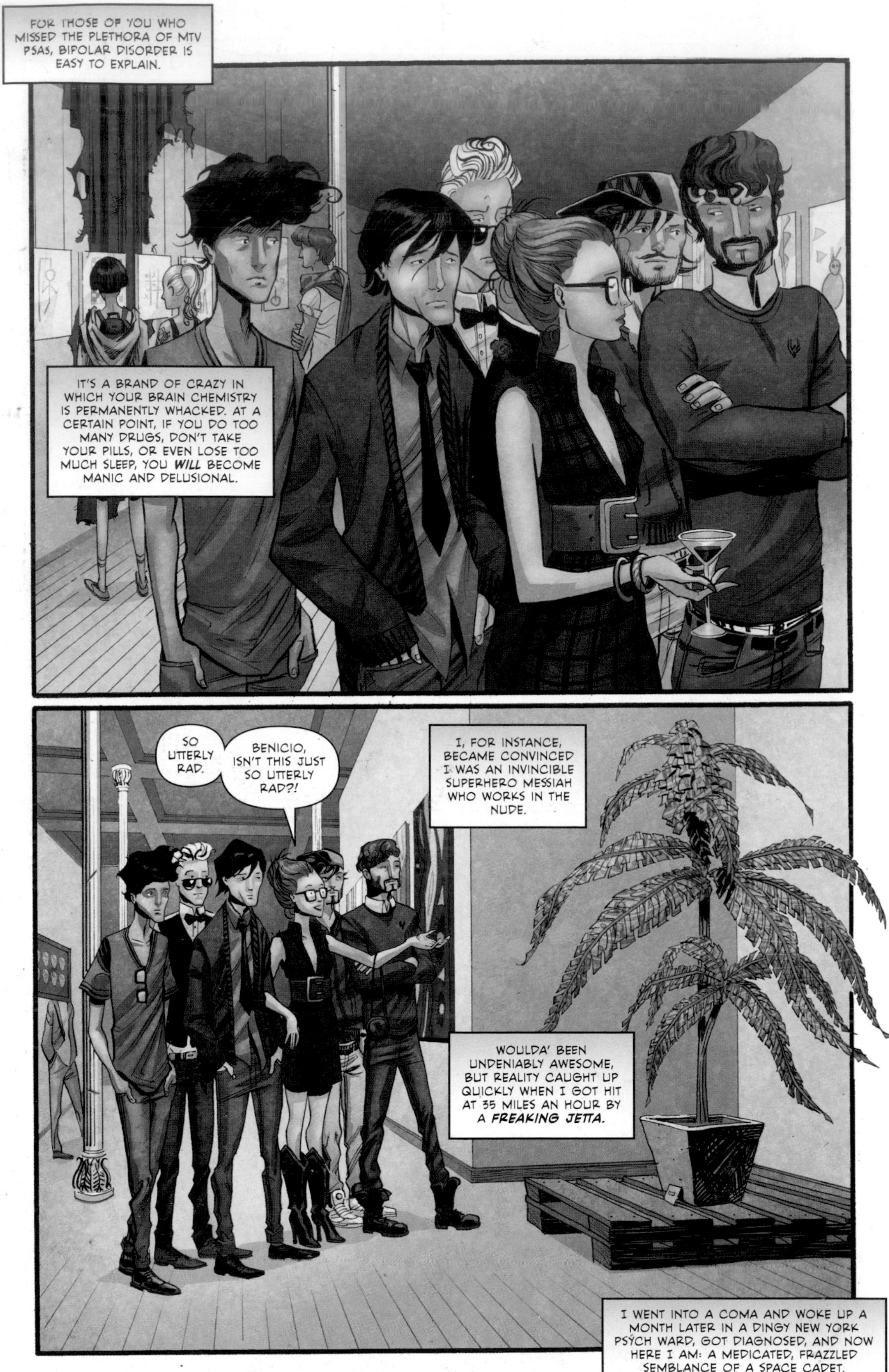
FOR THOSE OF YOU WHO MISSED THE PLETHORA OF MTV PSAS, BIPOLAR DISORDER IS EASY TO EXPLAIN.
IT'S A BRAND OF CRAZY IN WHICH YOUR BRAIN CHEMISTRY IS PERMANENTLY WHACKED. AT A CERTAIN POINT, IF YOU DO TOO MANY DRUGS, DON'T TAKE YOUR PILLS, OR EVEN LOSE TOO MUCH SLEEP, YOU *WILL* BECOME MANIC AND DELUSIONAL.
BENICIO, ISN'T THIS JUST SO UTTERLY RAD?!
SO UTTERLY RAD.
I, FOR INSTANCE, BECAME CONVINCED I WAS AN INVINCIBLE SUPERHERO MESSIAH WHO WORKS IN THE NUDE.
WOULDA' BEEN UNDENIABLY AWESOME, BUT REALITY CAUGHT UP QUICKLY WHEN I GOT HIT AT 35 MILES AN HOUR BY A *FREAKING JETTA.*
I WENT INTO A COMA AND WOKE UP A MONTH LATER IN A DINGY NEW YORK PSYCH WARD, GOT DIAGNOSED, AND NOW HERE I AM: A MEDICATED, FRAZZLED SEMBLANCE OF A SPACE CADET.

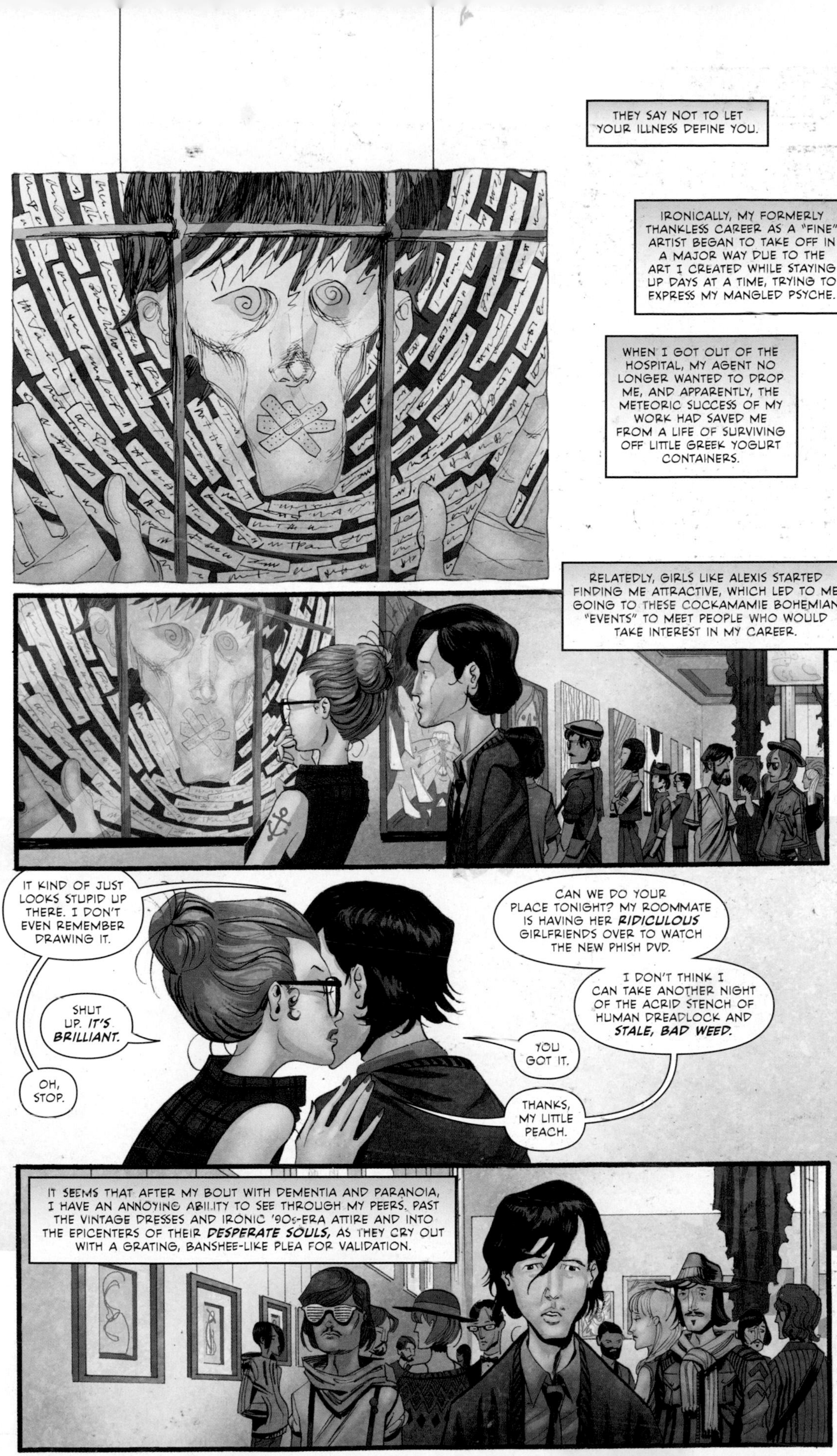
THEY SAY NOT TO LET YOUR ILLNESS DEFINE YOU.
IRONICALLY, MY FORMERLY THANKLESS CAREER AS A "FINE" ARTIST BEGAN TO TAKE OFF IN A MAJOR WAY DUE TO THE ART I CREATED WHILE STAYING UP DAYS AT A TIME, TRYING TO EXPRESS MY MANGLED PSYCHE.
WHEN I GOT OUT OF THE HOSPITAL, MY AGENT NO LONGER WANTED TO DROP ME, AND APPARENTLY, THE METEORIC SUCCESS OF MY WORK HAD SAVED ME FROM A LIFE OF SURVIVING OFF LITTLE GREEK YOGURT CONTAINERS.
RELATEDLY, GIRLS LIKE ALEXIS STARTED FINDING ME ATTRACTIVE, WHICH LED TO ME GOING TO THESE COCKAMAMIE BOHEMIAN "EVENTS" TO MEET PEOPLE WHO WOULD TAKE INTEREST IN MY CAREER.
IT KIND OF JUST LOOKS STUPID UP THERE. I DON'T EVEN REMEMBER DRAWING IT.
SHUT UP. *IT'S* ***BRILLIANT.***
OH, STOP.
CAN WE DO YOUR PLACE TONIGHT? MY ROOMMATE IS HAVING HER ***RIDICULOUS*** GIRLFRIENDS OVER TO WATCH THE NEW PHISH DVD.
I DON'T THINK I CAN TAKE ANOTHER NIGHT OF THE ACRID STENCH OF HUMAN DREADLOCK AND ***STALE, BAD WEED.***
YOU GOT IT.
THANKS, MY LITTLE PEACH.
IT SEEMS THAT AFTER MY BOUT WITH DEMENTIA AND PARANOIA, I HAVE AN ANNOYING ABILITY TO SEE THROUGH MY PEERS. PAST THE VINTAGE DRESSES AND IRONIC '90s-ERA ATTIRE AND INTO THE EPICENTERS OF THEIR ***DESPERATE SOULS,*** AS THEY CRY OUT WITH A GRATING, BANSHEE-LIKE PLEA FOR VALIDATION.

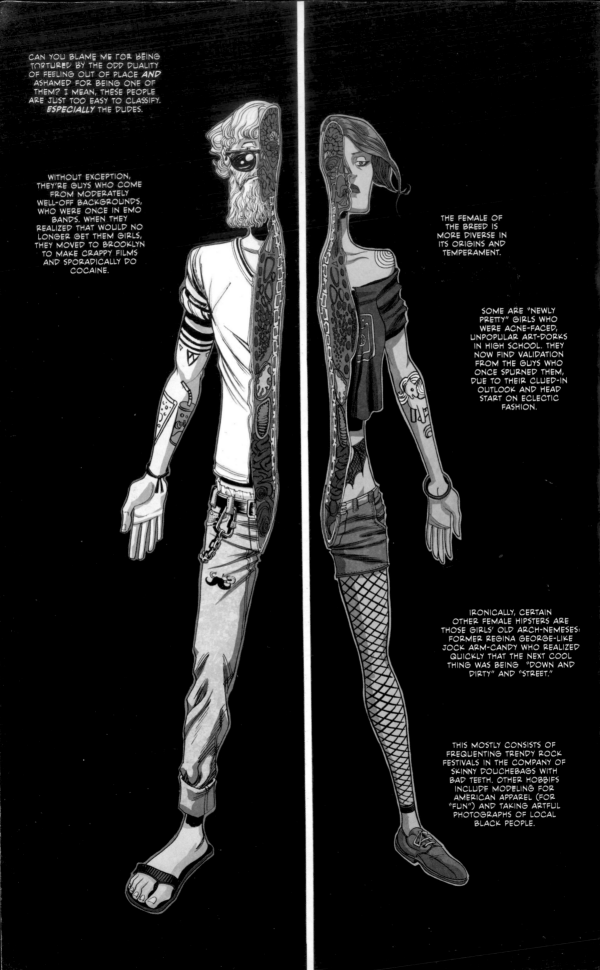

CAN YOU BLAME ME FOR BEING TORTURED BY THE ODD DUALITY OF FEELING OUT OF PLACE *AND* ASHAMED FOR BEING ONE OF THEM? I MEAN, THESE PEOPLE ARE JUST TOO EASY TO CLASSIFY. *ESPECIALLY* THE DUDES.

WITHOUT EXCEPTION, THEY'RE GUYS WHO COME FROM MODERATELY WELL-OFF BACKGROUNDS, WHO WERE ONCE IN EMO BANDS. WHEN THEY REALIZED THAT WOULD NO LONGER GET THEM GIRLS, THEY MOVED TO BROOKLYN TO MAKE CRAPPY FILMS AND SPORADICALLY DO COCAINE.

THE FEMALE OF THE BREED IS MORE DIVERSE IN ITS ORIGINS AND TEMPERAMENT.

SOME ARE "NEWLY PRETTY" GIRLS WHO WERE ACNE-FACED, UNPOPULAR ART-DORKS IN HIGH SCHOOL. THEY NOW FIND VALIDATION FROM THE GUYS WHO ONCE SPURNED THEM, DUE TO THEIR CLUED-IN OUTLOOK AND HEAD START ON ECLECTIC FASHION.

IRONICALLY, CERTAIN OTHER FEMALE HIPSTERS ARE THOSE GIRLS' OLD ARCH-NEMESES: FORMER REGINA GEORGE-LIKE JOCK ARM-CANDY WHO REALIZED QUICKLY THAT THE NEXT COOL THING WAS BEING "DOWN AND DIRTY" AND "STREET."

THIS MOSTLY CONSISTS OF FREQUENTING TRENDY ROCK FESTIVALS IN THE COMPANY OF SKINNY DOUCHEBAGS WITH BAD TEETH. OTHER HOBBIES INCLUDE MODELING FOR AMERICAN APPAREL (FOR "FUN") AND TAKING ARTFUL PHOTOGRAPHS OF LOCAL BLACK PEOPLE.

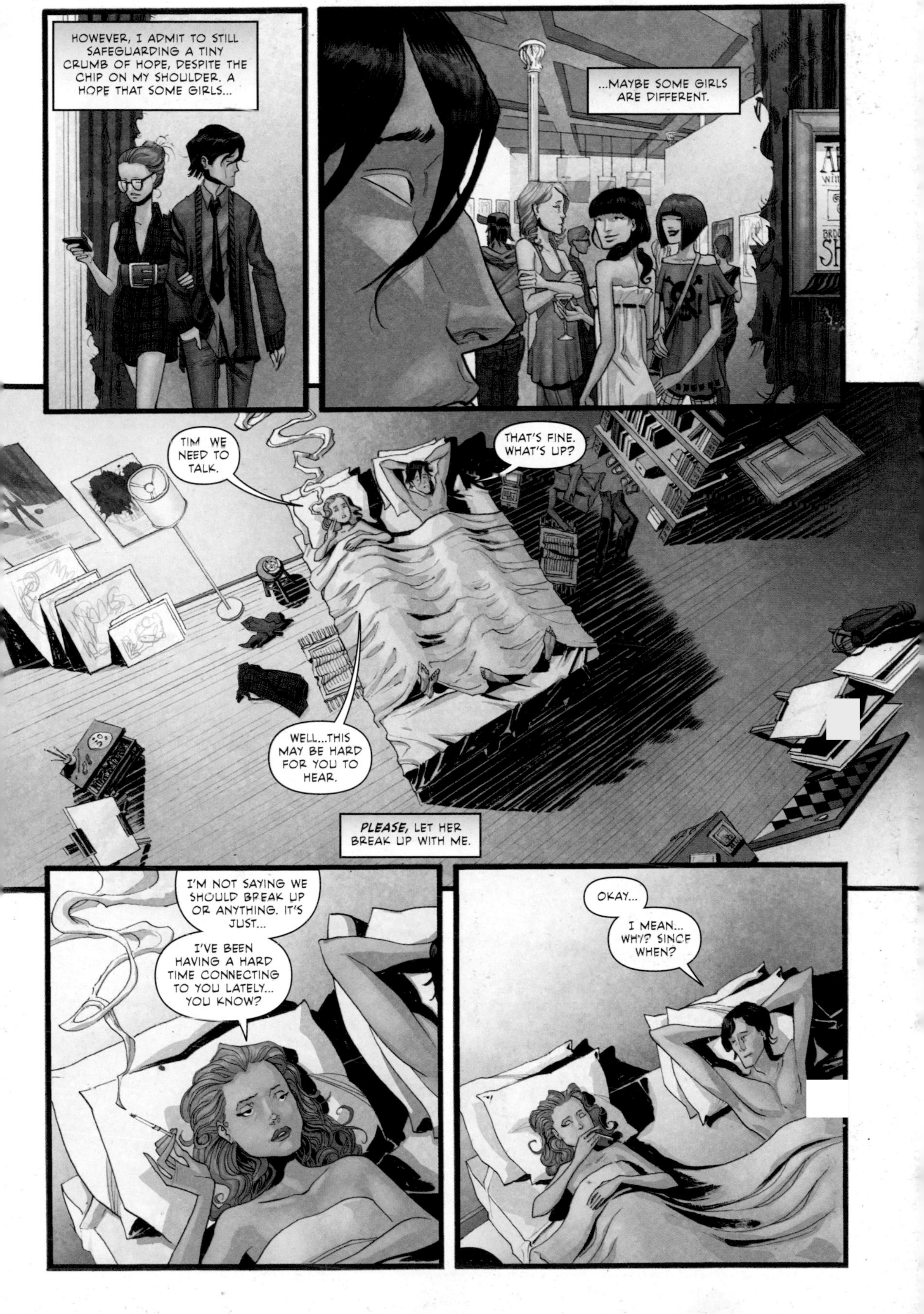
HOWEVER, I ADMIT TO STILL SAFEGUARDING A TINY CRUMB OF HOPE, DESPITE THE CHIP ON MY SHOULDER. A HOPE THAT SOME GIRLS...
...MAYBE SOME GIRLS ARE DIFFERENT.
TIM WE NEED TO TALK.
THAT'S FINE. WHAT'S UP?
WELL...THIS MAY BE HARD FOR YOU TO HEAR.
PLEASE, LET HER BREAK UP WITH ME.
I'M NOT SAYING WE SHOULD BREAK UP OR ANYTHING. IT'S JUST...
I'VE BEEN HAVING A HARD TIME CONNECTING TO YOU LATELY... YOU KNOW?
OKAY...
I MEAN... WHY? SINCE WHEN?

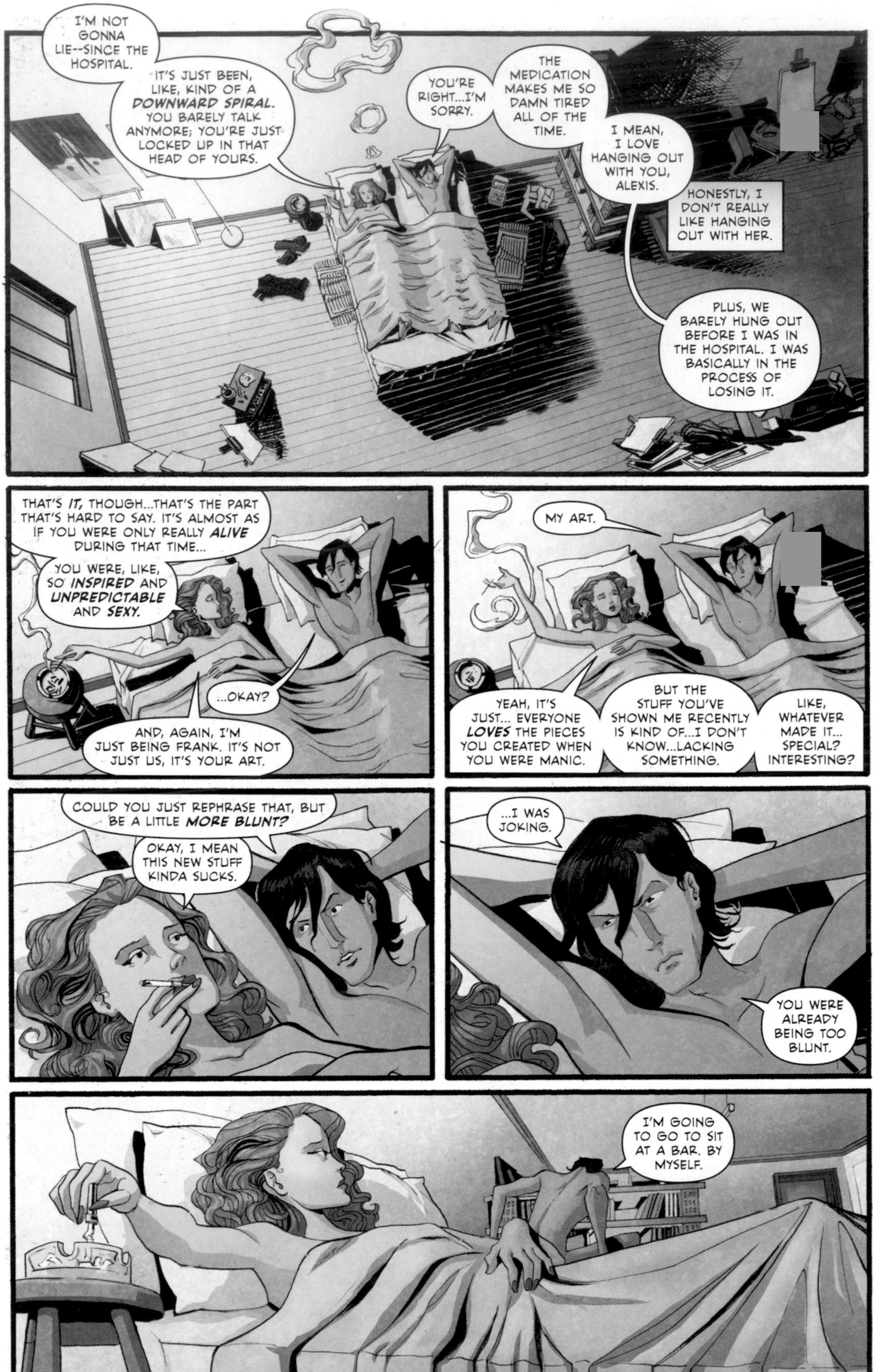
I'M NOT GONNA LIE--SINCE THE HOSPITAL.
IT'S JUST BEEN, LIKE, KIND OF A DOWNWARD SPIRAL. YOU BARELY TALK ANYMORE; YOU'RE JUST LOCKED UP IN THAT HEAD OF YOURS.
YOU'RE RIGHT...I'M SORRY.
THE MEDICATION MAKES ME SO DAMN TIRED ALL OF THE TIME.
I MEAN, I LOVE HANGING OUT WITH YOU, ALEXIS.
HONESTLY, I DON'T REALLY LIKE HANGING OUT WITH HER.
PLUS, WE BARELY HUNG OUT BEFORE I WAS IN THE HOSPITAL. I WAS BASICALLY IN THE PROCESS OF LOSING IT.
THAT'S IT, THOUGH...THAT'S THE PART THAT'S HARD TO SAY. IT'S ALMOST AS IF YOU WERE ONLY REALLY ALIVE DURING THAT TIME...
YOU WERE, LIKE, SO INSPIRED AND UNPREDICTABLE AND SEXY.
...OKAY?
AND, AGAIN, I'M JUST BEING FRANK. IT'S NOT JUST US, IT'S YOUR ART.
MY ART.
YEAH, IT'S JUST... EVERYONE LOVES THE PIECES YOU CREATED WHEN YOU WERE MANIC.
BUT THE STUFF YOU'VE SHOWN ME RECENTLY IS KIND OF...I DON'T KNOW...LACKING SOMETHING.
LIKE, WHATEVER MADE IT... SPECIAL? INTERESTING?
COULD YOU JUST REPHRASE THAT, BUT BE A LITTLE MORE BLUNT?
OKAY, I MEAN THIS NEW STUFF KINDA SUCKS.
...I WAS JOKING.
YOU WERE ALREADY BEING TOO BLUNT.
I'M GOING TO GO TO SIT AT A BAR. BY MYSELF.

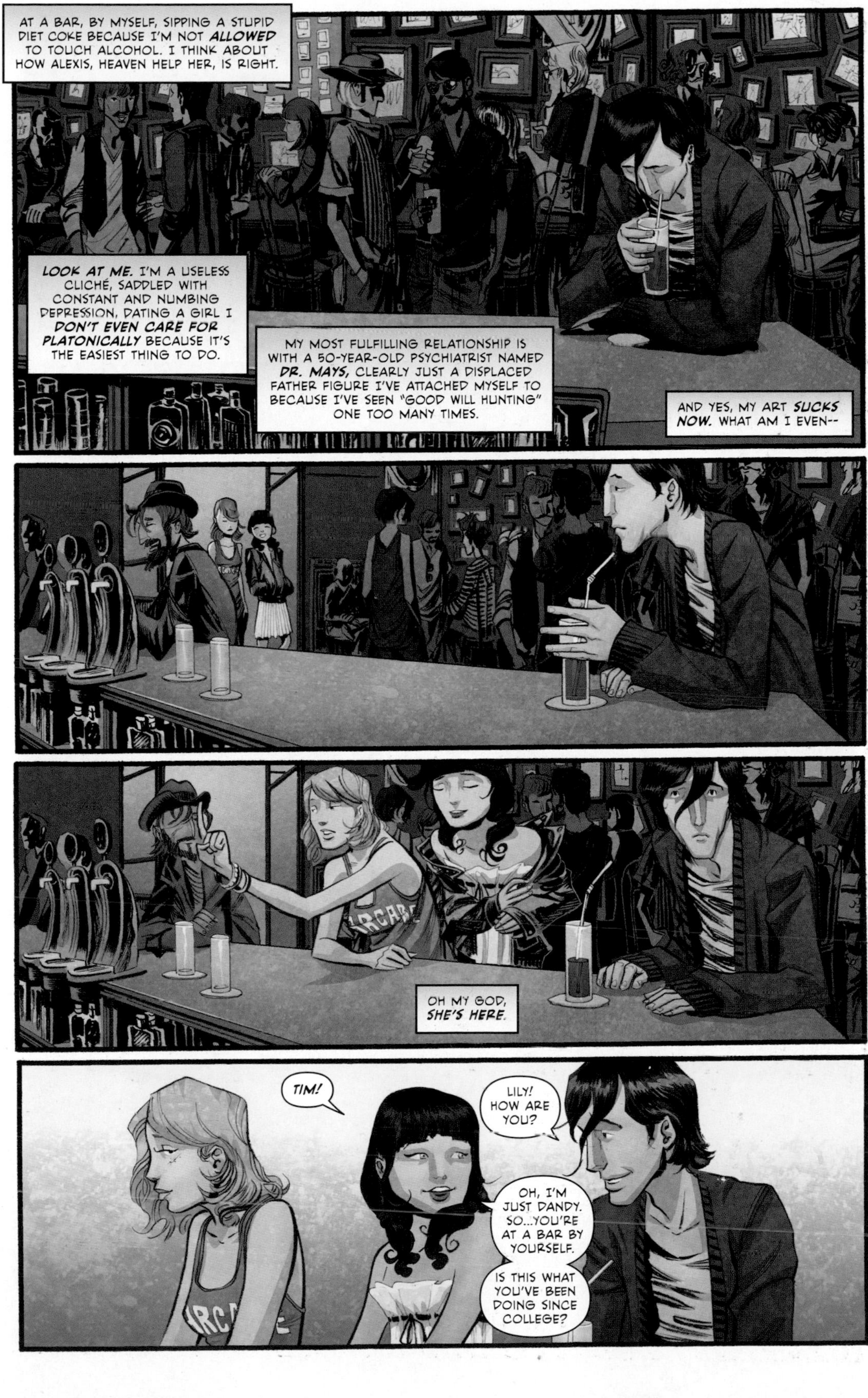
AT A BAR, BY MYSELF, SIPPING A STUPID DIET COKE BECAUSE I'M NOT *ALLOWED* TO TOUCH ALCOHOL. I THINK ABOUT HOW ALEXIS, HEAVEN HELP HER, IS RIGHT.
LOOK AT ME. I'M A USELESS CLICHÉ, SADDLED WITH CONSTANT AND NUMBING DEPRESSION, DATING A GIRL I *DON'T EVEN CARE FOR PLATONICALLY* BECAUSE IT'S THE EASIEST THING TO DO.
MY MOST FULFILLING RELATIONSHIP IS WITH A 50-YEAR-OLD PSYCHIATRIST NAMED *DR. MAYS,* CLEARLY JUST A DISPLACED FATHER FIGURE I'VE ATTACHED MYSELF TO BECAUSE I'VE SEEN "GOOD WILL HUNTING" ONE TOO MANY TIMES.
AND YES, MY ART *SUCKS NOW.* WHAT AM I EVEN--
OH MY GOD, *SHE'S HERE.*
TIM!
LILY! HOW ARE YOU?
OH, I'M JUST DANDY. SO...YOU'RE AT A BAR BY YOURSELF.
IS THIS WHAT YOU'VE BEEN DOING SINCE COLLEGE?

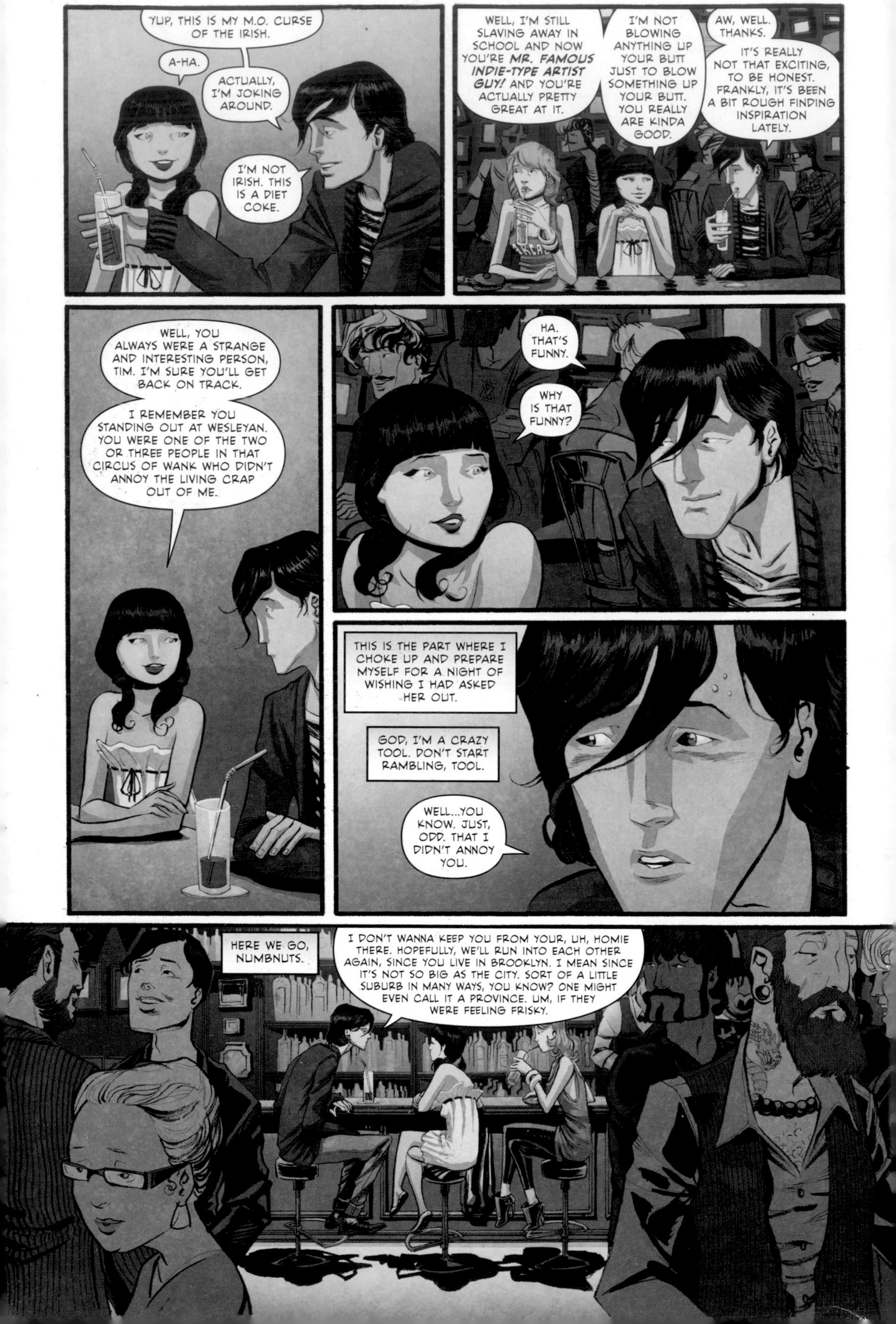

YUP, THIS IS MY M.O. CURSE OF THE IRISH.
A-HA.
ACTUALLY, I'M JOKING AROUND.
I'M NOT IRISH. THIS IS A DIET COKE.
WELL, I'M STILL SLAVING AWAY IN SCHOOL AND NOW YOU'RE *MR. FAMOUS INDIE-TYPE ARTIST GUY!* AND YOU'RE ACTUALLY PRETTY GREAT AT IT.
I'M NOT BLOWING ANYTHING UP YOUR BUTT JUST TO BLOW SOMETHING UP YOUR BUTT. YOU REALLY ARE KINDA GOOD.
AW, WELL. THANKS.
IT'S REALLY NOT THAT EXCITING, TO BE HONEST. FRANKLY, IT'S BEEN A BIT ROUGH FINDING INSPIRATION LATELY.
WELL, YOU ALWAYS WERE A STRANGE AND INTERESTING PERSON, TIM. I'M SURE YOU'LL GET BACK ON TRACK.
I REMEMBER YOU STANDING OUT AT WESLEYAN. YOU WERE ONE OF THE TWO OR THREE PEOPLE IN THAT CIRCUS OF WANK WHO DIDN'T ANNOY THE LIVING CRAP OUT OF ME..
HA. THAT'S FUNNY.
WHY IS THAT FUNNY?
THIS IS THE PART WHERE I CHOKE UP AND PREPARE MYSELF FOR A NIGHT OF WISHING I HAD ASKED HER OUT.
GOD, I'M A CRAZY TOOL. DON'T START RAMBLING, TOOL.
WELL...YOU KNOW. JUST, ODD. THAT I DIDN'T ANNOY YOU.
HERE WE GO, NUMBNUTS.
I DON'T WANNA KEEP YOU FROM YOUR, UH, HOMIE THERE. HOPEFULLY, WE'LL RUN INTO EACH OTHER AGAIN, SINCE YOU LIVE IN BROOKLYN. I MEAN SINCE IT'S NOT SO BIG AS THE CITY. SORT OF A LITTLE SUBURB IN MANY WAYS, YOU KNOW? ONE MIGHT EVEN CALL IT A PROVINCE. UM, IF THEY WERE FEELING FRISKY.

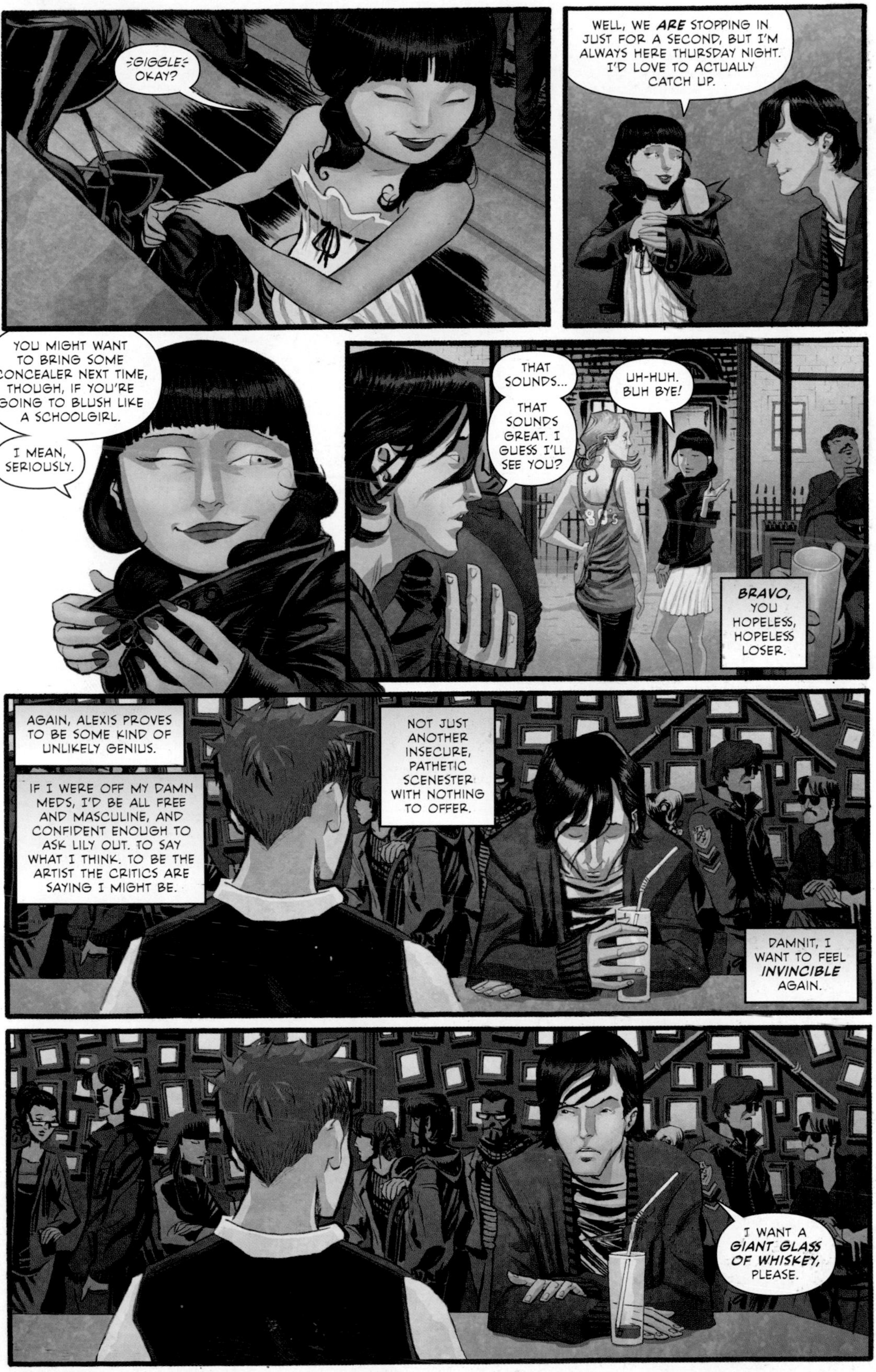

=GIGGLE= OKAY?
WELL, WE ARE STOPPING IN JUST FOR A SECOND, BUT I'M ALWAYS HERE THURSDAY NIGHT. I'D LOVE TO ACTUALLY CATCH UP.
YOU MIGHT WANT TO BRING SOME CONCEALER NEXT TIME, THOUGH, IF YOU'RE GOING TO BLUSH LIKE A SCHOOLGIRL.
I MEAN, SERIOUSLY.
THAT SOUNDS...
THAT SOUNDS GREAT. I GUESS I'LL SEE YOU?
UH-HUH. BUH BYE!
80's
BRAVO, YOU HOPELESS, HOPELESS LOSER.
AGAIN, ALEXIS PROVES TO BE SOME KIND OF UNLIKELY GENIUS.
IF I WERE OFF MY DAMN MEDS, I'D BE ALL FREE AND MASCULINE, AND CONFIDENT ENOUGH TO ASK LILY OUT. TO SAY WHAT I THINK. TO BE THE ARTIST THE CRITICS ARE SAYING I MIGHT BE.
NOT JUST ANOTHER INSECURE, PATHETIC SCENESTER WITH NOTHING TO OFFER.
DAMNIT, I WANT TO FEEL INVINCIBLE AGAIN.
I WANT A GIANT GLASS OF WHISKEY, PLEASE.

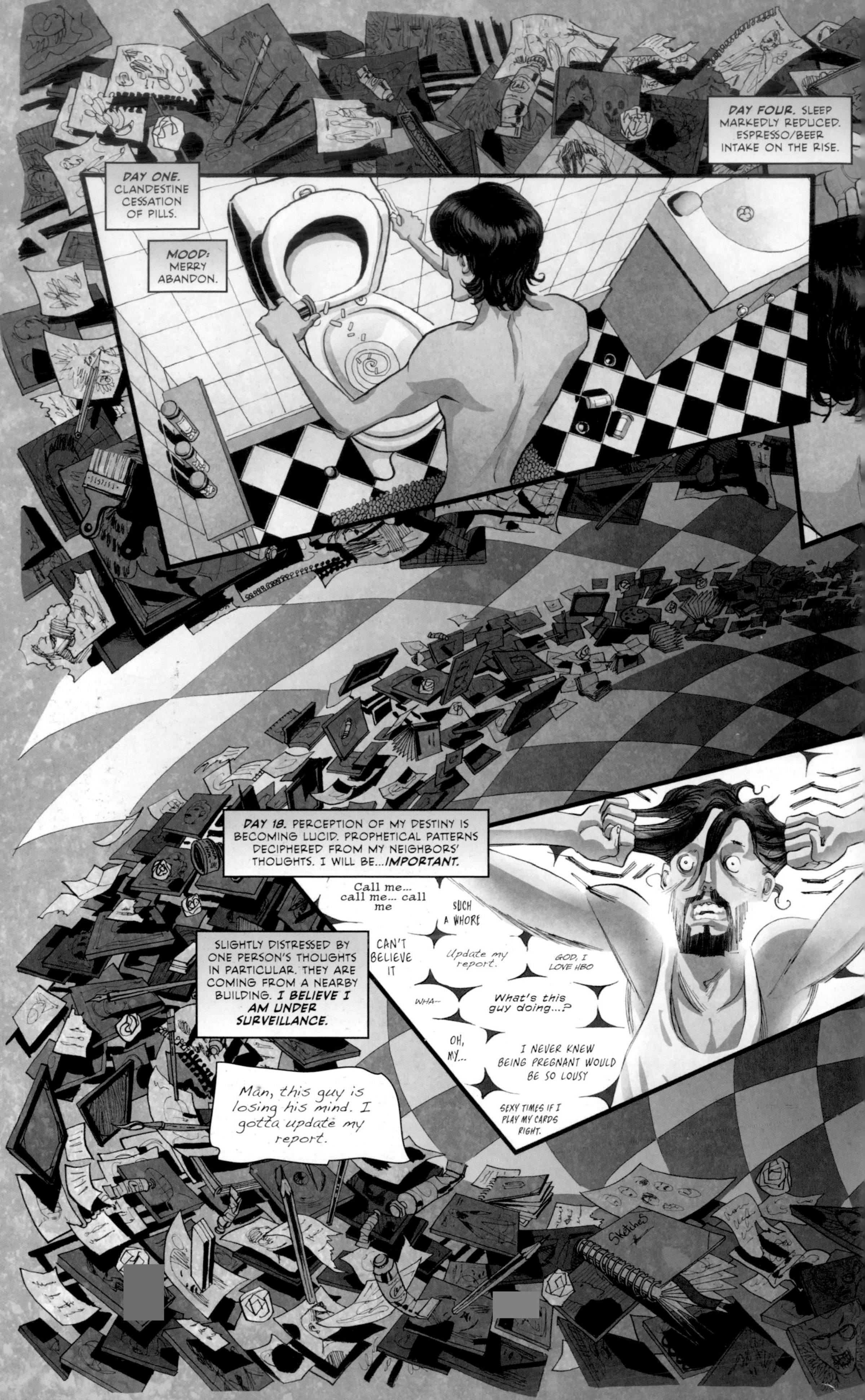

DAY ONE. CLANDESTINE CESSATION OF PILLS.
MOOD: MERRY ABANDON.
DAY FOUR. SLEEP MARKEDLY REDUCED. ESPRESSO/BEER INTAKE ON THE RISE.
DAY 18. PERCEPTION OF MY DESTINY IS BECOMING LUCID. PROPHETICAL PATTERNS DECIPHERED FROM MY NEIGHBORS' THOUGHTS. I WILL BE...IMPORTANT.
Call me... call me... call me
SUCH A WHORE
CAN'T BELIEVE IT
Update my report.
GOD, I LOVE HBO
WHA--
What's this guy doing...?
OH, MY...
I NEVER KNEW BEING PREGNANT WOULD BE SO LOUSY
SEXY TIMES IF I PLAY MY CARDS RIGHT.
SLIGHTLY DISTRESSED BY ONE PERSON'S THOUGHTS IN PARTICULAR. THEY ARE COMING FROM A NEARBY BUILDING. I BELIEVE I AM UNDER SURVEILLANCE.
Man, this guy is losing his mind. I gotta update my report.
Sketches

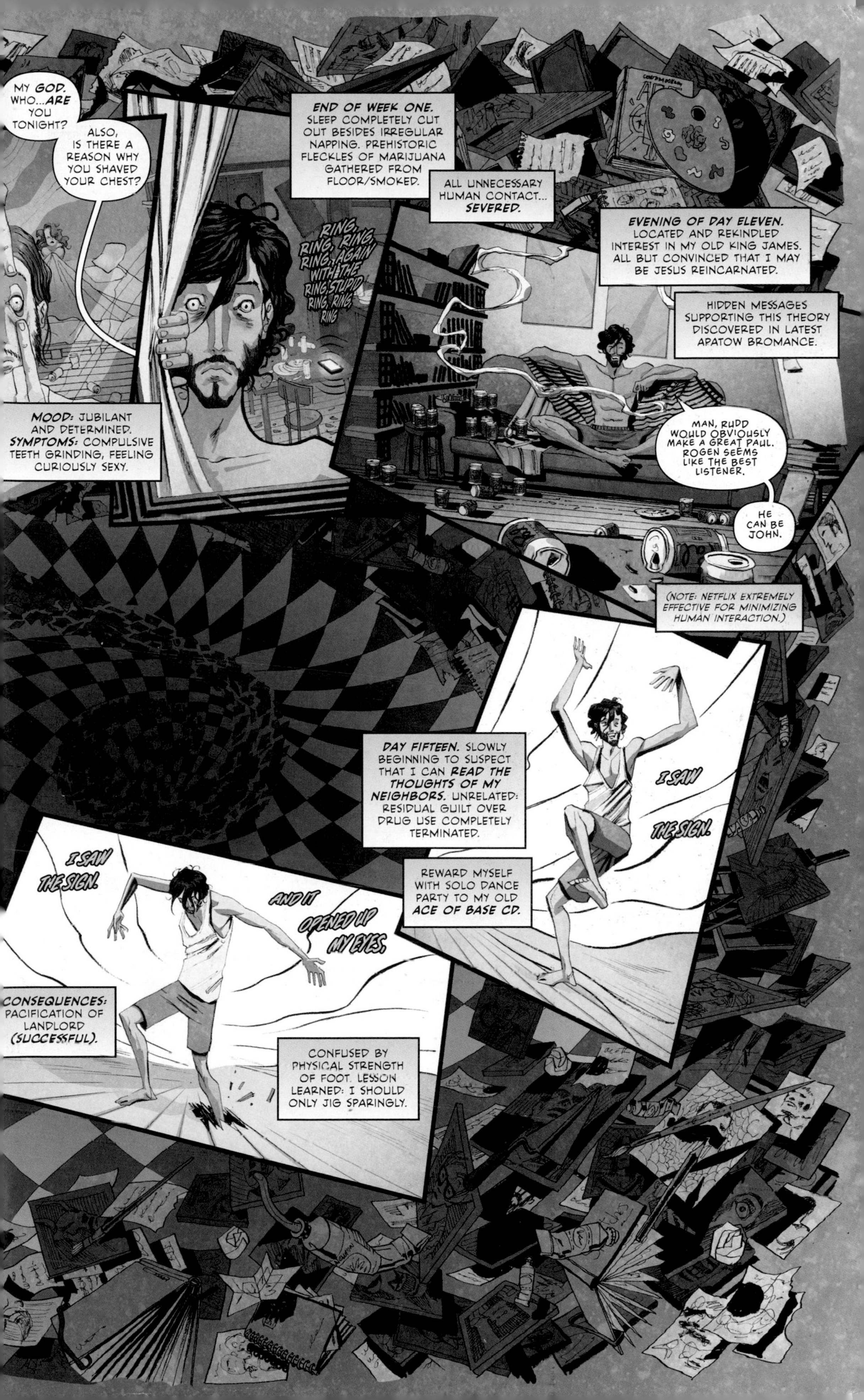
MY GOD. WHO...ARE YOU TONIGHT?
ALSO, IS THERE A REASON WHY YOU SHAVED YOUR CHEST?
END OF WEEK ONE. SLEEP COMPLETELY CUT OUT BESIDES IRREGULAR NAPPING. PREHISTORIC FLECKLES OF MARIJUANA GATHERED FROM FLOOR/SMOKED.
RING, RING, RING, AGAIN WITH THE RING, STUPID RING, RING, RING
MOOD: JUBILANT AND DETERMINED. SYMPTOMS: COMPULSIVE TEETH GRINDING, FEELING CURIOUSLY SEXY.
ALL UNNECESSARY HUMAN CONTACT... SEVERED.
EVENING OF DAY ELEVEN. LOCATED AND REKINDLED INTEREST IN MY OLD KING JAMES. ALL BUT CONVINCED THAT I MAY BE JESUS REINCARNATED.
HIDDEN MESSAGES SUPPORTING THIS THEORY DISCOVERED IN LATEST APATOW BROMANCE.
MAN, RUDD WOULD OBVIOUSLY MAKE A GREAT PAUL. ROGEN SEEMS LIKE THE BEST LISTENER.
HE CAN BE JOHN.
(NOTE: NETFLIX EXTREMELY EFFECTIVE FOR MINIMIZING HUMAN INTERACTION.)
DAY FIFTEEN. SLOWLY BEGINNING TO SUSPECT THAT I CAN READ THE THOUGHTS OF MY NEIGHBORS. UNRELATED: RESIDUAL GUILT OVER DRUG USE COMPLETELY TERMINATED.
I SAW THE SIGN.
REWARD MYSELF WITH SOLO DANCE PARTY TO MY OLD ACE OF BASE CD.
I SAW THE SIGN.
AND IT OPENED UP MY EYES.
CONSEQUENCES: PACIFICATION OF LANDLORD (SUCCESSFUL).
CONFUSED BY PHYSICAL STRENGTH OF FOOT. LESSON LEARNED: I SHOULD ONLY JIG SPARINGLY.

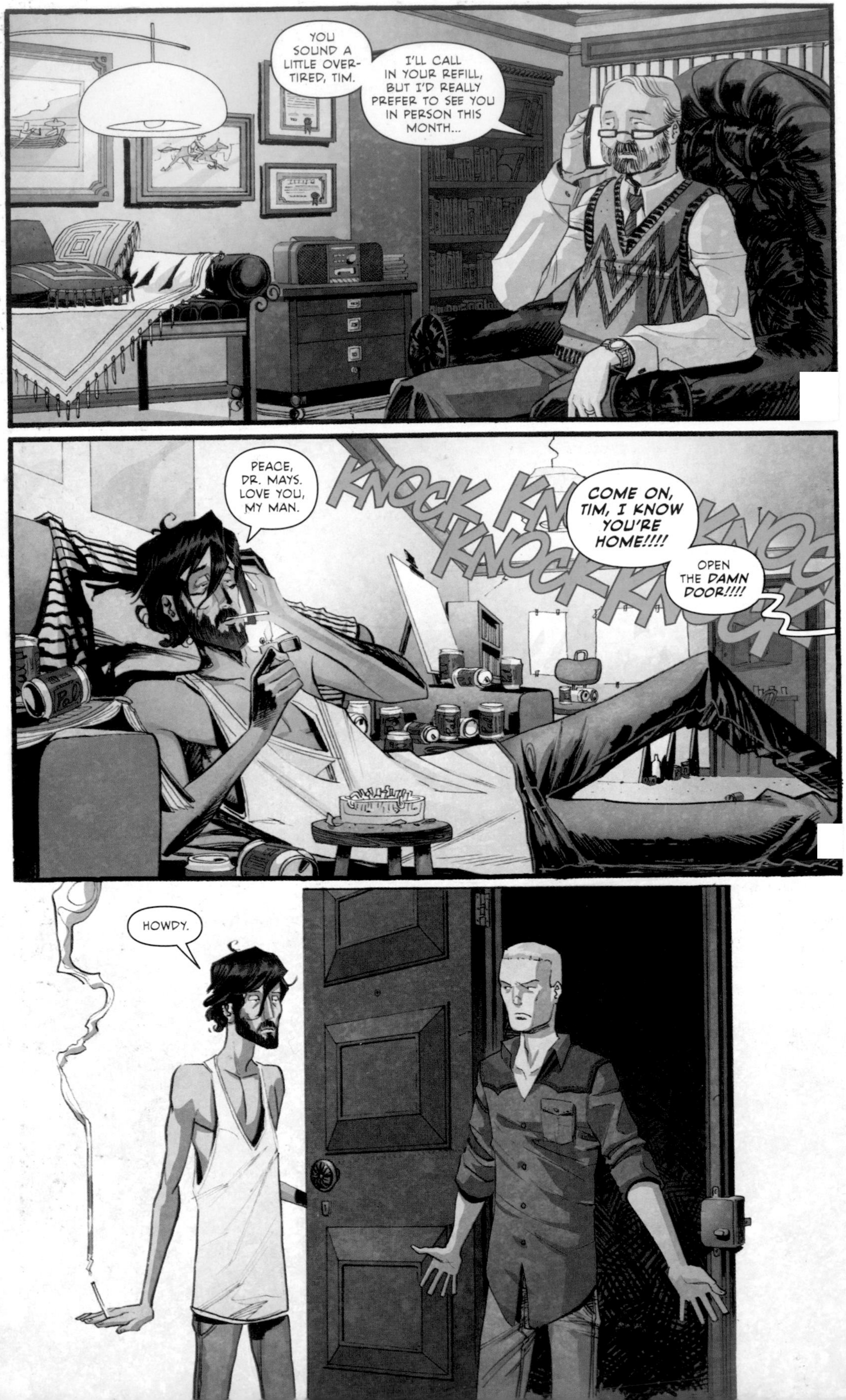
YOU SOUND A LITTLE OVER-TIRED, TIM.
I'LL CALL IN YOUR REFILL, BUT I'D REALLY PREFER TO SEE YOU IN PERSON THIS MONTH...
PEACE, DR. MAYS. LOVE YOU, MY MAN.
KNOCK KNOCK KNOCK KNOCK KNOCK
COME ON, TIM, I KNOW YOU'RE HOME!!!!
OPEN THE DAMN DOOR!!!!
HOWDY.

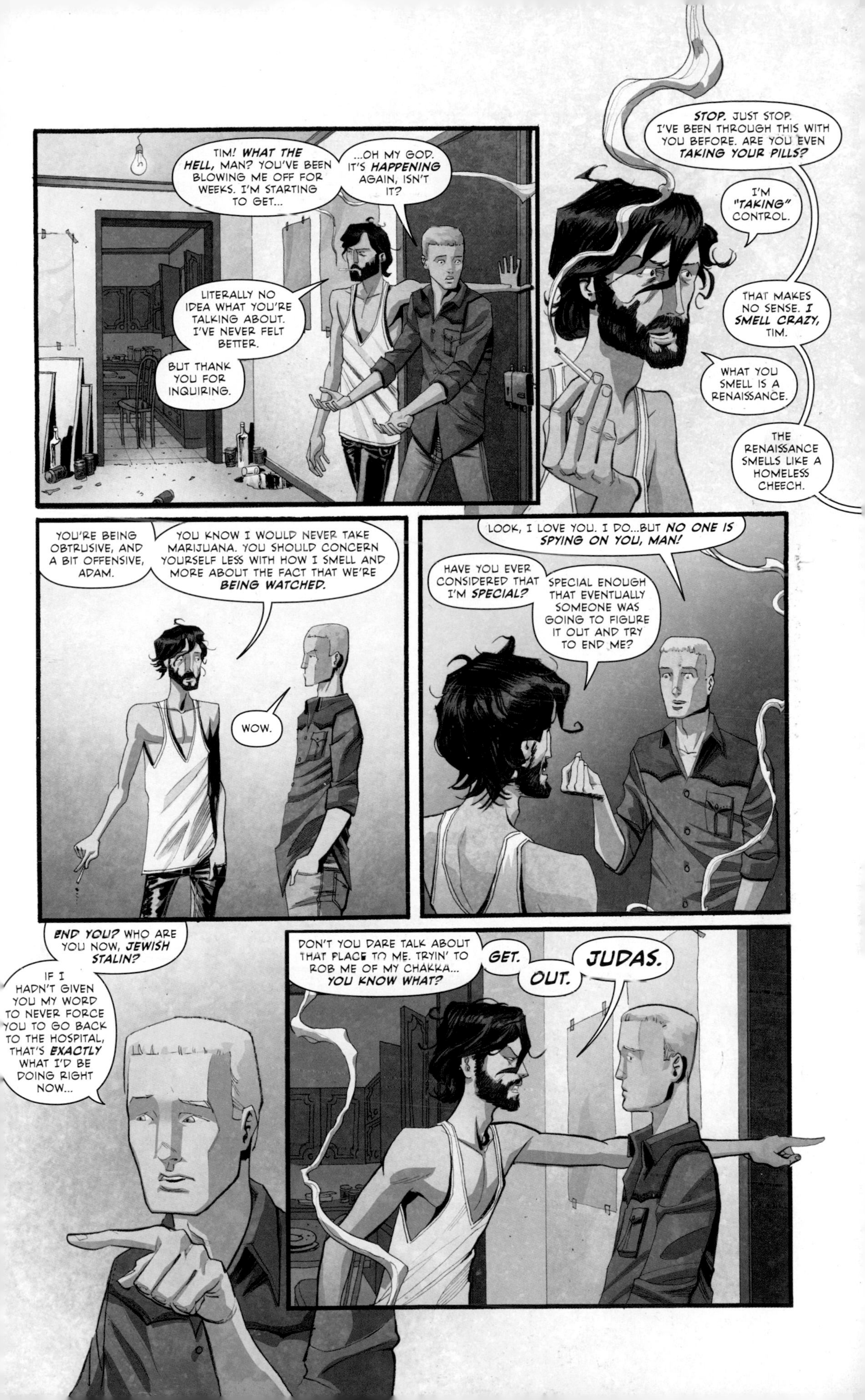
TIM! WHAT THE HELL, MAN? YOU'VE BEEN BLOWING ME OFF FOR WEEKS. I'M STARTING TO GET...
...OH MY GOD. IT'S HAPPENING AGAIN, ISN'T IT?
LITERALLY NO IDEA WHAT YOU'RE TALKING ABOUT. I'VE NEVER FELT BETTER.
BUT THANK YOU FOR INQUIRING.
STOP. JUST STOP. I'VE BEEN THROUGH THIS WITH YOU BEFORE. ARE YOU EVEN TAKING YOUR PILLS?
I'M "TAKING" CONTROL.
THAT MAKES NO SENSE. I SMELL CRAZY, TIM.
WHAT YOU SMELL IS A RENAISSANCE.
THE RENAISSANCE SMELLS LIKE A HOMELESS CHEECH.
YOU'RE BEING OBTRUSIVE, AND A BIT OFFENSIVE, ADAM.
YOU KNOW I WOULD NEVER TAKE MARIJUANA. YOU SHOULD CONCERN YOURSELF LESS WITH HOW I SMELL AND MORE ABOUT THE FACT THAT WE'RE BEING WATCHED.
WOW.
LOOK, I LOVE YOU. I DO...BUT NO ONE IS SPYING ON YOU, MAN!
HAVE YOU EVER CONSIDERED THAT I'M SPECIAL?
SPECIAL ENOUGH THAT EVENTUALLY SOMEONE WAS GOING TO FIGURE IT OUT AND TRY TO END ME?
END YOU? WHO ARE YOU NOW, JEWISH STALIN?
IF I HADN'T GIVEN YOU MY WORD TO NEVER FORCE YOU TO GO BACK TO THE HOSPITAL, THAT'S EXACTLY WHAT I'D BE DOING RIGHT NOW...
DON'T YOU DARE TALK ABOUT THAT PLACE TO ME. TRYIN' TO ROB ME OF MY CHAKKA... YOU KNOW WHAT?
GET.
OUT.
JUDAS.

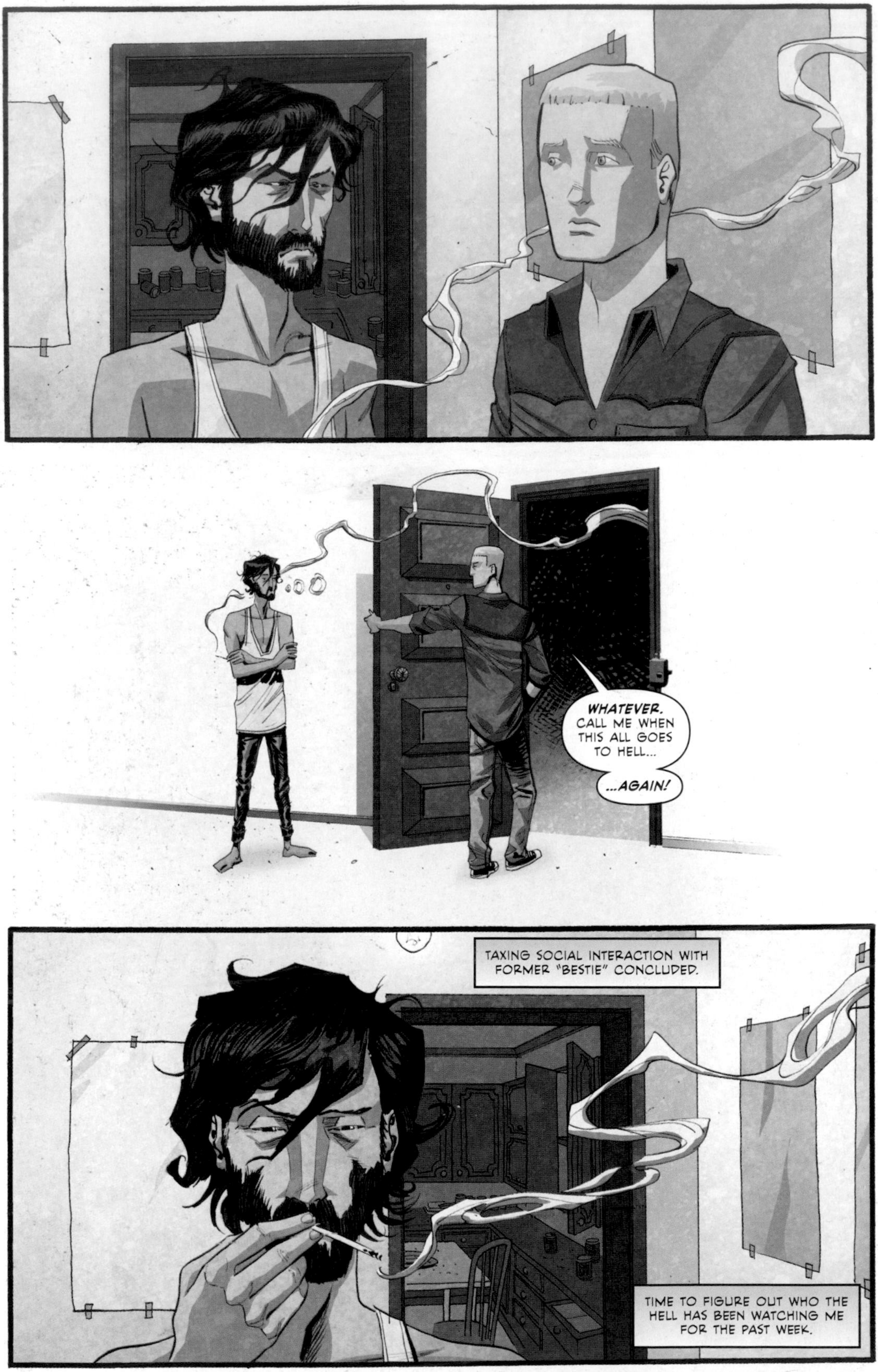
WHATEVER. CALL ME WHEN THIS ALL GOES TO HELL...
...AGAIN!
TAXING SOCIAL INTERACTION WITH FORMER "BESTIE" CONCLUDED.
TIME TO FIGURE OUT WHO THE HELL HAS BEEN WATCHING ME FOR THE PAST WEEK.

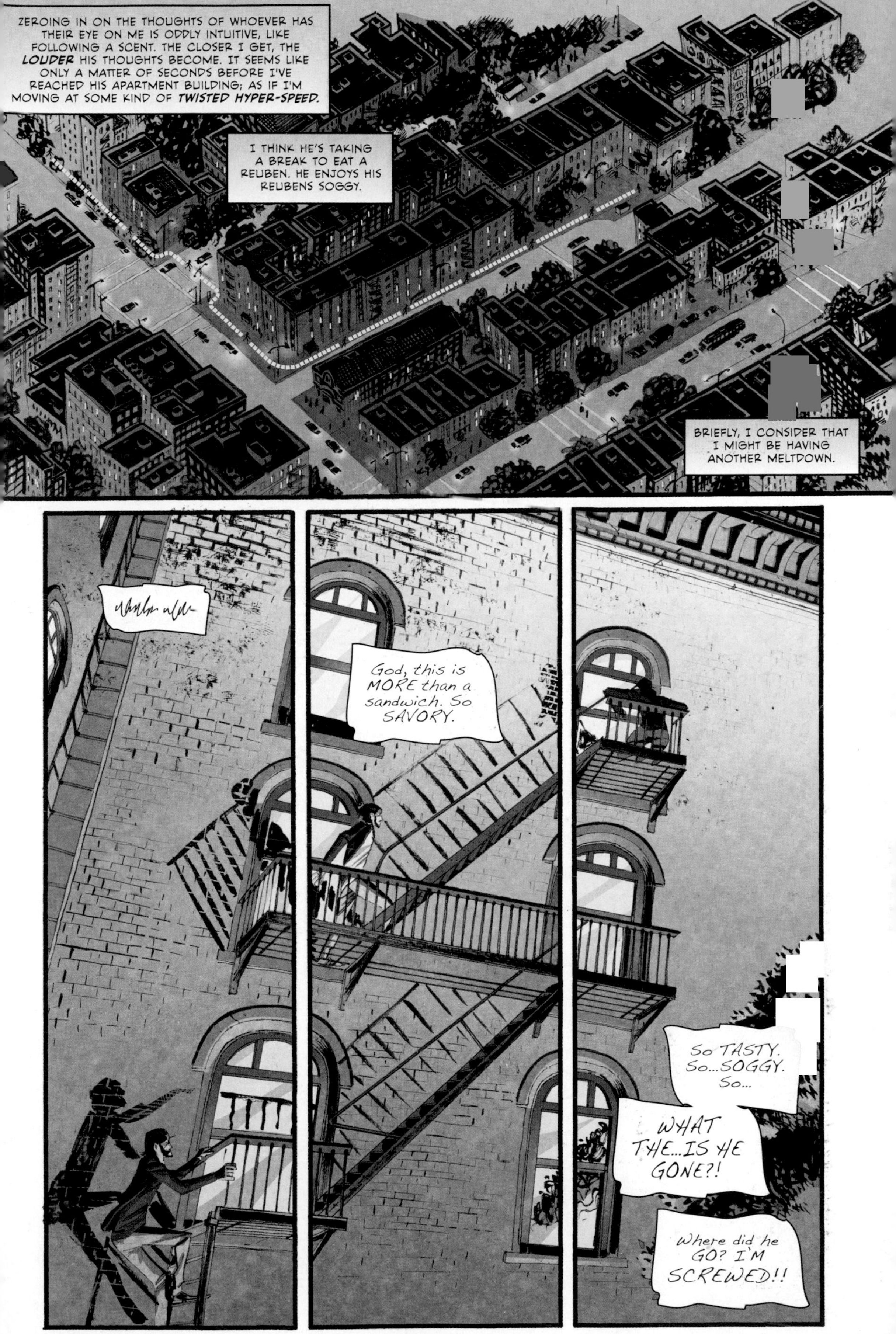
ZEROING IN ON THE THOUGHTS OF WHOEVER HAS THEIR EYE ON ME IS ODDLY INTUITIVE, LIKE FOLLOWING A SCENT. THE CLOSER I GET, THE LOUDER HIS THOUGHTS BECOME. IT SEEMS LIKE ONLY A MATTER OF SECONDS BEFORE I'VE REACHED HIS APARTMENT BUILDING; AS IF I'M MOVING AT SOME KIND OF TWISTED HYPER-SPEED.
I THINK HE'S TAKING A BREAK TO EAT A REUBEN. HE ENJOYS HIS REUBENS SOGGY.
BRIEFLY, I CONSIDER THAT I MIGHT BE HAVING ANOTHER MELTDOWN.
God, this is MORE than a sandwich. So SAVORY.
So TASTY. So...SOGGY. So...
WHAT THE...IS HE GONE?!
Where did he GO? I'M SCREWED!!

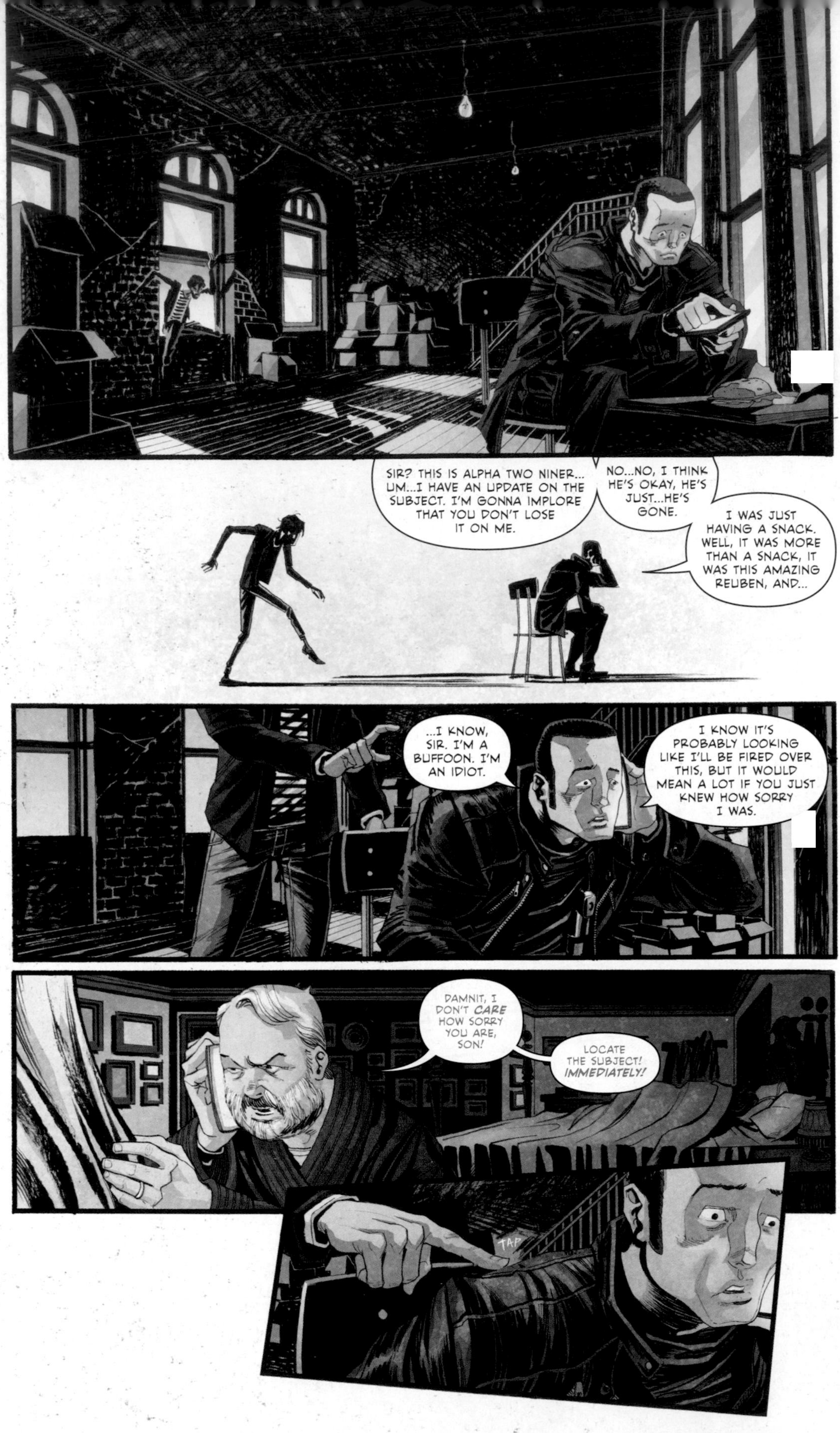
SIR? THIS IS ALPHA TWO NINER... UM...I HAVE AN UPDATE ON THE SUBJECT. I'M GONNA IMPLORE THAT YOU DON'T LOSE IT ON ME.
NO...NO, I THINK HE'S OKAY, HE'S JUST...HE'S GONE.
I WAS JUST HAVING A SNACK. WELL, IT WAS MORE THAN A SNACK, IT WAS THIS AMAZING REUBEN, AND...
...I KNOW, SIR. I'M A BUFFOON. I'M AN IDIOT.
I KNOW IT'S PROBABLY LOOKING LIKE I'LL BE FIRED OVER THIS, BUT IT WOULD MEAN A LOT IF YOU JUST KNEW HOW SORRY I WAS.
DAMNIT, I DON'T *CARE* HOW SORRY YOU ARE, SON!
LOCATE THE SUBJECT! *IMMEDIATELY!*
TAP

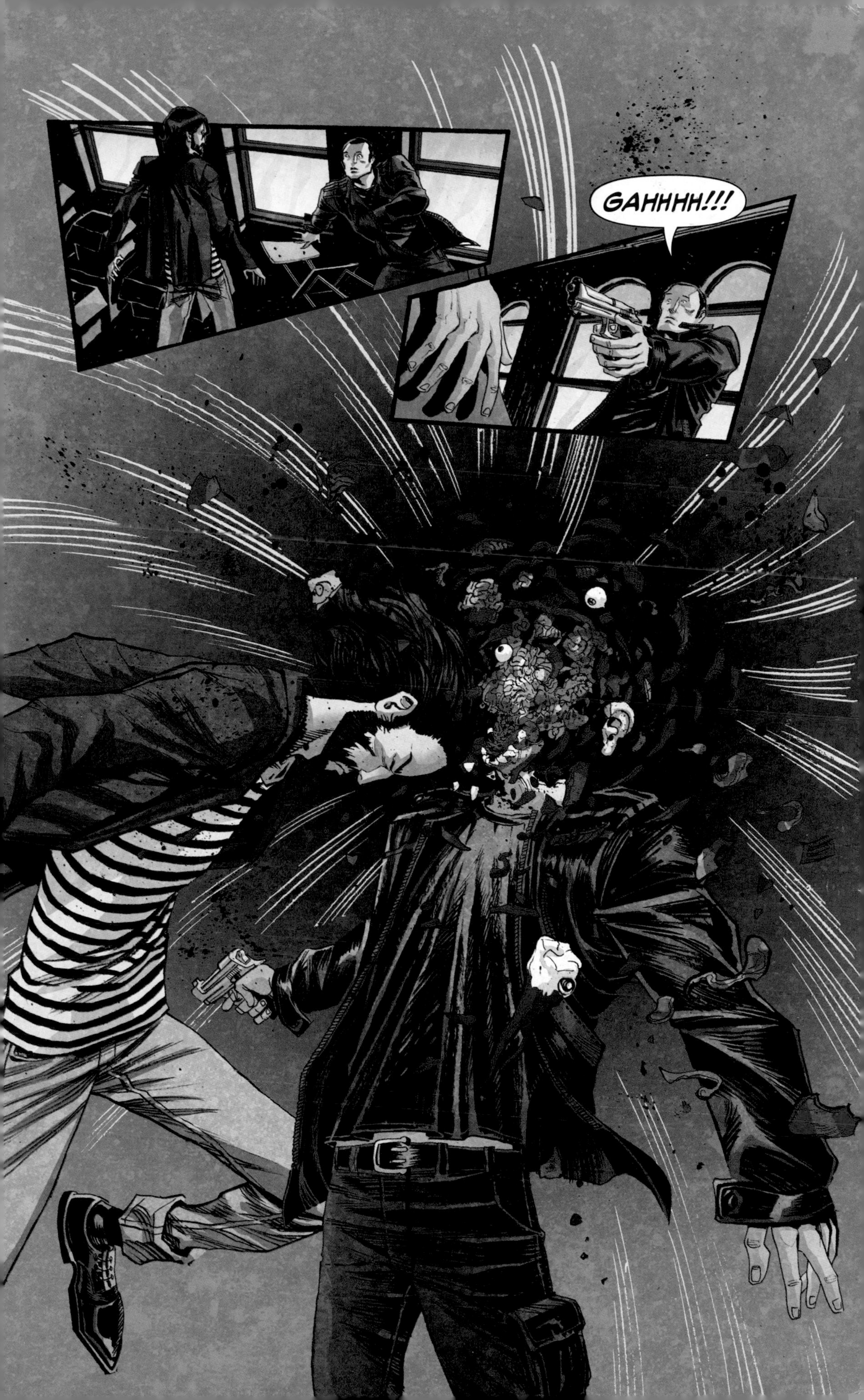
GAHHHH!!!

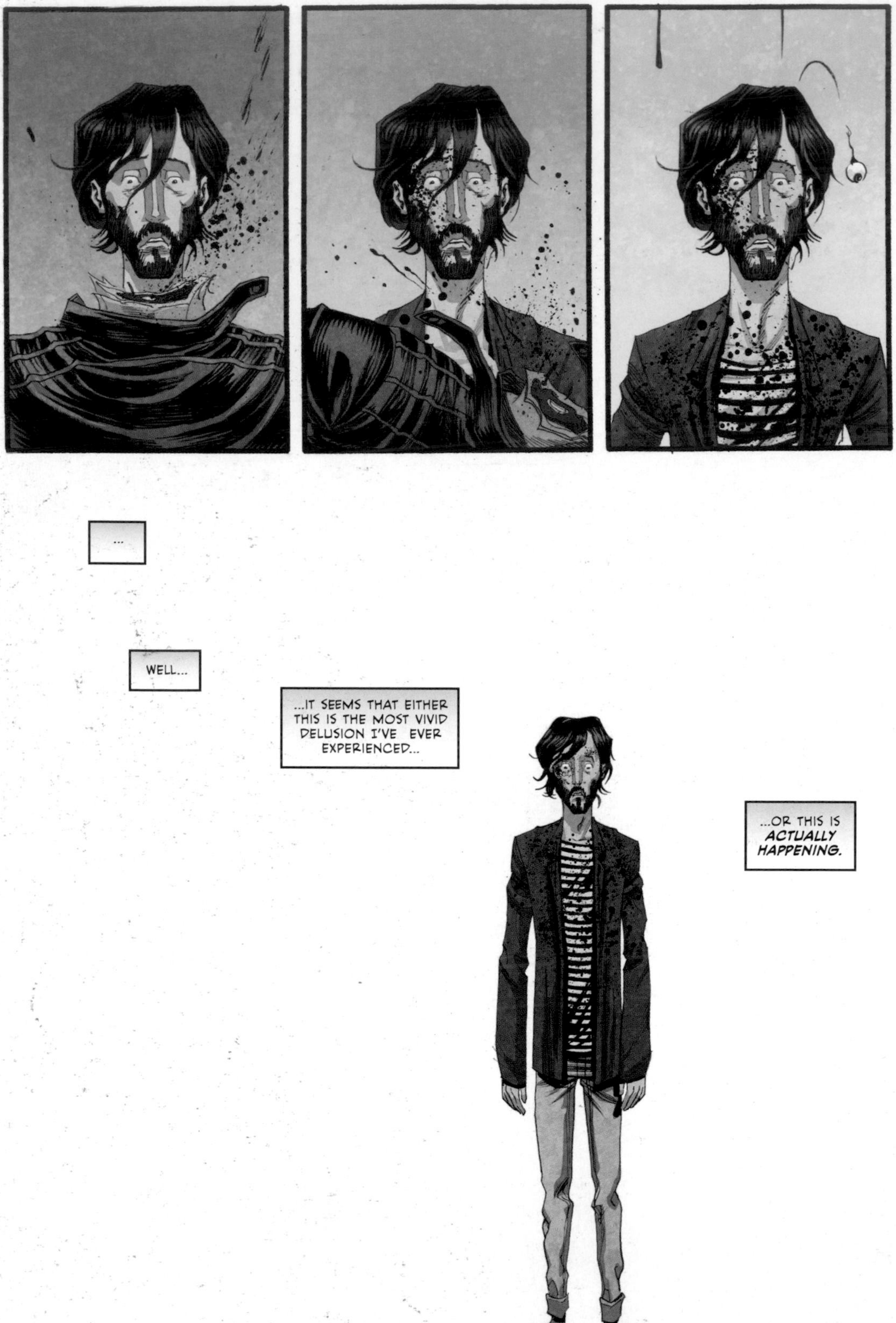
...
WELL...
...IT SEEMS THAT EITHER THIS IS THE MOST VIVID DELUSION I'VE EVER EXPERIENCED...
...OR THIS IS *ACTUALLY HAPPENING.*

"POLARITY"

THIS IS THE SOUND OF FEELING NUMB TO THE CIRCUS AROUND ME
VULTURES PECKING OUT MY EYES, THIS CULTURE ASTOUNDS ME
BUILT ON THE BACKS OF THOSE WITH HEARTS, THE SHALLOW SIMPLISTIC
THIS BROOKLYN NIGHT IS FRAUGHT WITH FIENDS
AND THEY'RE CANNIBALISTIC

NO MOTIVATION
IT'S IN A PRETTY LITTLE PILL
NO MOTIVATION
I'M THE ONLY ONE WITH...

MY POLARITY
IT'S WHAT I HIDE TO KEEP ME NORMAL
ITS SEVERITY
THE ENDLESS SHADE OF DARKNESS DEEP IN
MY POLARITY
IT'S WHAT I HIDE TO KEEP ME NORMAL
ITS SEVERITY
THE ENDLESS SHADE OF DARKNESS DEEP IN

NO MOTIVATION
IT'S IN A PRETTY LITTLE PILL
NO MOTIVATION
I'M THE ONLY ONE WITH

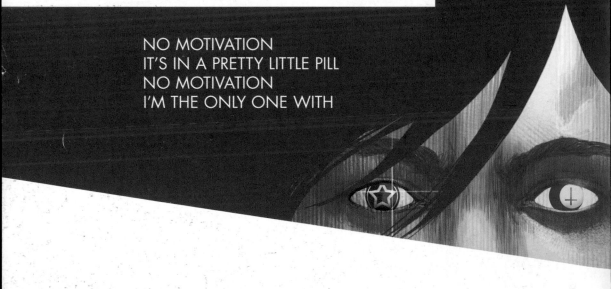

VULTURES PECKING OUT MY EYES,
YEAH THE CULTURE ASTOUNDS ME

NO MOTIVATION
IT'S IN A PRETTY LITTLE PILL
NO MOTIVATION
I'M THE ONLY ONE WITH...

MY POLARITY
IT'S WHAT I HIDE TO KEEP ME NORMAL
ITS SEVERITY
THE ENDLESS SHADE OF DARKNESS DEEP IN
MY POLARITY
IT'S WHAT I HIDE TO KEEP ME NORMAL
ITS SEVERITY
THE ENDLESS SHADE OF DARKNESS DEEP IN ME

AND THE IRONY OF IT ALL
IS THAT IRONY HOLDS NO MEANING
AND THE IRONY OF IT ALL
IS THAT IRONY HOLDS NO MEANING
NO MEANING, NO MEANING
NO MEANING TO ME

"...THAT'S ALL I'LL NEED TO LOSE IT."

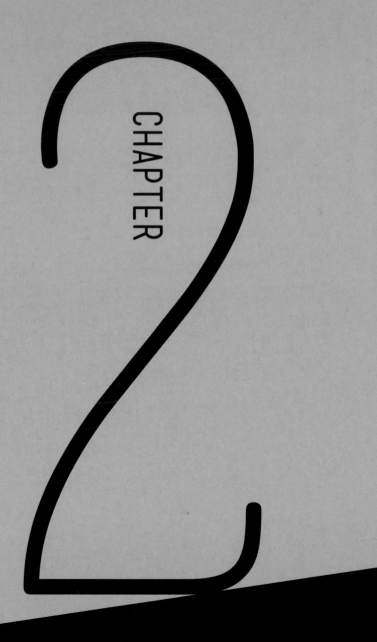

CHAPTER

2

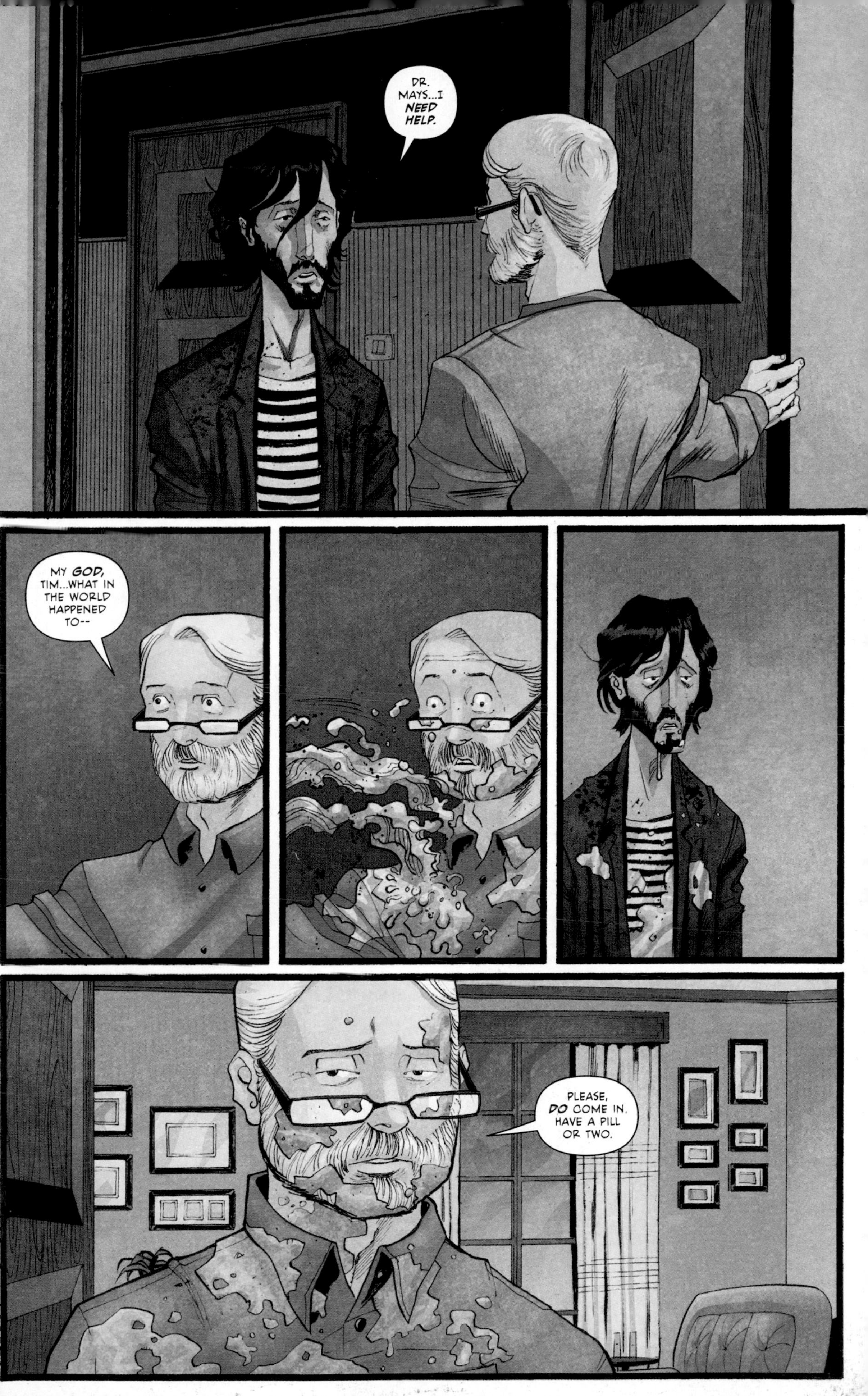
DR. MAYS...I NEED HELP.
MY GOD, TIM...WHAT IN THE WORLD HAPPENED TO--
PLEASE, DO COME IN. HAVE A PILL OR TWO.

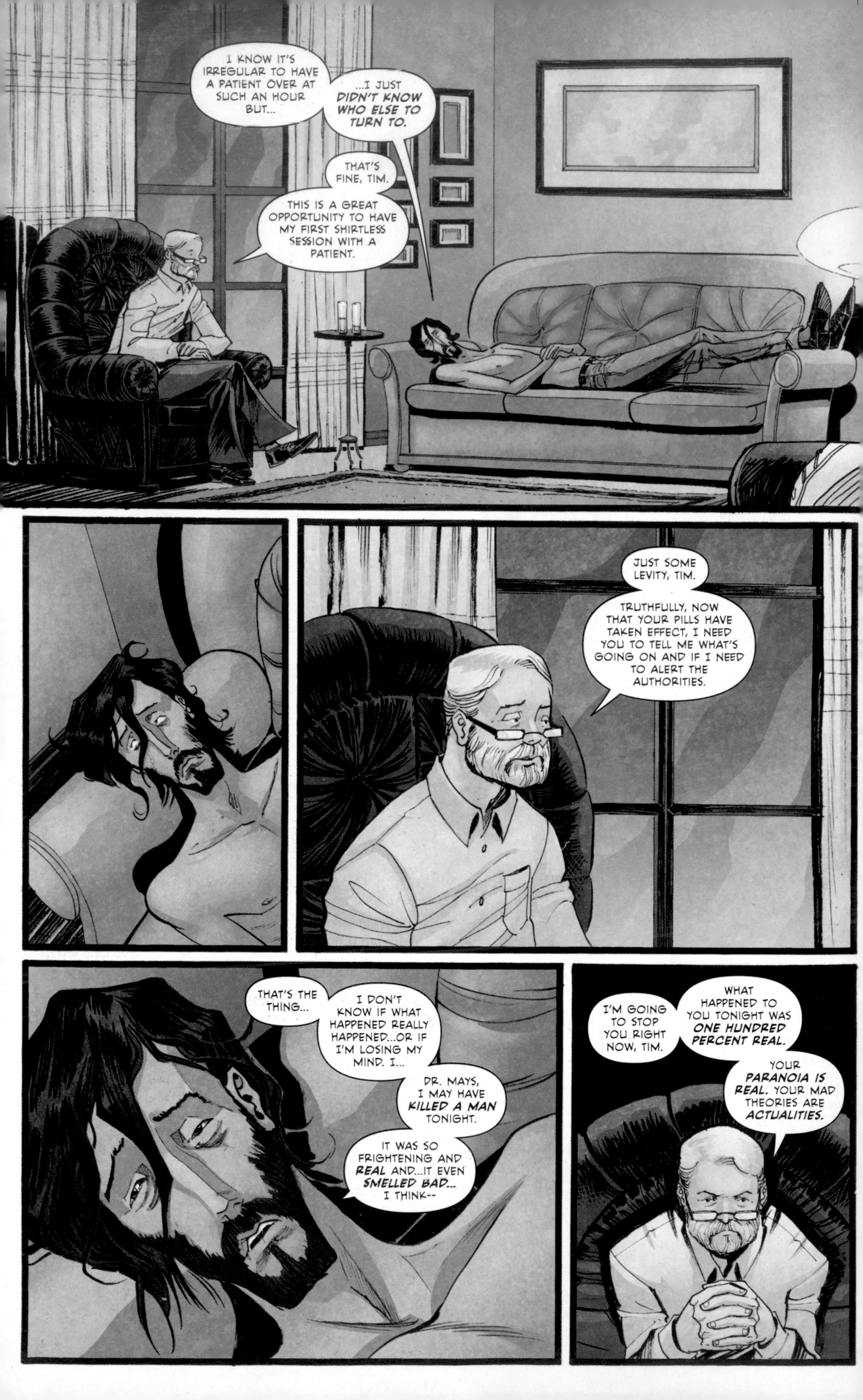
I KNOW IT'S IRREGULAR TO HAVE A PATIENT OVER AT SUCH AN HOUR BUT...
...I JUST DIDN'T KNOW WHO ELSE TO TURN TO.
THAT'S FINE, TIM.
THIS IS A GREAT OPPORTUNITY TO HAVE MY FIRST SHIRTLESS SESSION WITH A PATIENT.
JUST SOME LEVITY, TIM.
TRUTHFULLY, NOW THAT YOUR PILLS HAVE TAKEN EFFECT, I NEED YOU TO TELL ME WHAT'S GOING ON AND IF I NEED TO ALERT THE AUTHORITIES.
THAT'S THE THING...
I DON'T KNOW IF WHAT HAPPENED REALLY HAPPENED...OR IF I'M LOSING MY MIND. I...
DR. MAYS, I MAY HAVE KILLED A MAN TONIGHT.
IT WAS SO FRIGHTENING AND REAL AND...IT EVEN SMELLED BAD... I THINK--
I'M GOING TO STOP YOU RIGHT NOW, TIM.
WHAT HAPPENED TO YOU TONIGHT WAS ONE HUNDRED PERCENT REAL.
YOUR PARANOIA IS REAL. YOUR MAD THEORIES ARE ACTUALITIES.

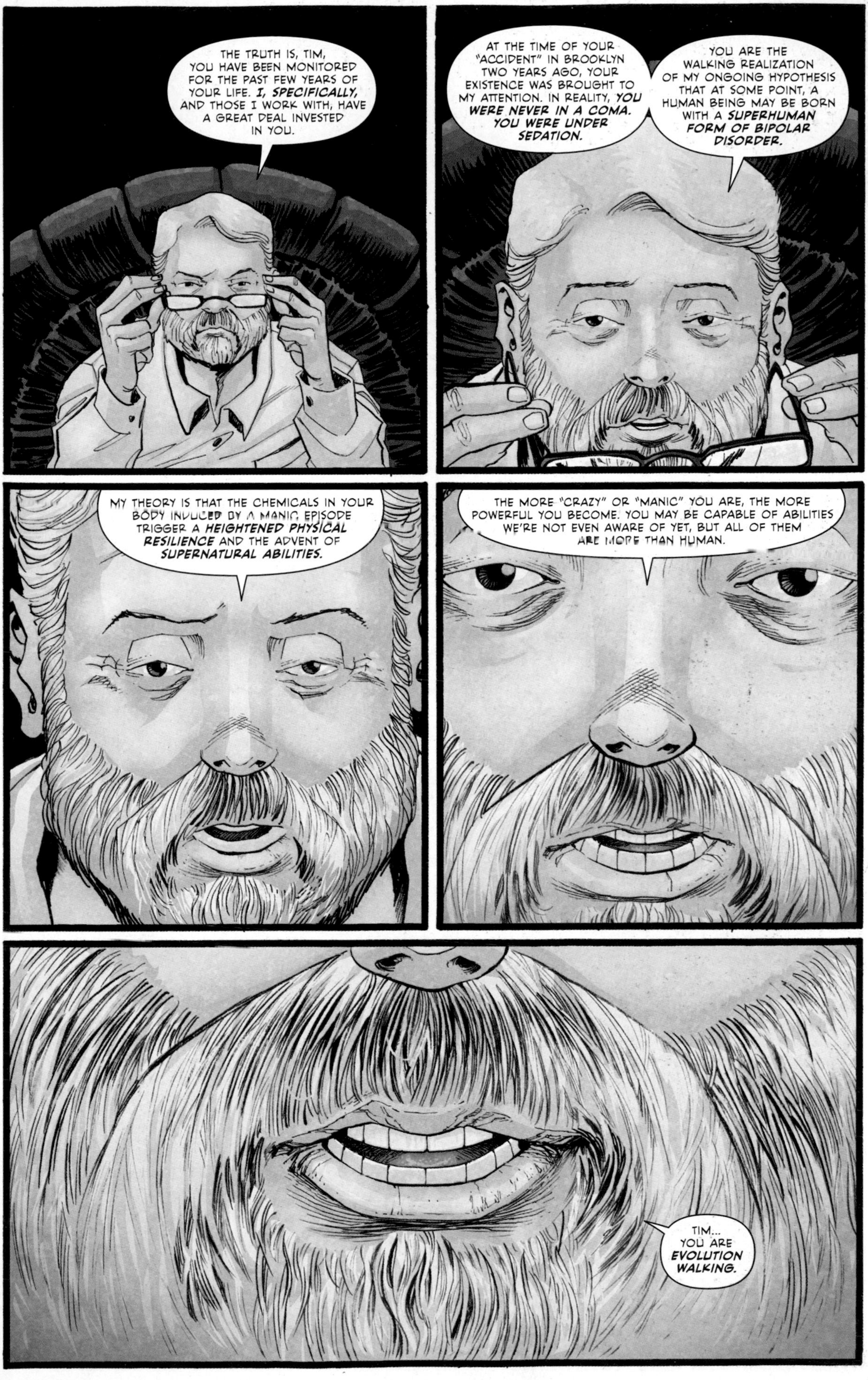
THE TRUTH IS, TIM, YOU HAVE BEEN MONITORED FOR THE PAST FEW YEARS OF YOUR LIFE. *I, SPECIFICALLY,* AND THOSE I WORK WITH, HAVE A GREAT DEAL INVESTED IN YOU.
AT THE TIME OF YOUR "ACCIDENT" IN BROOKLYN TWO YEARS AGO, YOUR EXISTENCE WAS BROUGHT TO MY ATTENTION. IN REALITY, *YOU WERE NEVER IN A COMA. YOU WERE UNDER SEDATION.*
YOU ARE THE WALKING REALIZATION OF MY ONGOING HYPOTHESIS THAT AT SOME POINT, A HUMAN BEING MAY BE BORN WITH A *SUPERHUMAN FORM OF BIPOLAR DISORDER.*
MY THEORY IS THAT THE CHEMICALS IN YOUR BODY INDUCED BY A MANIC EPISODE TRIGGER A *HEIGHTENED PHYSICAL RESILIENCE* AND THE ADVENT OF *SUPERNATURAL ABILITIES.*
THE MORE "CRAZY" OR "MANIC" YOU ARE, THE MORE POWERFUL YOU BECOME. YOU MAY BE CAPABLE OF ABILITIES WE'RE NOT EVEN AWARE OF YET, BUT ALL OF THEM ARE MORE THAN HUMAN.
TIM... YOU ARE *EVOLUTION WALKING.*

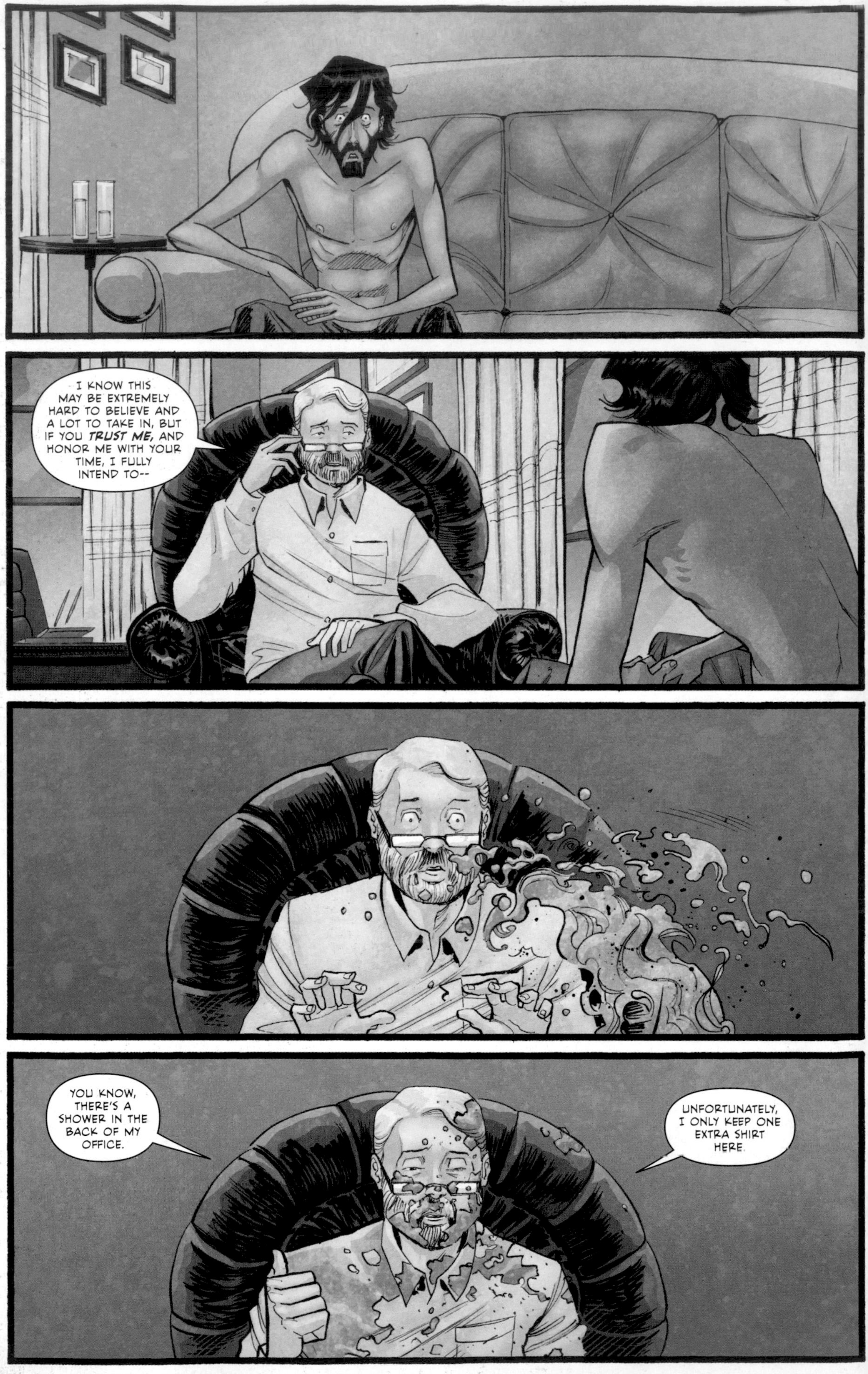
I KNOW THIS MAY BE EXTREMELY HARD TO BELIEVE AND A LOT TO TAKE IN, BUT IF YOU *TRUST ME,* AND HONOR ME WITH YOUR TIME, I FULLY INTEND TO--
YOU KNOW, THERE'S A SHOWER IN THE BACK OF MY OFFICE.
UNFORTUNATELY, I ONLY KEEP ONE EXTRA SHIRT HERE.

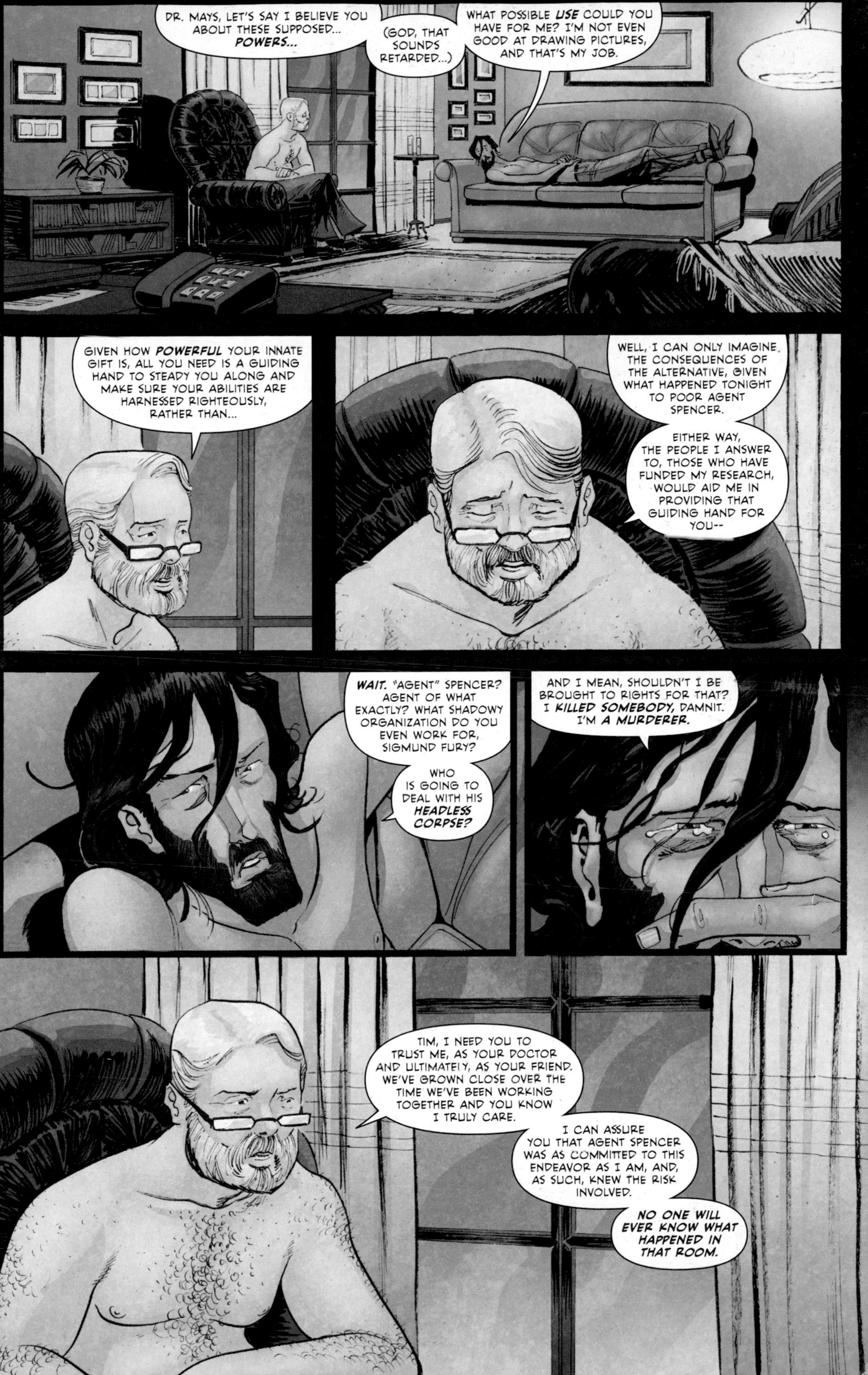
DR. MAYS, LET'S SAY I BELIEVE YOU ABOUT THESE SUPPOSED... POWERS...
(GOD, THAT SOUNDS RETARDED...)
WHAT POSSIBLE USE COULD YOU HAVE FOR ME? I'M NOT EVEN GOOD AT DRAWING PICTURES, AND THAT'S MY JOB.
GIVEN HOW POWERFUL YOUR INNATE GIFT IS, ALL YOU NEED IS A GUIDING HAND TO STEADY YOU ALONG AND MAKE SURE YOUR ABILITIES ARE HARNESSED RIGHTEOUSLY, RATHER THAN...
WELL, I CAN ONLY IMAGINE THE CONSEQUENCES OF THE ALTERNATIVE, GIVEN WHAT HAPPENED TONIGHT TO POOR AGENT SPENCER.
EITHER WAY, THE PEOPLE I ANSWER TO, THOSE WHO HAVE FUNDED MY RESEARCH, WOULD AID ME IN PROVIDING THAT GUIDING HAND FOR YOU--
WAIT. "AGENT" SPENCER? AGENT OF WHAT EXACTLY? WHAT SHADOWY ORGANIZATION DO YOU EVEN WORK FOR, SIGMUND FURY?
WHO IS GOING TO DEAL WITH HIS HEADLESS CORPSE?
AND I MEAN, SHOULDN'T I BE BROUGHT TO RIGHTS FOR THAT? I KILLED SOMEBODY, DAMNIT. I'M A MURDERER.
TIM, I NEED YOU TO TRUST ME, AS YOUR DOCTOR AND ULTIMATELY, AS YOUR FRIEND. WE'VE GROWN CLOSE OVER THE TIME WE'VE BEEN WORKING TOGETHER AND YOU KNOW I TRULY CARE.
I CAN ASSURE YOU THAT AGENT SPENCER WAS AS COMMITTED TO THIS ENDEAVOR AS I AM, AND, AS SUCH, KNEW THE RISK INVOLVED.
NO ONE WILL EVER KNOW WHAT HAPPENED IN THAT ROOM.

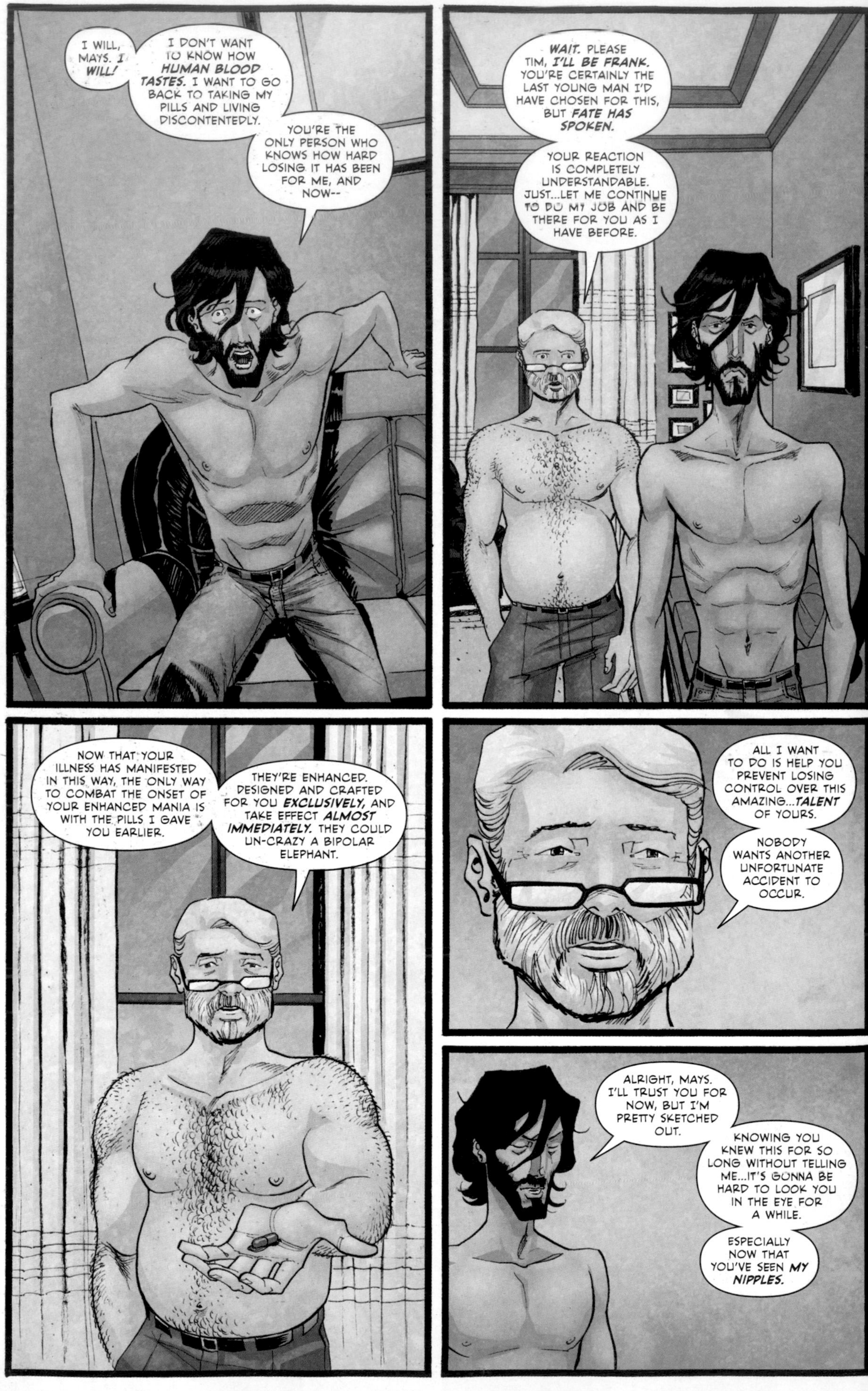
I WILL, MAYS. I WILL!
I DON'T WANT TO KNOW HOW HUMAN BLOOD TASTES. I WANT TO GO BACK TO TAKING MY PILLS AND LIVING DISCONTENTEDLY.
YOU'RE THE ONLY PERSON WHO KNOWS HOW HARD LOSING IT HAS BEEN FOR ME, AND NOW--
WAIT. PLEASE TIM, I'LL BE FRANK. YOU'RE CERTAINLY THE LAST YOUNG MAN I'D HAVE CHOSEN FOR THIS, BUT FATE HAS SPOKEN.
YOUR REACTION IS COMPLETELY UNDERSTANDABLE. JUST...LET ME CONTINUE TO DO MY JOB AND BE THERE FOR YOU AS I HAVE BEFORE.
NOW THAT YOUR ILLNESS HAS MANIFESTED IN THIS WAY, THE ONLY WAY TO COMBAT THE ONSET OF YOUR ENHANCED MANIA IS WITH THE PILLS I GAVE YOU EARLIER.
THEY'RE ENHANCED. DESIGNED AND CRAFTED FOR YOU EXCLUSIVELY, AND TAKE EFFECT ALMOST IMMEDIATELY. THEY COULD UN-CRAZY A BIPOLAR ELEPHANT.
ALL I WANT TO DO IS HELP YOU PREVENT LOSING CONTROL OVER THIS AMAZING...TALENT OF YOURS.
NOBODY WANTS ANOTHER UNFORTUNATE ACCIDENT TO OCCUR.
ALRIGHT, MAYS. I'LL TRUST YOU FOR NOW, BUT I'M PRETTY SKETCHED OUT.
KNOWING YOU KNEW THIS FOR SO LONG WITHOUT TELLING ME...IT'S GONNA BE HARD TO LOOK YOU IN THE EYE FOR A WHILE.
ESPECIALLY NOW THAT YOU'VE SEEN MY NIPPLES.

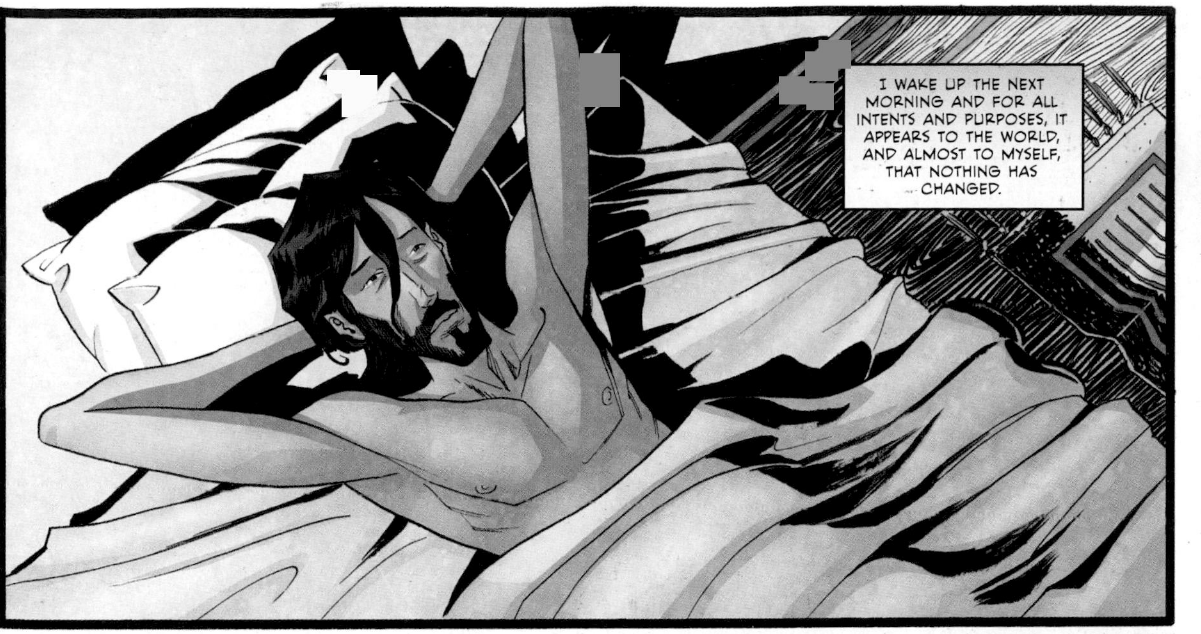
I WAKE UP THE NEXT MORNING AND FOR ALL INTENTS AND PURPOSES, IT APPEARS TO THE WORLD, AND ALMOST TO MYSELF, THAT NOTHING HAS CHANGED.

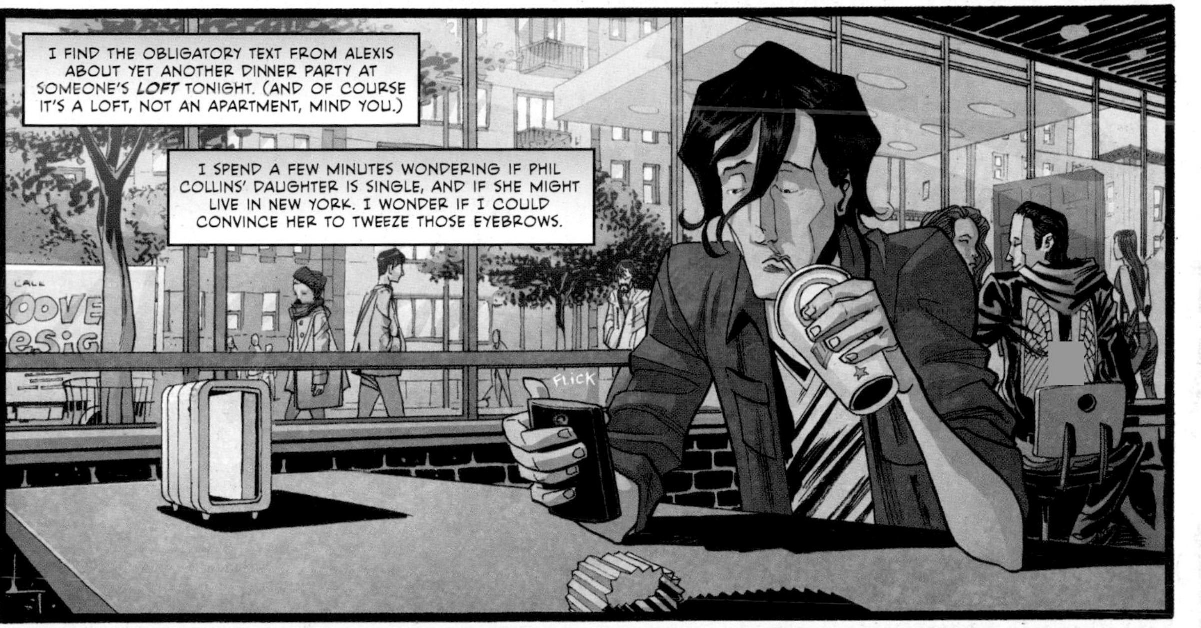
I FIND THE OBLIGATORY TEXT FROM ALEXIS ABOUT YET ANOTHER DINNER PARTY AT SOMEONE'S *LOFT* TONIGHT. (AND OF COURSE IT'S A LOFT, NOT AN APARTMENT, MIND YOU.)
I SPEND A FEW MINUTES WONDERING IF PHIL COLLINS' DAUGHTER IS SINGLE, AND IF SHE MIGHT LIVE IN NEW YORK. I WONDER IF I COULD CONVINCE HER TO TWEEZE THOSE EYEBROWS.
FLICK

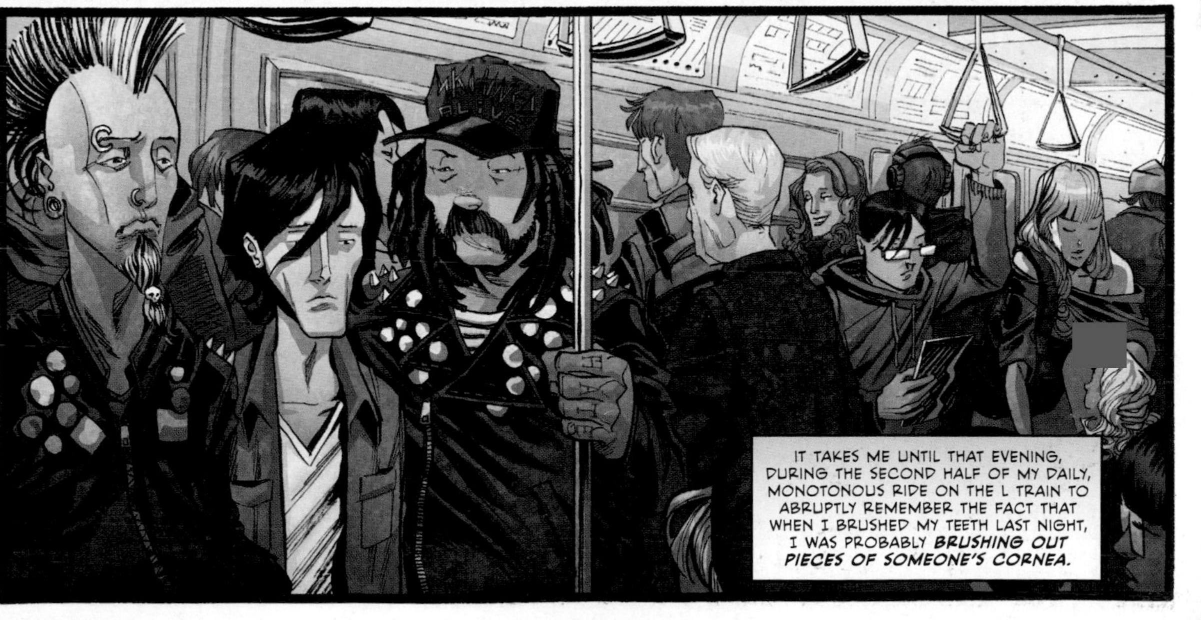
IT TAKES ME UNTIL THAT EVENING, DURING THE SECOND HALF OF MY DAILY, MONOTONOUS RIDE ON THE L TRAIN TO ABRUPTLY REMEMBER THE FACT THAT WHEN I BRUSHED MY TEETH LAST NIGHT, I WAS PROBABLY ***BRUSHING OUT PIECES OF SOMEONE'S CORNEA.***

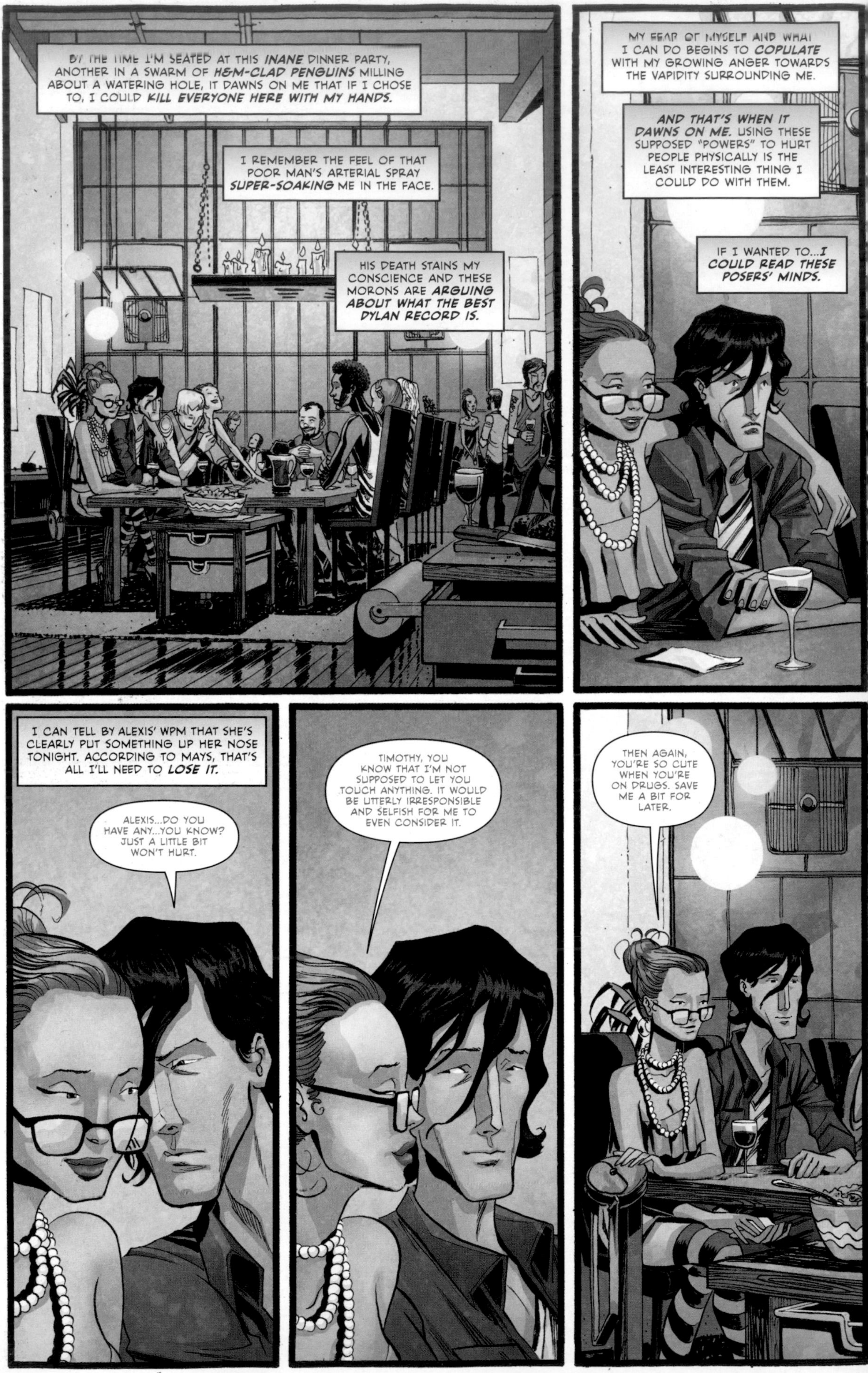
BY THE TIME I'M SEATED AT THIS INANE DINNER PARTY, ANOTHER IN A SWARM OF H&M-CLAD PENGUINS MILLING ABOUT A WATERING HOLE, IT DAWNS ON ME THAT IF I CHOSE TO, I COULD KILL EVERYONE HERE WITH MY HANDS.
I REMEMBER THE FEEL OF THAT POOR MAN'S ARTERIAL SPRAY SUPER-SOAKING ME IN THE FACE.
HIS DEATH STAINS MY CONSCIENCE AND THESE MORONS ARE ARGUING ABOUT WHAT THE BEST DYLAN RECORD IS.
MY FEAR OF MYSELF AND WHAT I CAN DO BEGINS TO COPULATE WITH MY GROWING ANGER TOWARDS THE VAPIDITY SURROUNDING ME.
AND THAT'S WHEN IT DAWNS ON ME. USING THESE SUPPOSED "POWERS" TO HURT PEOPLE PHYSICALLY IS THE LEAST INTERESTING THING I COULD DO WITH THEM.
IF I WANTED TO...I COULD READ THESE POSERS' MINDS.
I CAN TELL BY ALEXIS' WPM THAT SHE'S CLEARLY PUT SOMETHING UP HER NOSE TONIGHT. ACCORDING TO MAYS, THAT'S ALL I'LL NEED TO LOSE IT.
ALEXIS...DO YOU HAVE ANY...YOU KNOW? JUST A LITTLE BIT WON'T HURT.
TIMOTHY, YOU KNOW THAT I'M NOT SUPPOSED TO LET YOU TOUCH ANYTHING. IT WOULD BE UTTERLY IRRESPONSIBLE AND SELFISH FOR ME TO EVEN CONSIDER IT.
THEN AGAIN, YOU'RE SO CUTE WHEN YOU'RE ON DRUGS. SAVE ME A BIT FOR LATER.

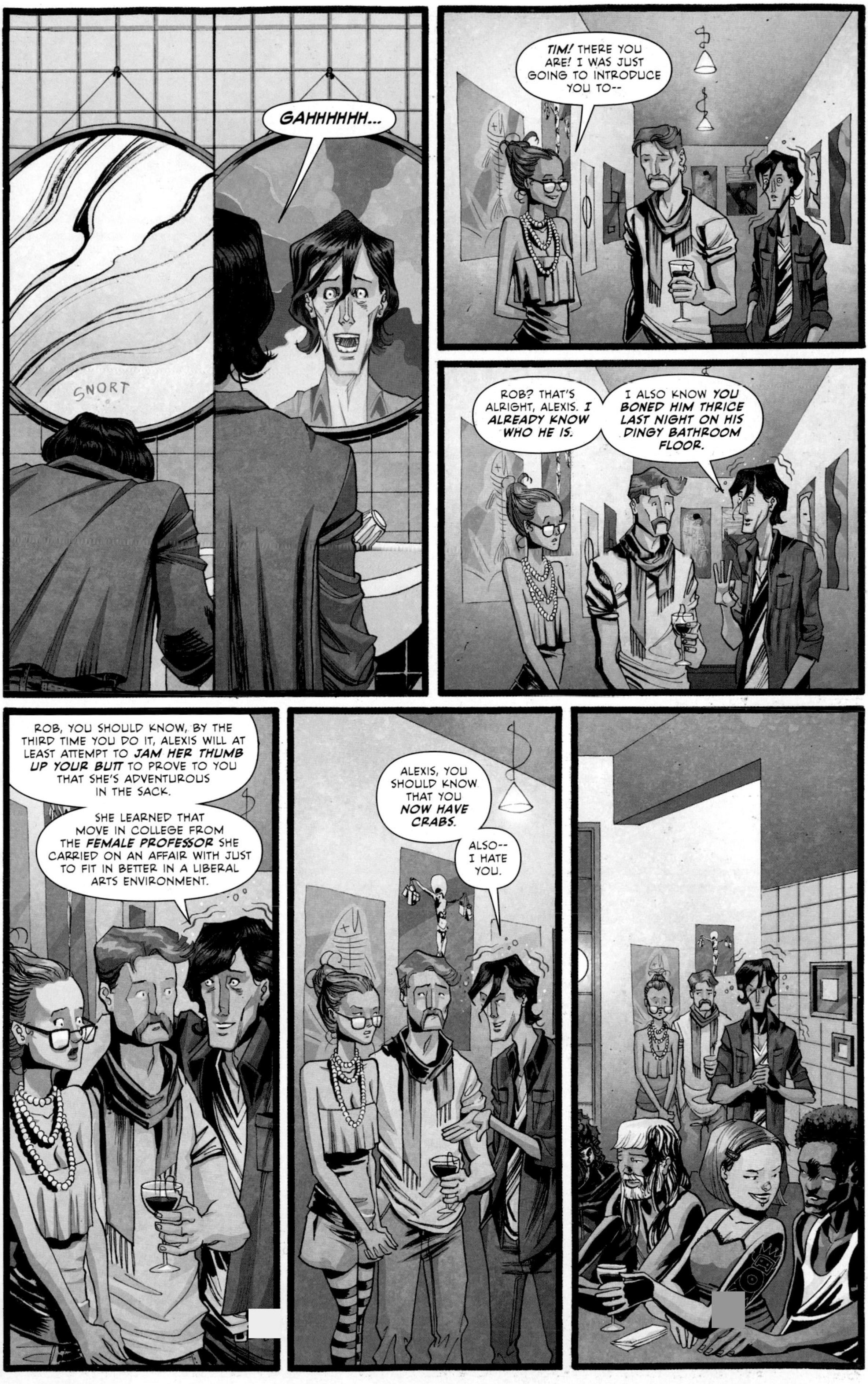
GAHHHHHH...
SNORT
TIM! THERE YOU ARE! I WAS JUST GOING TO INTRODUCE YOU TO--
ROB? THAT'S ALRIGHT, ALEXIS. I ALREADY KNOW WHO HE IS.
I ALSO KNOW YOU BONED HIM THRICE LAST NIGHT ON HIS DINGY BATHROOM FLOOR.
ROB, YOU SHOULD KNOW, BY THE THIRD TIME YOU DO IT, ALEXIS WILL AT LEAST ATTEMPT TO JAM HER THUMB UP YOUR BUTT TO PROVE TO YOU THAT SHE'S ADVENTUROUS IN THE SACK.
SHE LEARNED THAT MOVE IN COLLEGE FROM THE FEMALE PROFESSOR SHE CARRIED ON AN AFFAIR WITH JUST TO FIT IN BETTER IN A LIBERAL ARTS ENVIRONMENT.
ALEXIS, YOU SHOULD KNOW THAT YOU NOW HAVE CRABS.
ALSO-- I HATE YOU.

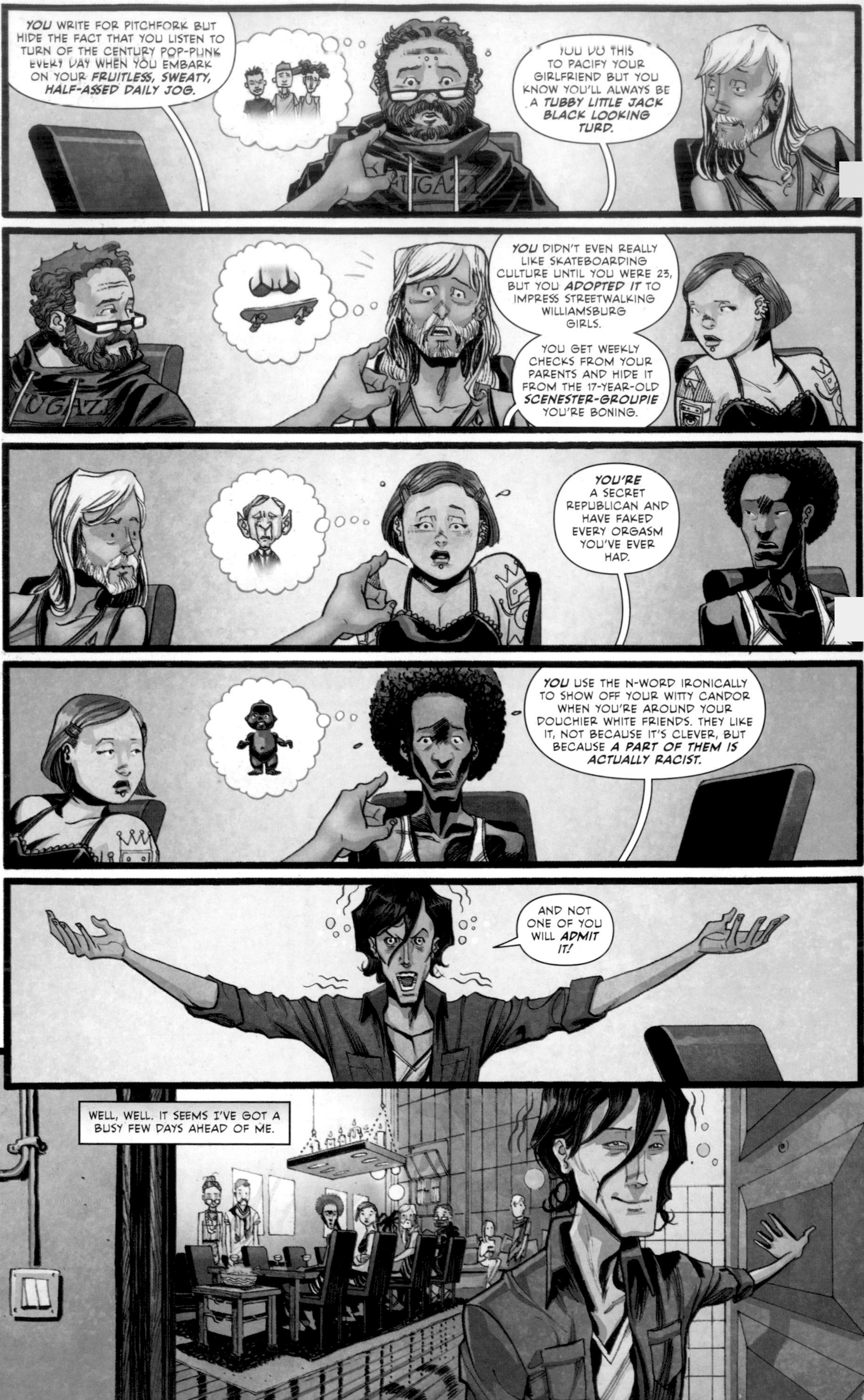

YOU WRITE FOR PITCHFORK BUT HIDE THE FACT THAT YOU LISTEN TO TURN OF THE CENTURY POP-PUNK EVERY DAY WHEN YOU EMBARK ON YOUR FRUITLESS, SWEATY, HALF-ASSED DAILY JOG.
YOU DO THIS TO PACIFY YOUR GIRLFRIEND BUT YOU KNOW YOU'LL ALWAYS BE A TUBBY LITTLE JACK BLACK LOOKING TURD.
FUGAZI
YOU DIDN'T EVEN REALLY LIKE SKATEBOARDING CULTURE UNTIL YOU WERE 23, BUT YOU ADOPTED IT TO IMPRESS STREETWALKING WILLIAMSBURG GIRLS.
YOU GET WEEKLY CHECKS FROM YOUR PARENTS AND HIDE IT FROM THE 17-YEAR-OLD SCENESTER-GROUPIE YOU'RE BONING.
YOU'RE A SECRET REPUBLICAN AND HAVE FAKED EVERY ORGASM YOU'VE EVER HAD.
YOU USE THE N-WORD IRONICALLY TO SHOW OFF YOUR WITTY CANDOR WHEN YOU'RE AROUND YOUR DOUCHIER WHITE FRIENDS. THEY LIKE IT, NOT BECAUSE IT'S CLEVER, BUT BECAUSE A PART OF THEM IS ACTUALLY RACIST.
AND NOT ONE OF YOU WILL ADMIT IT!
WELL, WELL. IT SEEMS I'VE GOT A BUSY FEW DAYS AHEAD OF ME.

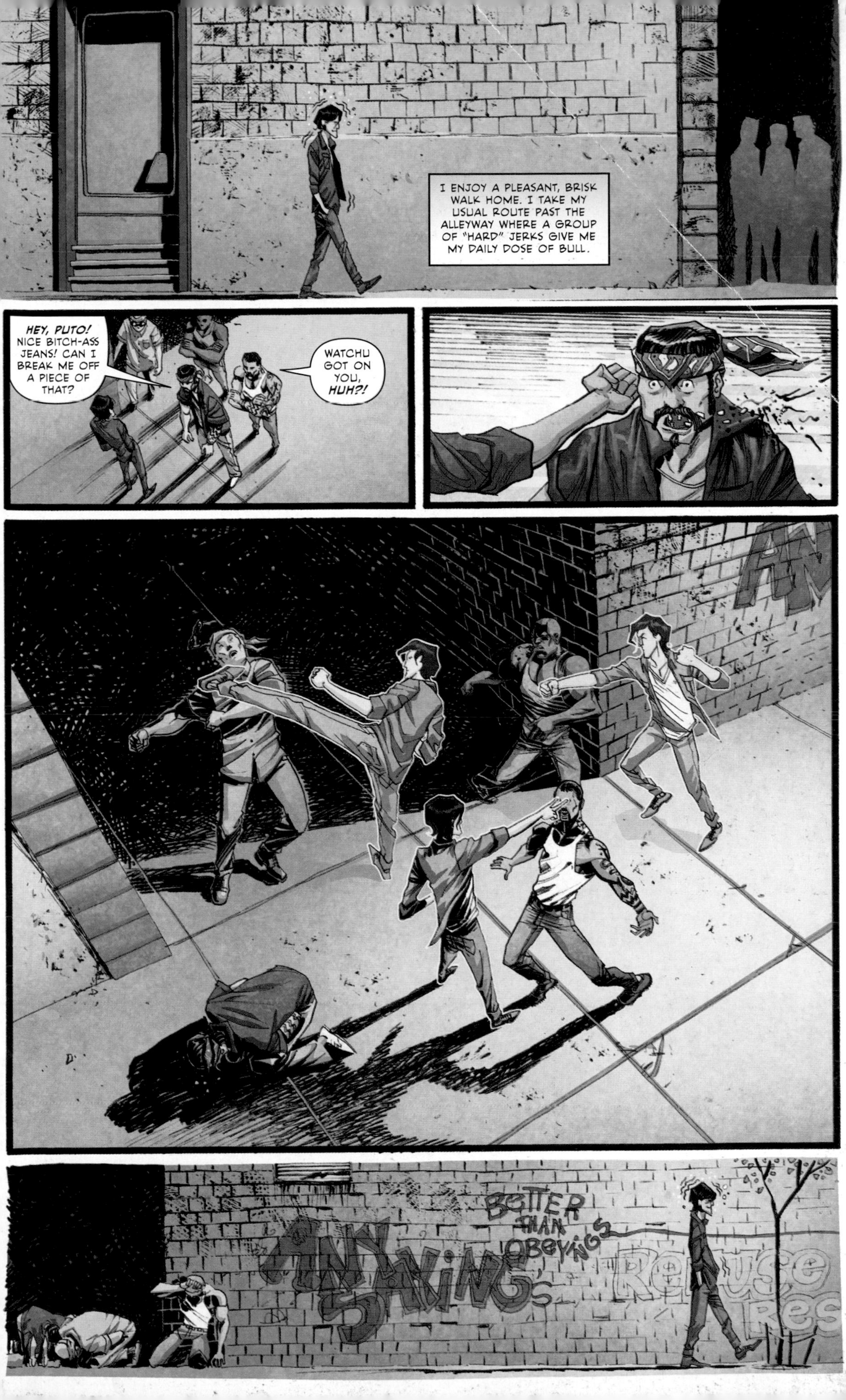

I ENJOY A PLEASANT, BRISK WALK HOME. I TAKE MY USUAL ROUTE PAST THE ALLEYWAY WHERE A GROUP OF "HARD" JERKS GIVE ME MY DAILY DOSE OF BULL.
HEY, PUTO! NICE BITCH-ASS JEANS! CAN I BREAK ME OFF A PIECE OF THAT?
WATCHU GOT ON YOU, *HUH?!*

I TAKE MAYS' PINK "SUPER-PILLS" THAT NIGHT AND BY THE NEXT DAY I'M FEELING AS SUBDUED AND INCOMPETENT AS EVER. TRYING TO PAINT IS ABOUT AS FUN AS WATCHING COMPETITIVE GOLF.

HMMMM.

AHH, SCREW IT.

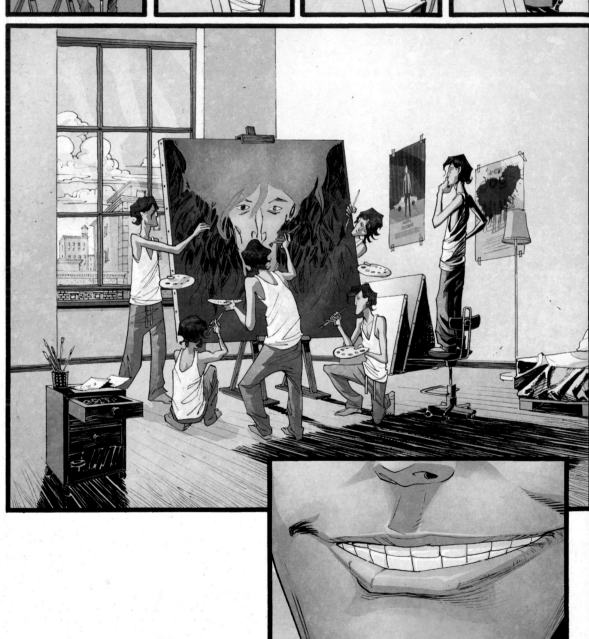

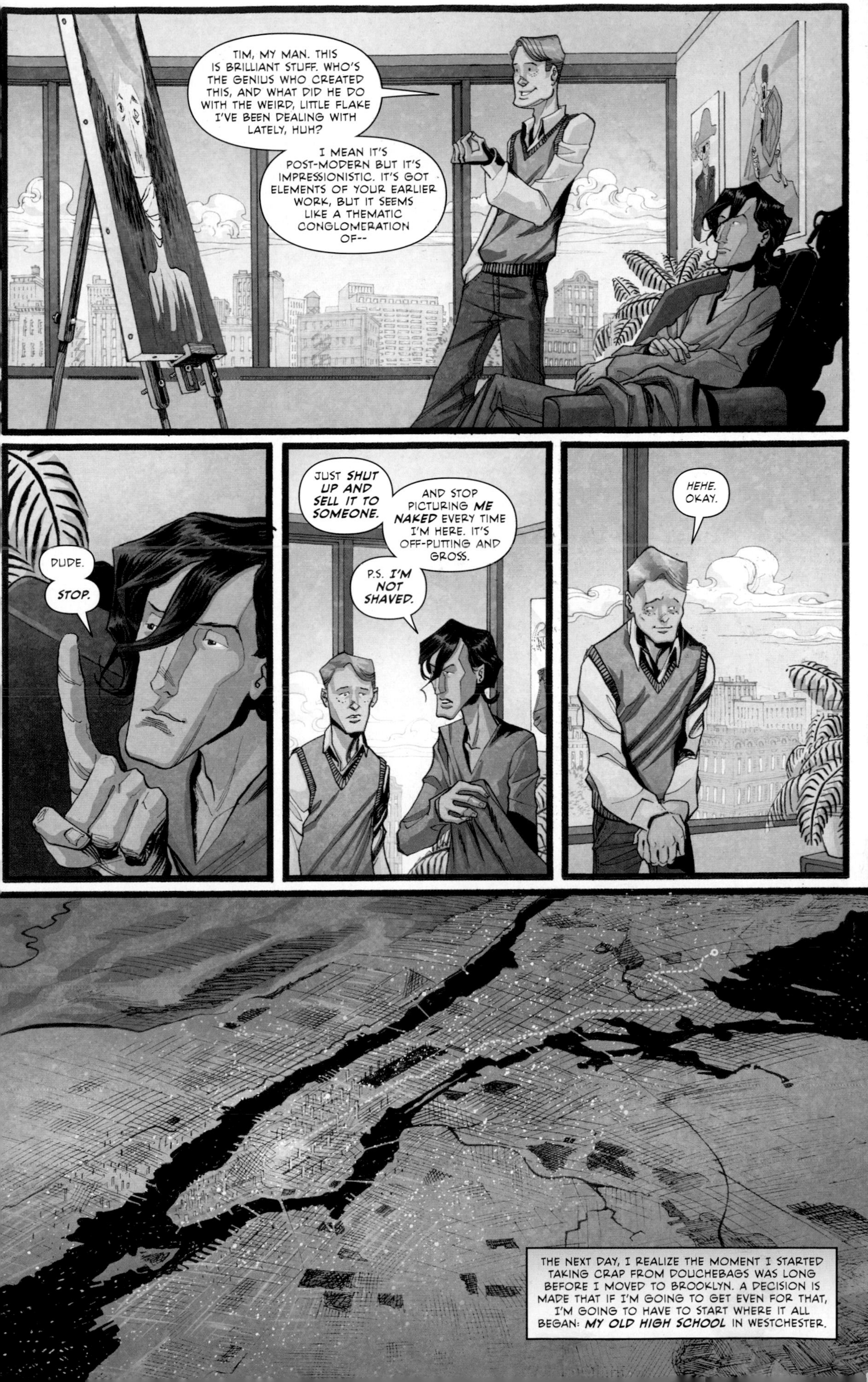
TIM, MY MAN. THIS IS BRILLIANT STUFF. WHO'S THE GENIUS WHO CREATED THIS, AND WHAT DID HE DO WITH THE WEIRD, LITTLE FLAKE I'VE BEEN DEALING WITH LATELY, HUH?
I MEAN IT'S POST-MODERN BUT IT'S IMPRESSIONISTIC. IT'S GOT ELEMENTS OF YOUR EARLIER WORK, BUT IT SEEMS LIKE A THEMATIC CONGLOMERATION OF--
DUDE.
STOP.
JUST SHUT UP AND SELL IT TO SOMEONE.
AND STOP PICTURING ME NAKED EVERY TIME I'M HERE. IT'S OFF-PUTTING AND GROSS.
P.S. I'M NOT SHAVED.
HEHE. OKAY.
THE NEXT DAY, I REALIZE THE MOMENT I STARTED TAKING CRAP FROM DOUCHEBAGS WAS LONG BEFORE I MOVED TO BROOKLYN. A DECISION IS MADE THAT IF I'M GOING TO GET EVEN FOR THAT, I'M GOING TO HAVE TO START WHERE IT ALL BEGAN: MY OLD HIGH SCHOOL IN WESTCHESTER.

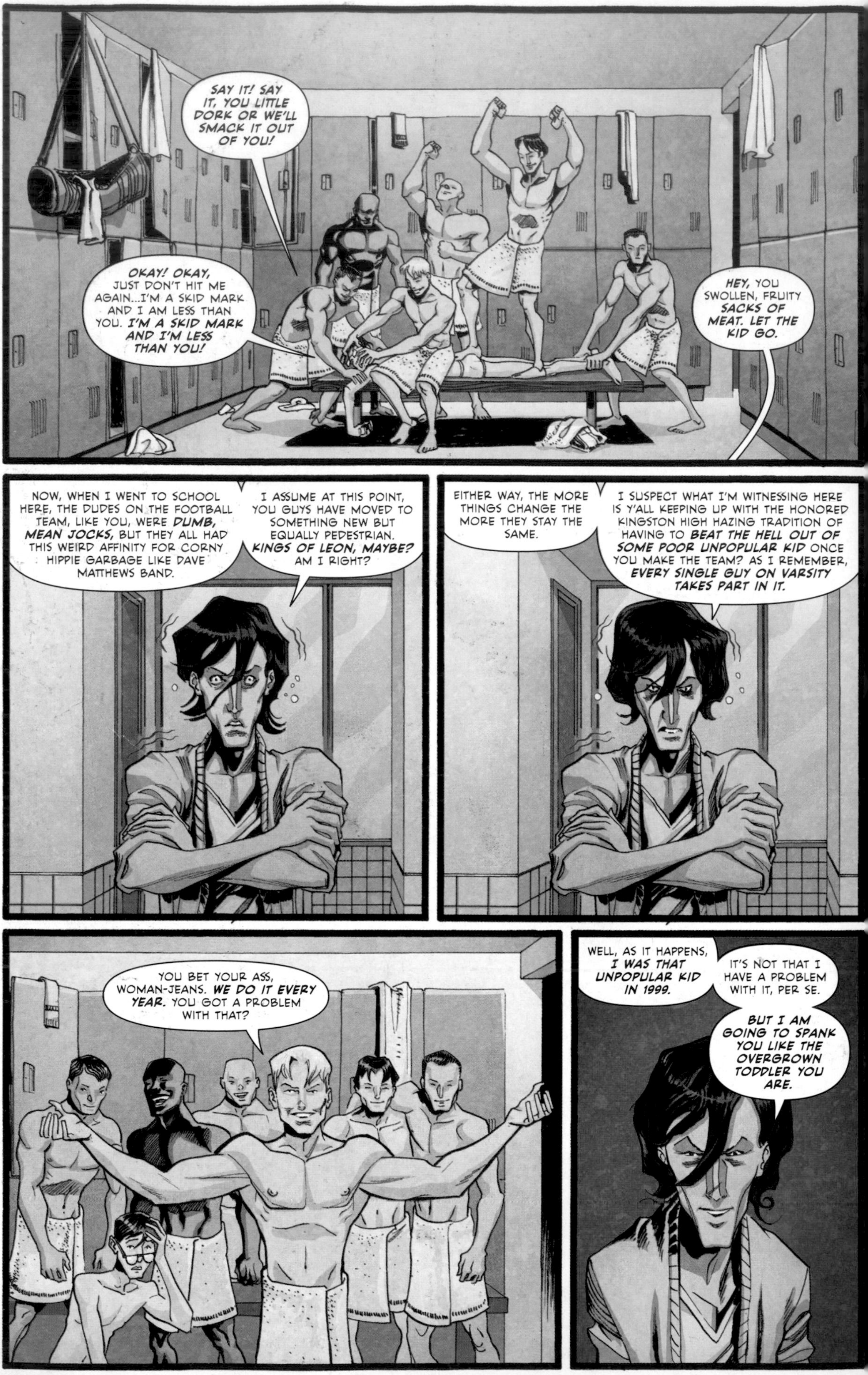
SAY IT! SAY IT, YOU LITTLE DORK OR WE'LL SMACK IT OUT OF YOU!
OKAY! OKAY, JUST DON'T HIT ME AGAIN...I'M A SKID MARK AND I AM LESS THAN YOU. I'M A SKID MARK AND I'M LESS THAN YOU!
HEY, YOU SWOLLEN, FRUITY SACKS OF MEAT. LET THE KID GO.
NOW, WHEN I WENT TO SCHOOL HERE, THE DUDES ON THE FOOTBALL TEAM, LIKE YOU, WERE DUMB, MEAN JOCKS, BUT THEY ALL HAD THIS WEIRD AFFINITY FOR CORNY HIPPIE GARBAGE LIKE DAVE MATTHEWS BAND.
I ASSUME AT THIS POINT, YOU GUYS HAVE MOVED TO SOMETHING NEW BUT EQUALLY PEDESTRIAN. KINGS OF LEON, MAYBE? AM I RIGHT?
EITHER WAY, THE MORE THINGS CHANGE THE MORE THEY STAY THE SAME.
I SUSPECT WHAT I'M WITNESSING HERE IS Y'ALL KEEPING UP WITH THE HONORED KINGSTON HIGH HAZING TRADITION OF HAVING TO BEAT THE HELL OUT OF SOME POOR UNPOPULAR KID ONCE YOU MAKE THE TEAM? AS I REMEMBER, EVERY SINGLE GUY ON VARSITY TAKES PART IN IT.
YOU BET YOUR ASS, WOMAN-JEANS. WE DO IT EVERY YEAR. YOU GOT A PROBLEM WITH THAT?
WELL, AS IT HAPPENS, I WAS THAT UNPOPULAR KID IN 1999.
IT'S NOT THAT I HAVE A PROBLEM WITH IT, PER SE.
BUT I AM GOING TO SPANK YOU LIKE THE OVERGROWN TODDLER YOU ARE.

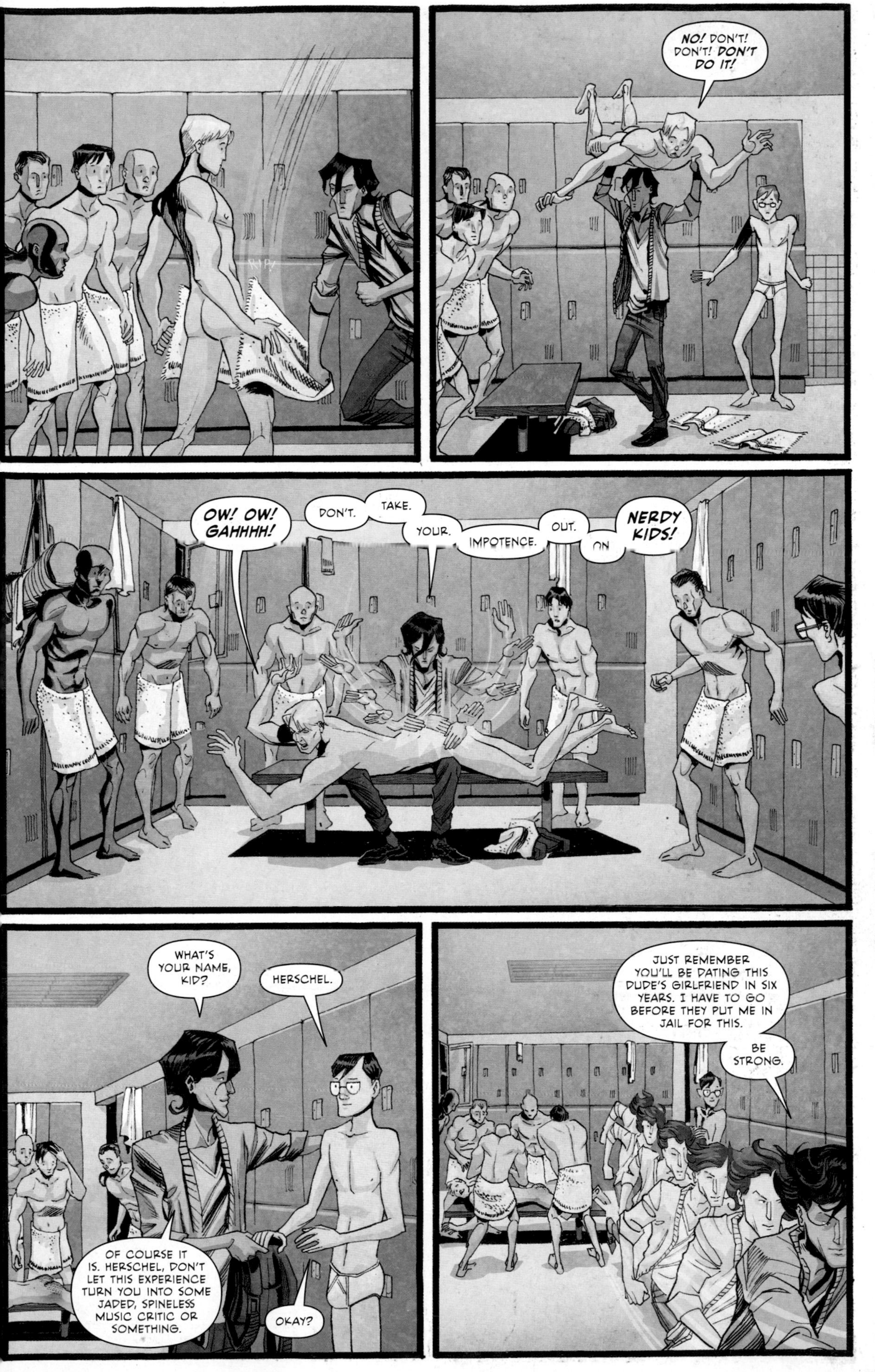
NO! DON'T! DON'T! DON'T DO IT!
OW! OW! GAHHHH!
DON'T.
TAKE.
YOUR.
IMPOTENCE.
OUT.
ON
NERDY KIDS!
WHAT'S YOUR NAME, KID?
HERSCHEL.
OF COURSE IT IS. HERSCHEL, DON'T LET THIS EXPERIENCE TURN YOU INTO SOME JADED, SPINELESS MUSIC CRITIC OR SOMETHING.
OKAY?
JUST REMEMBER YOU'LL BE DATING THIS DUDE'S GIRLFRIEND IN SIX YEARS. I HAVE TO GO BEFORE THEY PUT ME IN JAIL FOR THIS.
BE STRONG.

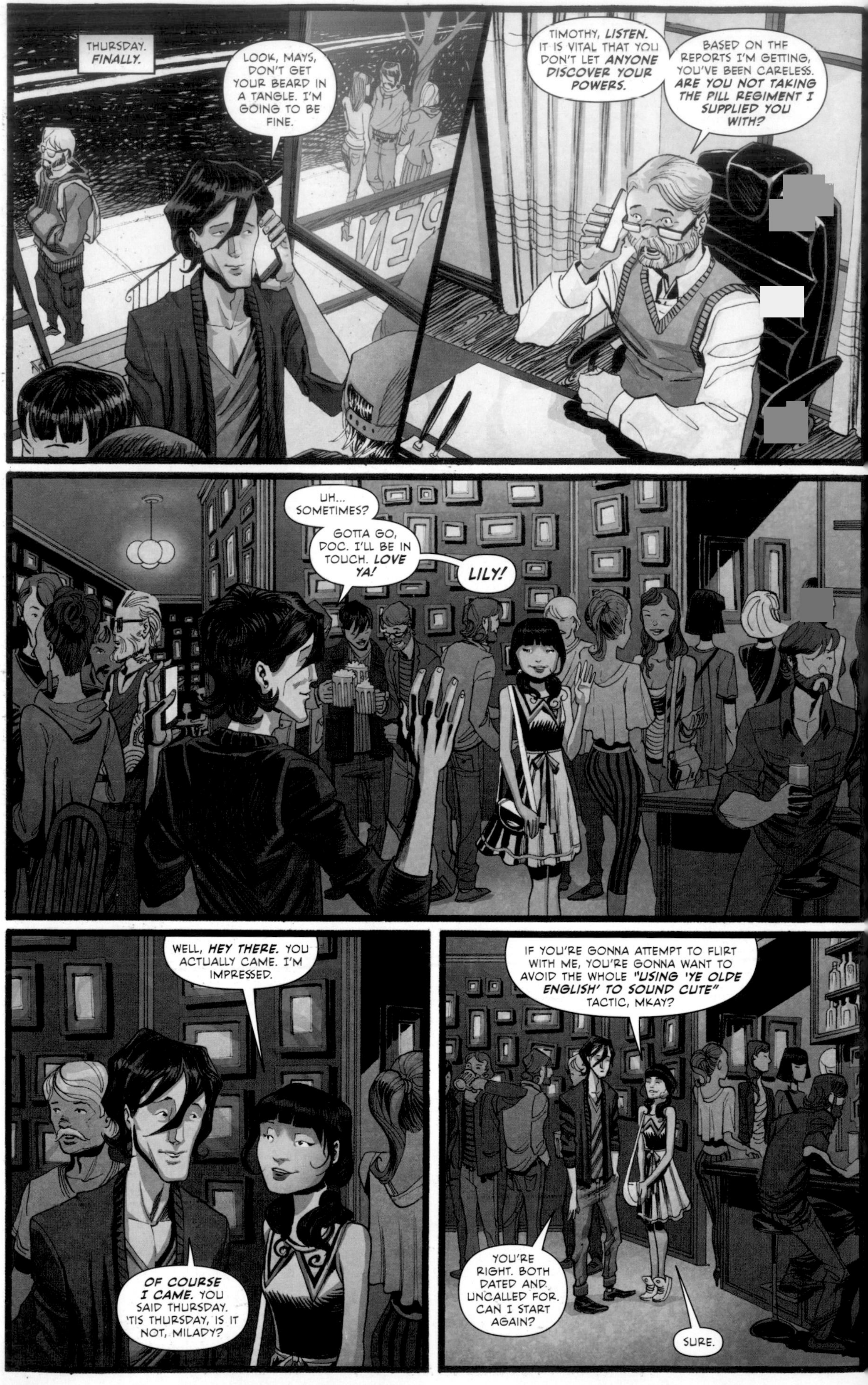
THURSDAY. FINALLY.
LOOK, MAYS, DON'T GET YOUR BEARD IN A TANGLE. I'M GOING TO BE FINE.
TIMOTHY, LISTEN. IT IS VITAL THAT YOU DON'T LET ANYONE DISCOVER YOUR POWERS.
BASED ON THE REPORTS I'M GETTING, YOU'VE BEEN CARELESS. ARE YOU NOT TAKING THE PILL REGIMENT I SUPPLIED YOU WITH?
UH... SOMETIMES?
GOTTA GO, DOC. I'LL BE IN TOUCH. LOVE YA!
LILY!
WELL, HEY THERE. YOU ACTUALLY CAME. I'M IMPRESSED.
OF COURSE I CAME. YOU SAID THURSDAY. 'TIS THURSDAY, IS IT NOT, MILADY?
IF YOU'RE GONNA ATTEMPT TO FLIRT WITH ME, YOU'RE GONNA WANT TO AVOID THE WHOLE "USING 'YE OLDE ENGLISH' TO SOUND CUTE" TACTIC, MKAY?
YOU'RE RIGHT. BOTH DATED AND UNCALLED FOR. CAN I START AGAIN?
SURE.

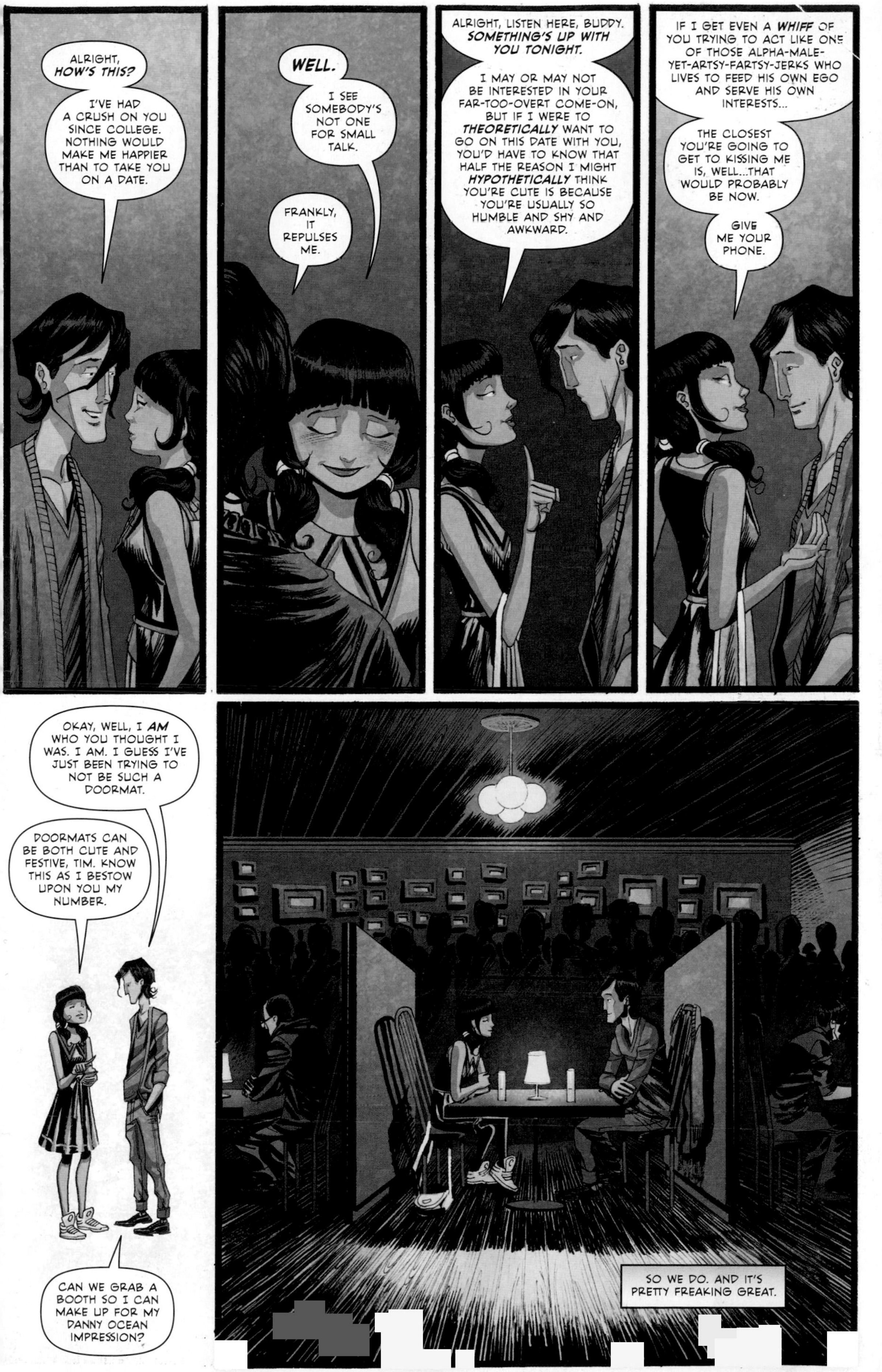
ALRIGHT, HOW'S THIS?
I'VE HAD A CRUSH ON YOU SINCE COLLEGE. NOTHING WOULD MAKE ME HAPPIER THAN TO TAKE YOU ON A DATE.
WELL.
I SEE SOMEBODY'S NOT ONE FOR SMALL TALK.
FRANKLY, IT REPULSES ME.
ALRIGHT, LISTEN HERE, BUDDY. SOMETHING'S UP WITH YOU TONIGHT.
I MAY OR MAY NOT BE INTERESTED IN YOUR FAR-TOO-OVERT COME-ON, BUT IF I WERE TO THEORETICALLY WANT TO GO ON THIS DATE WITH YOU, YOU'D HAVE TO KNOW THAT HALF THE REASON I MIGHT HYPOTHETICALLY THINK YOU'RE CUTE IS BECAUSE YOU'RE USUALLY SO HUMBLE AND SHY AND AWKWARD.
IF I GET EVEN A WHIFF OF YOU TRYING TO ACT LIKE ONE OF THOSE ALPHA-MALE-YET-ARTSY-FARTSY-JERKS WHO LIVES TO FEED HIS OWN EGO AND SERVE HIS OWN INTERESTS...
THE CLOSEST YOU'RE GOING TO GET TO KISSING ME IS, WELL...THAT WOULD PROBABLY BE NOW.
GIVE ME YOUR PHONE.
OKAY, WELL, I AM WHO YOU THOUGHT I WAS. I AM. I GUESS I'VE JUST BEEN TRYING TO NOT BE SUCH A DOORMAT.
DOORMATS CAN BE BOTH CUTE AND FESTIVE, TIM. KNOW THIS AS I BESTOW UPON YOU MY NUMBER.
CAN WE GRAB A BOOTH SO I CAN MAKE UP FOR MY DANNY OCEAN IMPRESSION?
SO WE DO. AND IT'S PRETTY FREAKING GREAT.

TALKING TO LILY AND GETTING A COUPLE PINK SUPER-PILLS IN ME GIVES ME PAUSE TO THINK ABOUT THESE PAST FEW DAYS, AND THE VERY WEIGHT OF IT HITS ME LIKE A PIANO FALLING OUT OF THE SKY.

WHETHER IT WAS SELF-DEFENSE OR NOT, *I TOOK A LIFE.* I HAVE TO MAKE AMENDS FOR THAT SOMEHOW.

IT'S NOT ENOUGH TO JUST PREVENT IT FROM HAPPENING AGAIN, EVEN WHEN MY ABILITIES *VERGE ON THE INFINITE.*

I ADMIT IT, I'VE BEEN ACTING LIKE A CRAZY JERK.

DESTINY PLACES THIS IMMENSE POWER IN MY LAP, AND I DO WHAT ANY OF THESE MORONIC SCENESTERS I HATE WOULD DO: USE IT TO OVERCOMPENSATE FOR FEELING LESS THAN EVERYONE.

THE ONLY THING THAT MAKES ME NOT LIKE THEM IS THAT PART OF ME, HOWEVER MINISCULE AND RESTRAINED, WANTS TO MAKE THIS WORLD A BETTER PLACE. PART OF ME ACTUALLY *CARES THAT IT SUCKS.*

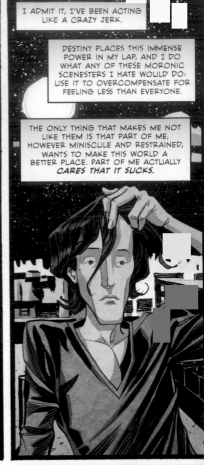

SUDDENLY, I REALIZE I'M SITTING PENSIVELY ON THE EDGE OF A TALL BUILDING, OVERLOOKING THE CITY AND PONDERING LIFE.

ONLY TWO TYPES OF PEOPLE DO THIS.

SUICIDE CASES...

...AND SUPERHEROES.

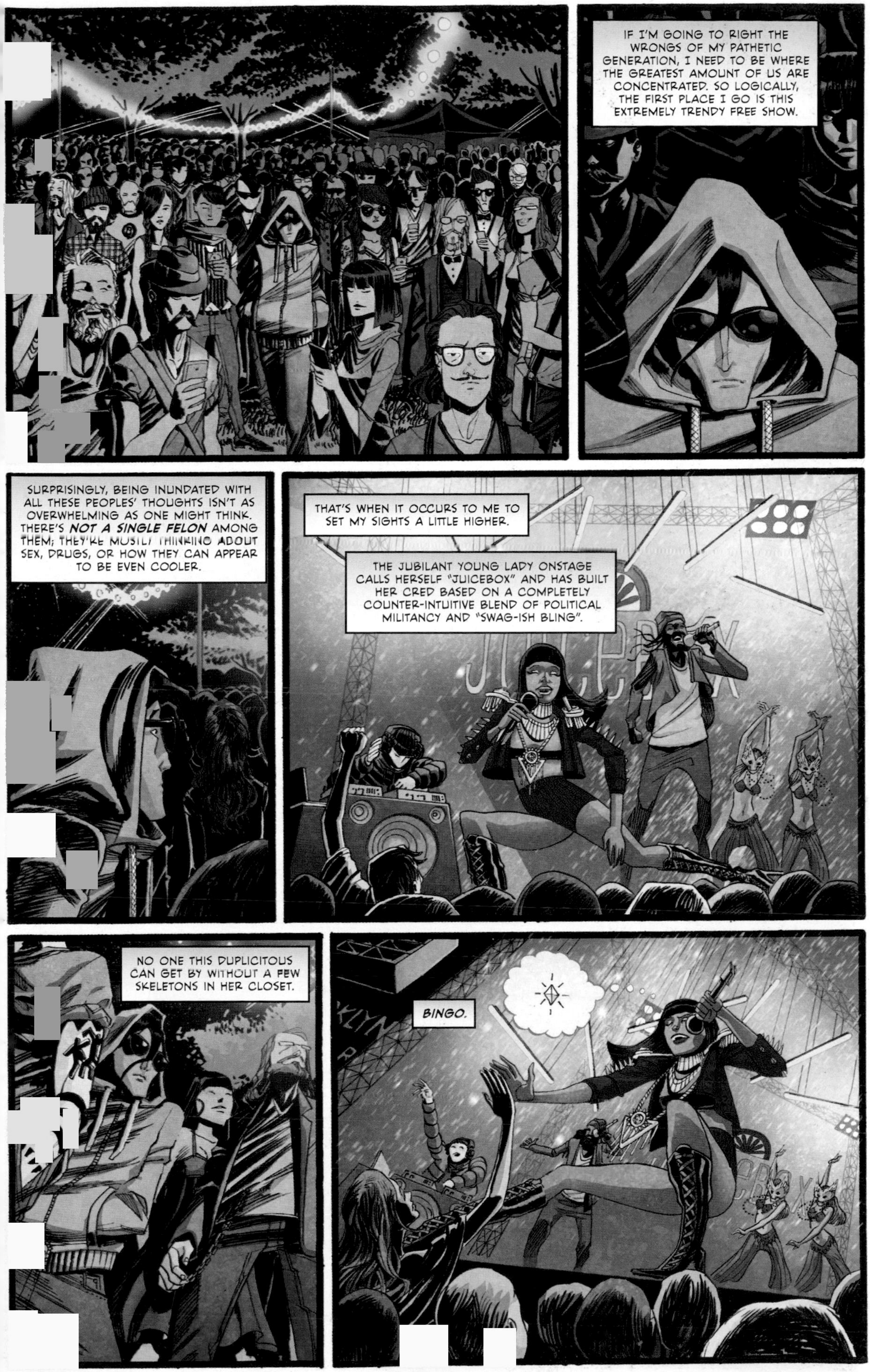
IF I'M GOING TO RIGHT THE WRONGS OF MY PATHETIC GENERATION, I NEED TO BE WHERE THE GREATEST AMOUNT OF US ARE CONCENTRATED. SO LOGICALLY, THE FIRST PLACE I GO IS THIS EXTREMELY TRENDY FREE SHOW.
SURPRISINGLY, BEING INUNDATED WITH ALL THESE PEOPLES' THOUGHTS ISN'T AS OVERWHELMING AS ONE MIGHT THINK. THERE'S ***NOT A SINGLE FELON*** AMONG THEM; THEY'RE MOSTLY THINKING ABOUT SEX, DRUGS, OR HOW THEY CAN APPEAR TO BE EVEN COOLER.
THAT'S WHEN IT OCCURS TO ME TO SET MY SIGHTS A LITTLE HIGHER.
THE JUBILANT YOUNG LADY ONSTAGE CALLS HERSELF "JUICEBOX" AND HAS BUILT HER CRED BASED ON A COMPLETELY COUNTER-INTUITIVE BLEND OF POLITICAL MILITANCY AND "SWAG-ISH BLING".
NO ONE THIS DUPLICITOUS CAN GET BY WITHOUT A FEW SKELETONS IN HER CLOSET.
BINGO.

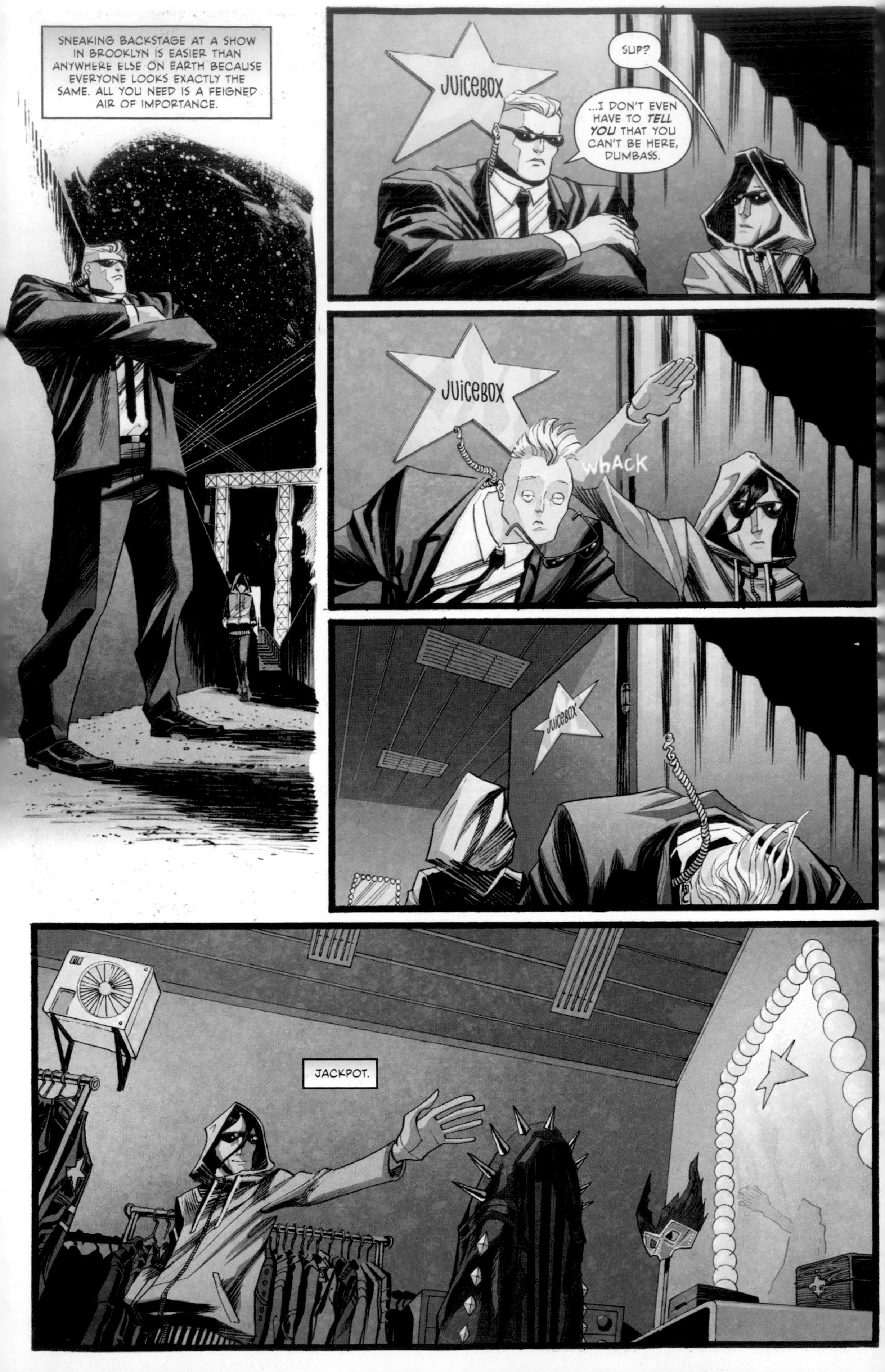
SNEAKING BACKSTAGE AT A SHOW IN BROOKLYN IS EASIER THAN ANYWHERE ELSE ON EARTH BECAUSE EVERYONE LOOKS EXACTLY THE SAME. ALL YOU NEED IS A FEIGNED AIR OF IMPORTANCE.
JUICEBOX
SUP?
...I DON'T EVEN HAVE TO TELL YOU THAT YOU CAN'T BE HERE, DUMBASS.
JUICEBOX
WHACK
JUICEBOX
JACKPOT.

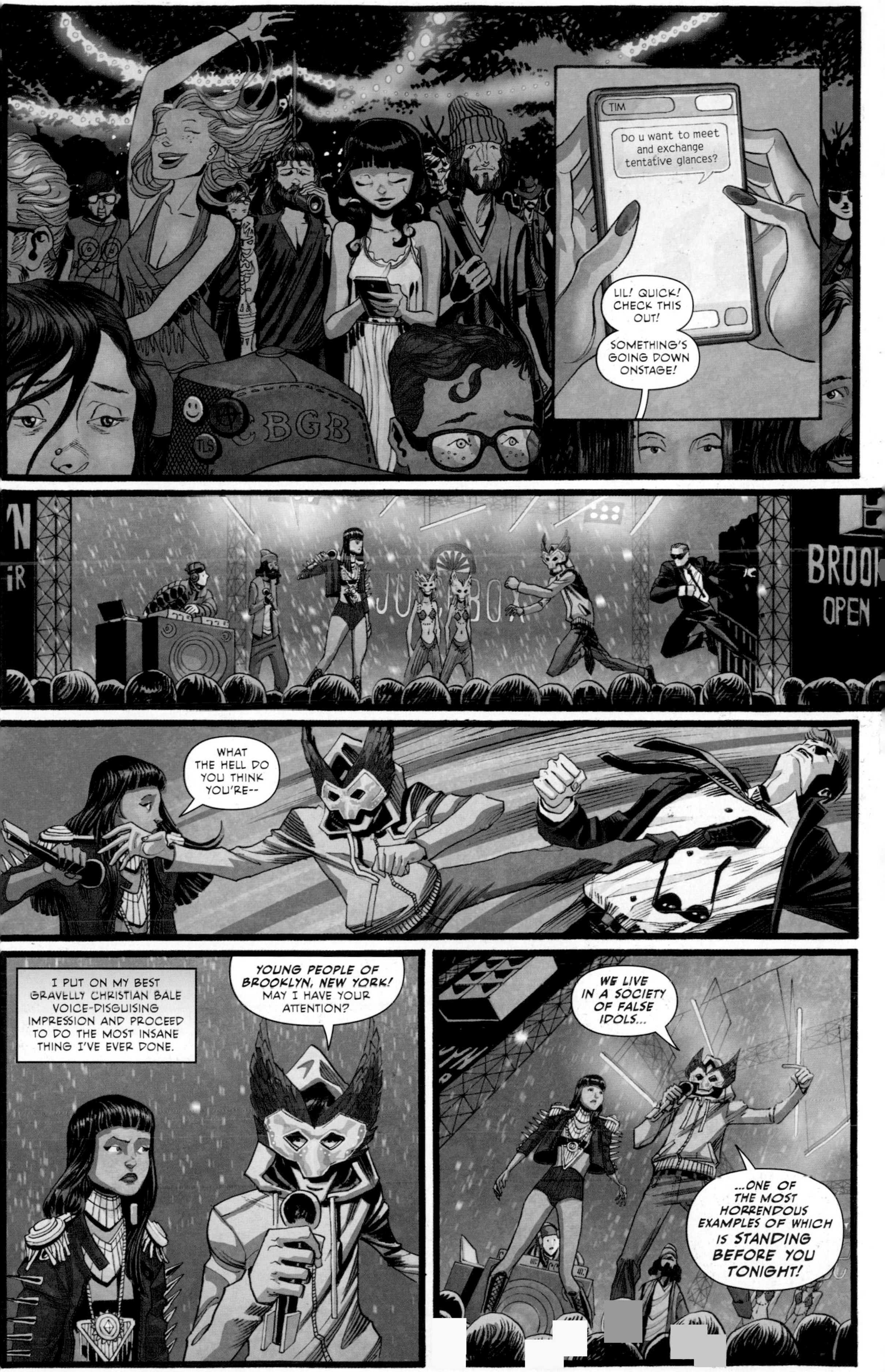
TIM
Do u want to meet and exchange tentative glances?
LIL! QUICK! CHECK THIS OUT!
SOMETHING'S GOING DOWN ONSTAGE!
CBGB
TLS
OPEN
WHAT THE HELL DO YOU THINK YOU'RE--
I PUT ON MY BEST GRAVELLY CHRISTIAN BALE VOICE-DISGUISING IMPRESSION AND PROCEED TO DO THE MOST INSANE THING I'VE EVER DONE.
YOUNG PEOPLE OF BROOKLYN, NEW YORK! MAY I HAVE YOUR ATTENTION?
WE LIVE IN A SOCIETY OF FALSE IDOLS...
...ONE OF THE MOST HORRENDOUS EXAMPLES OF WHICH IS STANDING BEFORE YOU TONIGHT!

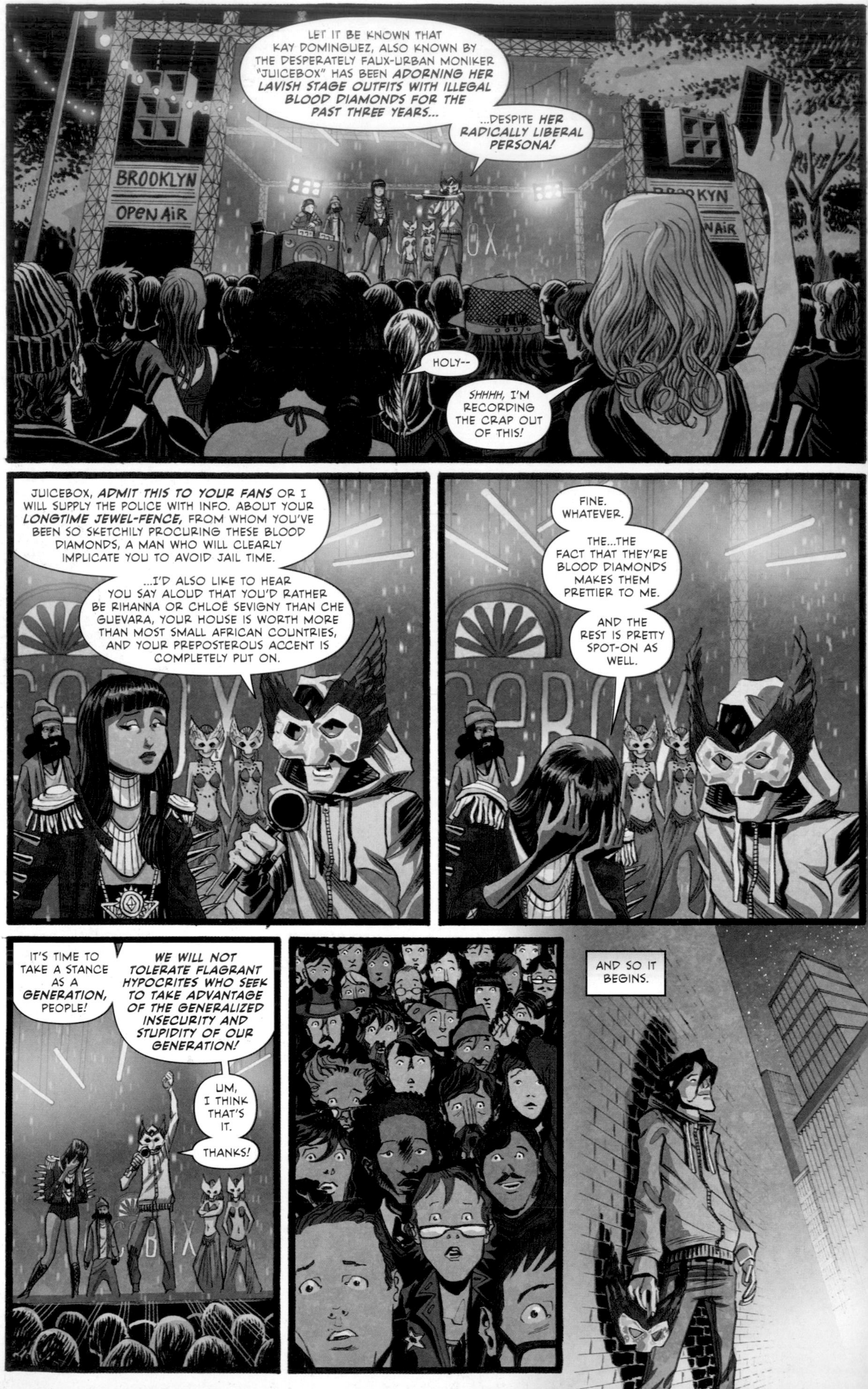
LET IT BE KNOWN THAT KAY DOMINGUEZ, ALSO KNOWN BY THE DESPERATELY FAUX-URBAN MONIKER "JUICEBOX" HAS BEEN ADORNING HER LAVISH STAGE OUTFITS WITH ILLEGAL BLOOD DIAMONDS FOR THE PAST THREE YEARS...
...DESPITE HER RADICALLY LIBERAL PERSONA!
BROOKLYN OPEN AIR
HOLY--
SHHHH, I'M RECORDING THE CRAP OUT OF THIS!
JUICEBOX, ADMIT THIS TO YOUR FANS OR I WILL SUPPLY THE POLICE WITH INFO. ABOUT YOUR LONGTIME JEWEL-FENCE, FROM WHOM YOU'VE BEEN SO SKETCHILY PROCURING THESE BLOOD DIAMONDS, A MAN WHO WILL CLEARLY IMPLICATE YOU TO AVOID JAIL TIME.
...I'D ALSO LIKE TO HEAR YOU SAY ALOUD THAT YOU'D RATHER BE RIHANNA OR CHLOË SEVIGNY THAN CHE GUEVARA, YOUR HOUSE IS WORTH MORE THAN MOST SMALL AFRICAN COUNTRIES, AND YOUR PREPOSTEROUS ACCENT IS COMPLETELY PUT ON.
FINE. WHATEVER.
THE...THE FACT THAT THEY'RE BLOOD DIAMONDS MAKES THEM PRETTIER TO ME.
AND THE REST IS PRETTY SPOT-ON AS WELL.
IT'S TIME TO TAKE A STANCE AS A GENERATION, PEOPLE!
WE WILL NOT TOLERATE FLAGRANT HYPOCRITES WHO SEEK TO TAKE ADVANTAGE OF THE GENERALIZED INSECURITY AND STUPIDITY OF OUR GENERATION!
UM, I THINK THAT'S IT.
THANKS!
AND SO IT BEGINS.

"MY BEST DAY"

MY BEST DAY I SECRETE THE TRUTH IN PINTS
TO BE FLUNG IN THE FACES OF THOSE I DISLIKE
I TELL THEM THEY'RE FAKE, THEY DESERVE PAIN

LUCIFER OUTDONE I'VE BESTED GOD
NO LONGER MEEK, NO FOOLISH FRAUD
I'M A HERO TO SOME AND A THREAT TO THE REST

MY BEST DAY

MY BEST DAY IT SWELLS WITH SWEET REVENGE
EVERY WASTED, USELESS MOMENT SPENT
ADDS UP TO A SUM, I CAN SPEND IN THE SUN

MY GREATEST FLAW IS MY SUPERHUMAN STRENGTH
FOUND A PATH TO WHERE JESUS AND LENNON WENT
HYPOCRISY ENDS AT THE EDGE OF MY BLADE

MY BEST DAY

SO I GUESS I'M NOT
JUST A WASTED YOUTH
A TWENTY SOMETHING FAILED PURSUIT

I'M A STAN LEE CREATION
I'M DIVINE VISITATION

AND THEY'LL ALL CRANE THEIR NECKS TO SWAY
TO THE BEAT OF MY BEST DAY

MY BEST DAY

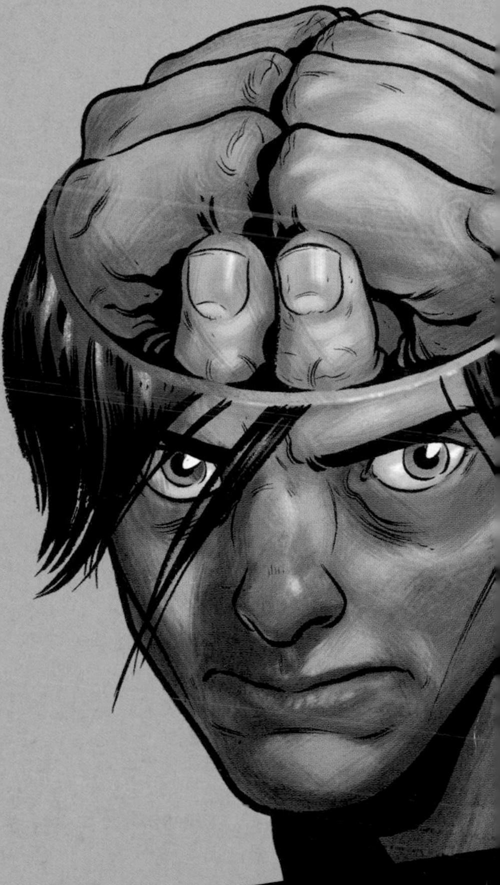

"I'M OFF THE DEEP END."

CHAPTER

3

WINTER. 1970.

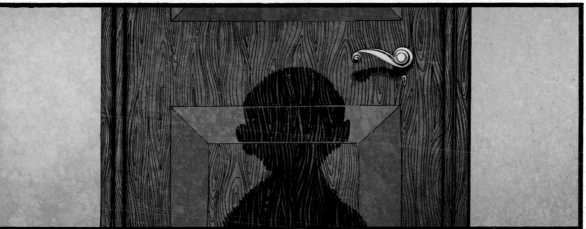

MOMMY? ARE YOU...*ARE YOU OKAY?*

SO YOU'VE COME FOR ME.

I KNEW YOU WOULD.

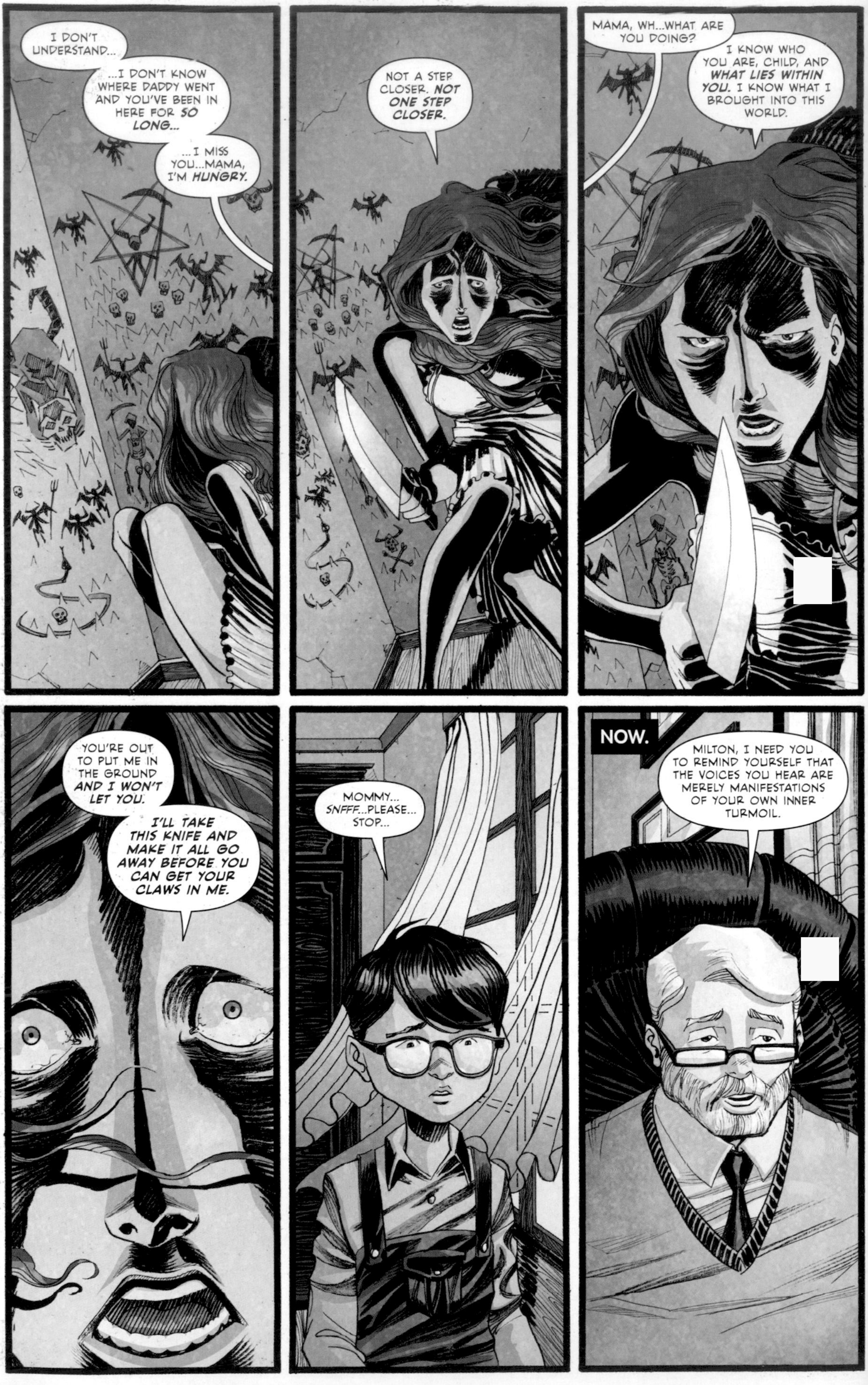
I DON'T UNDERSTAND...
...I DON'T KNOW WHERE DADDY WENT AND YOU'VE BEEN IN HERE FOR SO LONG...
...I MISS YOU...MAMA, I'M HUNGRY.
NOT A STEP CLOSER. NOT ONE STEP CLOSER.
MAMA, WH...WHAT ARE YOU DOING?
I KNOW WHO YOU ARE, CHILD, AND WHAT LIES WITHIN YOU. I KNOW WHAT I BROUGHT INTO THIS WORLD.
YOU'RE OUT TO PUT ME IN THE GROUND AND I WON'T LET YOU.
I'LL TAKE THIS KNIFE AND MAKE IT ALL GO AWAY BEFORE YOU CAN GET YOUR CLAWS IN ME.
MOMMY... SNFFF...PLEASE... STOP...
NOW.
MILTON, I NEED YOU TO REMIND YOURSELF THAT THE VOICES YOU HEAR ARE MERELY MANIFESTATIONS OF YOUR OWN INNER TURMOIL.

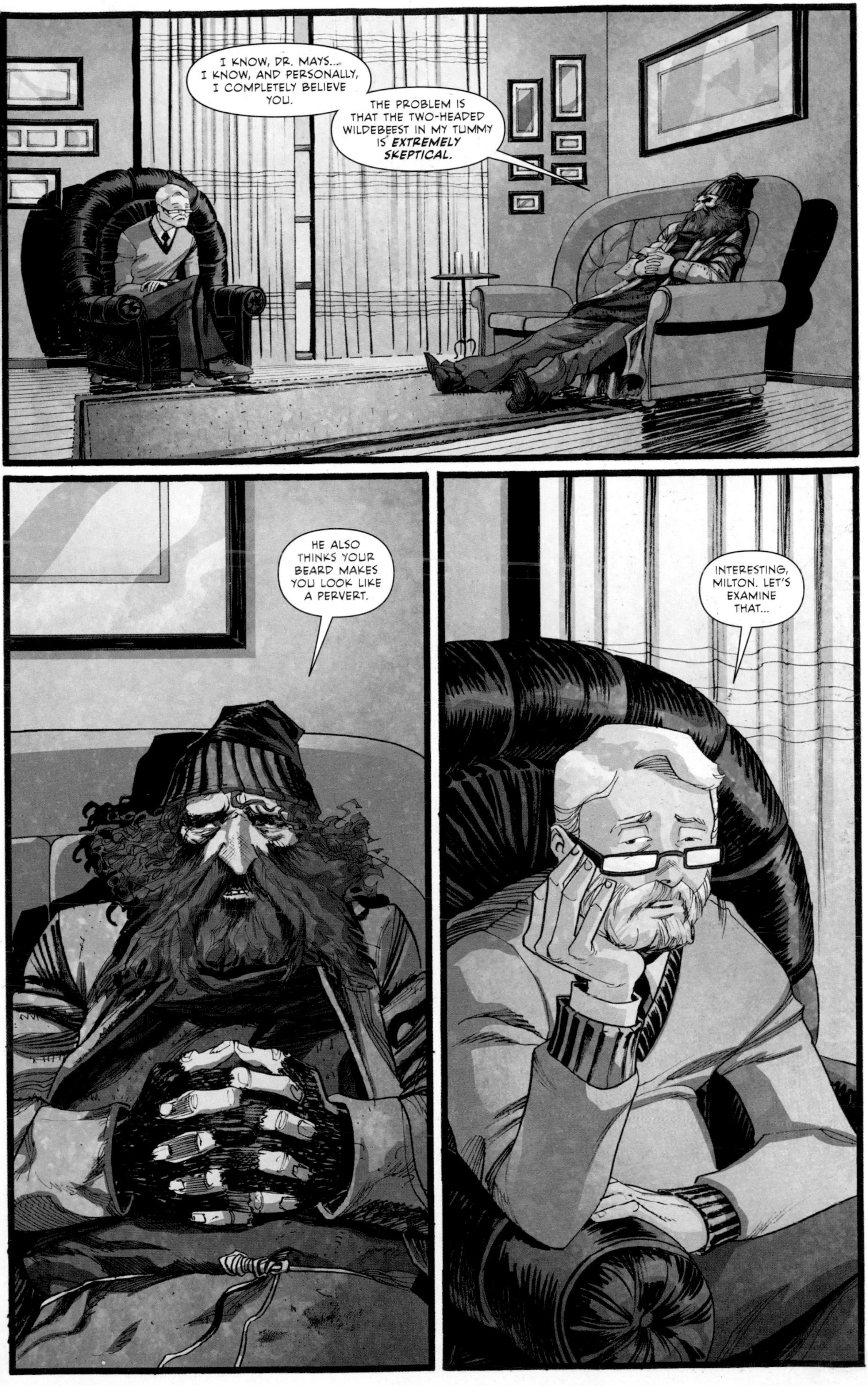
I KNOW, DR. MAYS... I KNOW, AND PERSONALLY, I COMPLETELY BELIEVE YOU.
THE PROBLEM IS THAT THE TWO-HEADED WILDEBEEST IN MY TUMMY IS *EXTREMELY SKEPTICAL.*
HE ALSO THINKS YOUR BEARD MAKES YOU LOOK LIKE A PERVERT.
INTERESTING, MILTON. LET'S EXAMINE THAT...

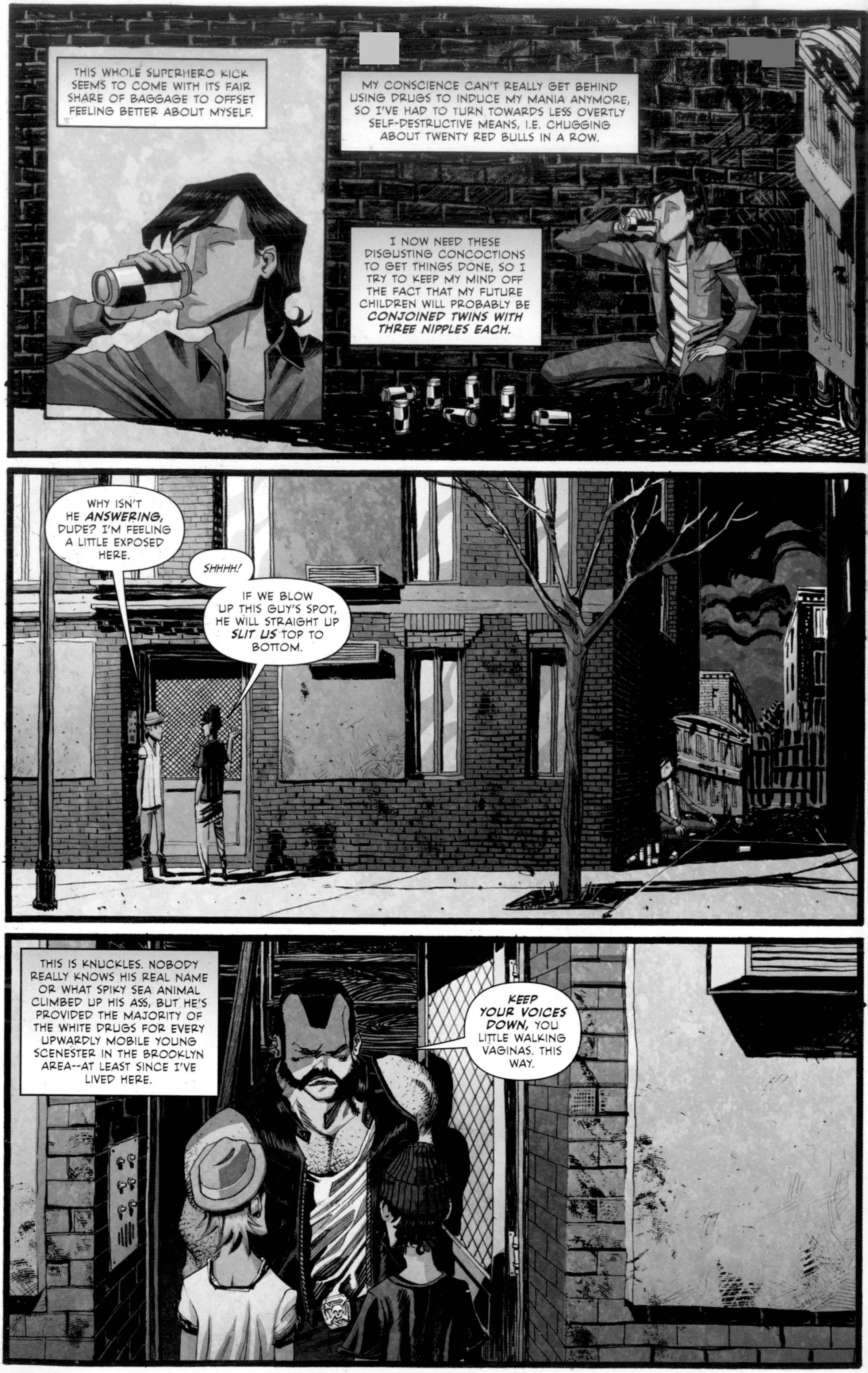
THIS WHOLE SUPERHERO KICK SEEMS TO COME WITH ITS FAIR SHARE OF BAGGAGE TO OFFSET FEELING BETTER ABOUT MYSELF.
MY CONSCIENCE CAN'T REALLY GET BEHIND USING DRUGS TO INDUCE MY MANIA ANYMORE, SO I'VE HAD TO TURN TOWARDS LESS OVERTLY SELF-DESTRUCTIVE MEANS, I.E. CHUGGING ABOUT TWENTY RED BULLS IN A ROW.
I NOW NEED THESE DISGUSTING CONCOCTIONS TO GET THINGS DONE, SO I TRY TO KEEP MY MIND OFF THE FACT THAT MY FUTURE CHILDREN WILL PROBABLY BE ***CONJOINED TWINS WITH THREE NIPPLES EACH.***
WHY ISN'T HE ***ANSWERING,*** DUDE? I'M FEELING A LITTLE EXPOSED HERE.
SHHHH!
IF WE BLOW UP THIS GUY'S SPOT, HE WILL STRAIGHT UP ***SLIT US*** TOP TO BOTTOM.
THIS IS KNUCKLES. NOBODY REALLY KNOWS HIS REAL NAME OR WHAT SPIKY SEA ANIMAL CLIMBED UP HIS ASS, BUT HE'S PROVIDED THE MAJORITY OF THE WHITE DRUGS FOR EVERY UPWARDLY MOBILE YOUNG SCENESTER IN THE BROOKLYN AREA--AT LEAST SINCE I'VE LIVED HERE.
KEEP YOUR VOICES DOWN, YOU LITTLE WALKING VAGINAS. THIS WAY.

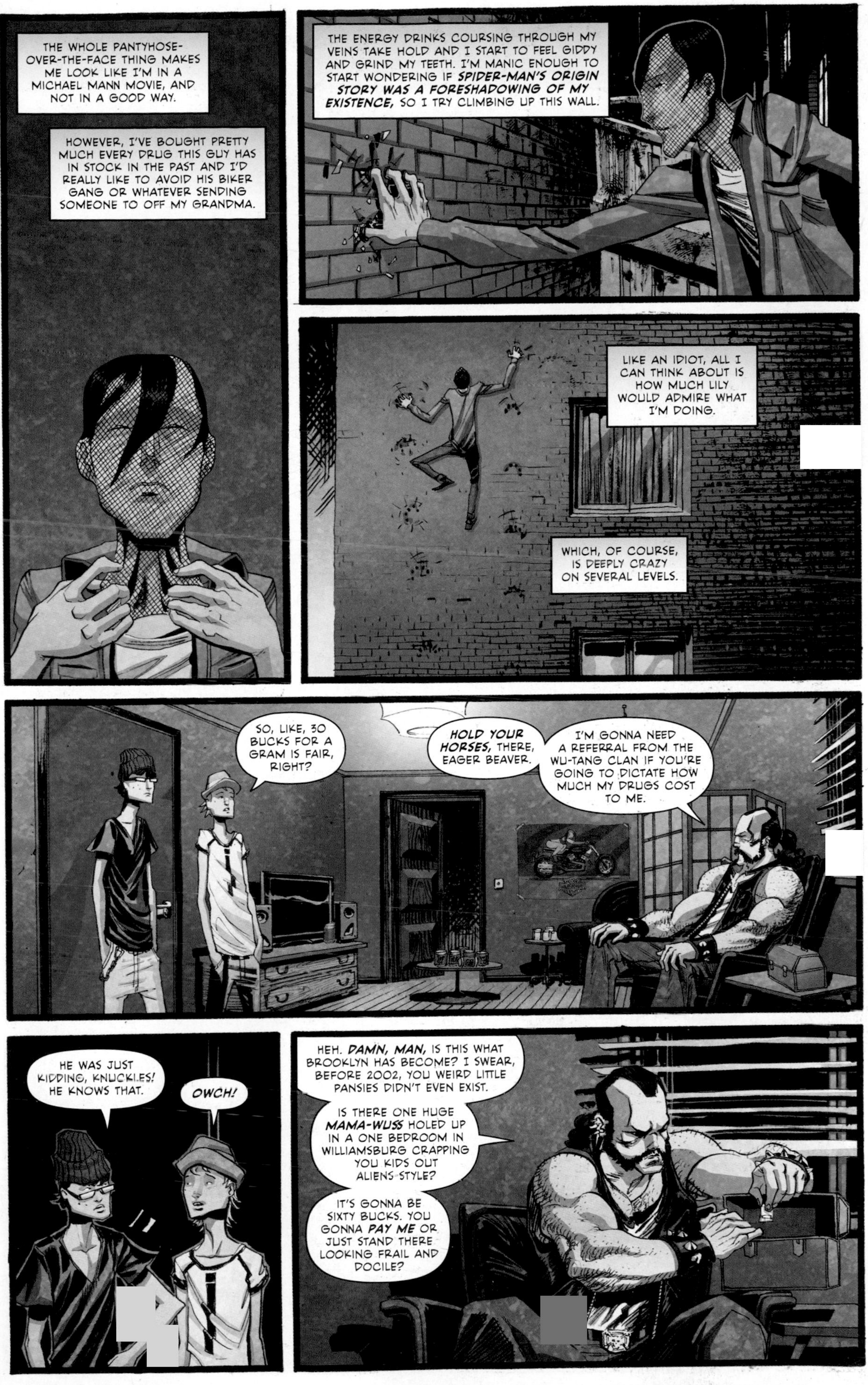
THE WHOLE PANTYHOSE-OVER-THE-FACE THING MAKES ME LOOK LIKE I'M IN A MICHAEL MANN MOVIE, AND NOT IN A GOOD WAY.
HOWEVER, I'VE BOUGHT PRETTY MUCH EVERY DRUG THIS GUY HAS IN STOCK IN THE PAST AND I'D REALLY LIKE TO AVOID HIS BIKER GANG OR WHATEVER SENDING SOMEONE TO OFF MY GRANDMA.
THE ENERGY DRINKS COURSING THROUGH MY VEINS TAKE HOLD AND I START TO FEEL GIDDY AND GRIND MY TEETH. I'M MANIC ENOUGH TO START WONDERING IF SPIDER-MAN'S ORIGIN STORY WAS A FORESHADOWING OF MY EXISTENCE, SO I TRY CLIMBING UP THIS WALL.
LIKE AN IDIOT, ALL I CAN THINK ABOUT IS HOW MUCH LILY WOULD ADMIRE WHAT I'M DOING.
WHICH, OF COURSE, IS DEEPLY CRAZY ON SEVERAL LEVELS.
SO, LIKE, 30 BUCKS FOR A GRAM IS FAIR, RIGHT?
HOLD YOUR HORSES, THERE, EAGER BEAVER.
I'M GONNA NEED A REFERRAL FROM THE WU-TANG CLAN IF YOU'RE GOING TO DICTATE HOW MUCH MY DRUGS COST TO ME.
HE WAS JUST KIDDING, KNUCKLES! HE KNOWS THAT.
OWCH!
HEH. DAMN, MAN, IS THIS WHAT BROOKLYN HAS BECOME? I SWEAR, BEFORE 2002, YOU WEIRD LITTLE PANSIES DIDN'T EVEN EXIST.
IS THERE ONE HUGE MAMA-WUSS HOLED UP IN A ONE BEDROOM IN WILLIAMSBURG CRAPPING YOU KIDS OUT ALIENS STYLE?
IT'S GONNA BE SIXTY BUCKS. YOU GONNA PAY ME OR JUST STAND THERE LOOKING FRAIL AND DOCILE?

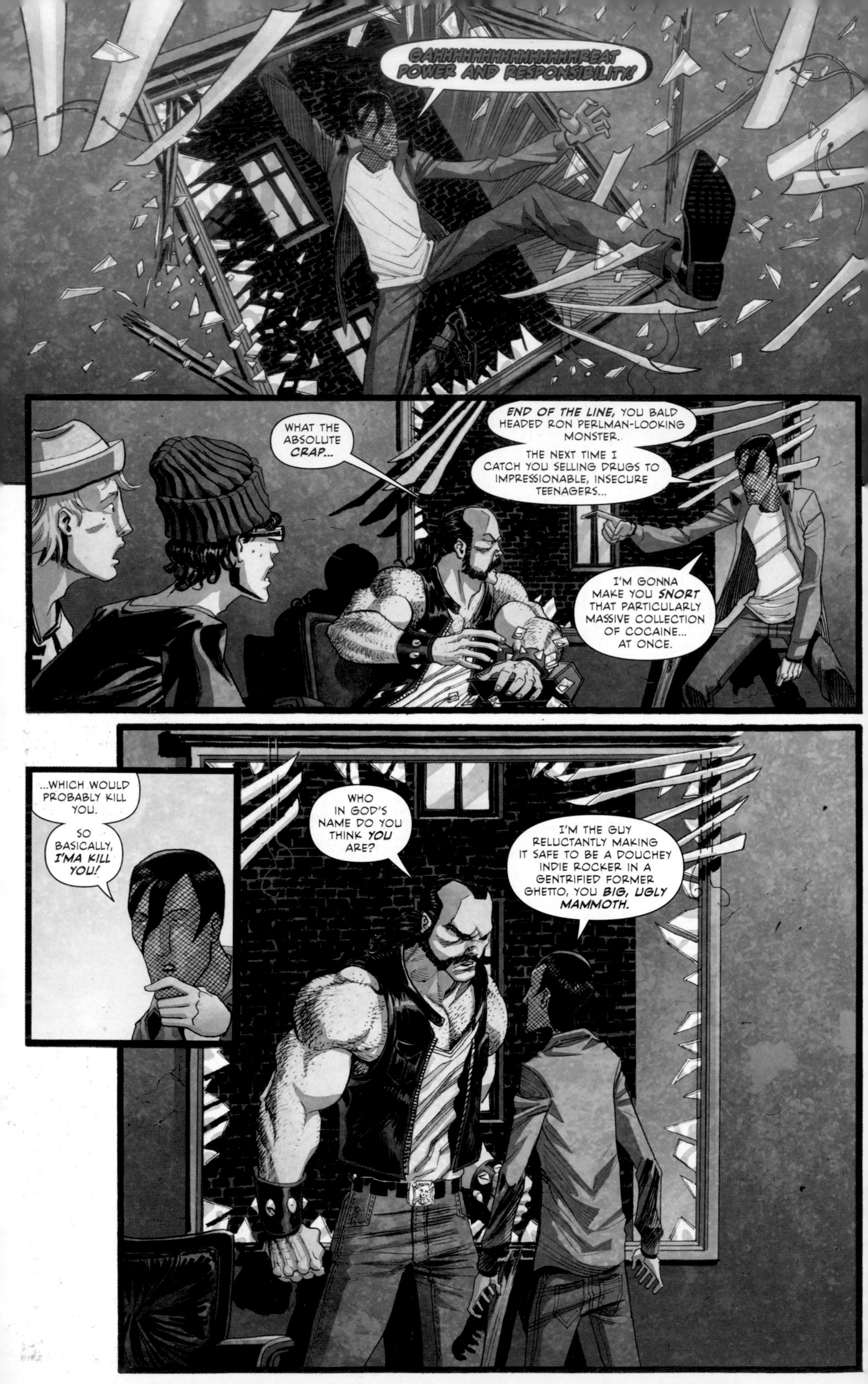
GAHHHHHHHHHHHHHHHHREAT POWER AND RESPONSIBILITY!
WHAT THE ABSOLUTE CRAP...
END OF THE LINE, YOU BALD HEADED RON PERLMAN-LOOKING MONSTER.
THE NEXT TIME I CATCH YOU SELLING DRUGS TO IMPRESSIONABLE, INSECURE TEENAGERS...
I'M GONNA MAKE YOU SNORT THAT PARTICULARLY MASSIVE COLLECTION OF COCAINE... AT ONCE.
...WHICH WOULD PROBABLY KILL YOU.
SO BASICALLY, I'MA KILL YOU!
WHO IN GOD'S NAME DO YOU THINK YOU ARE?
I'M THE GUY RELUCTANTLY MAKING IT SAFE TO BE A DOUCHEY INDIE ROCKER IN A GENTRIFIED FORMER GHETTO, YOU BIG, UGLY MAMMOTH.

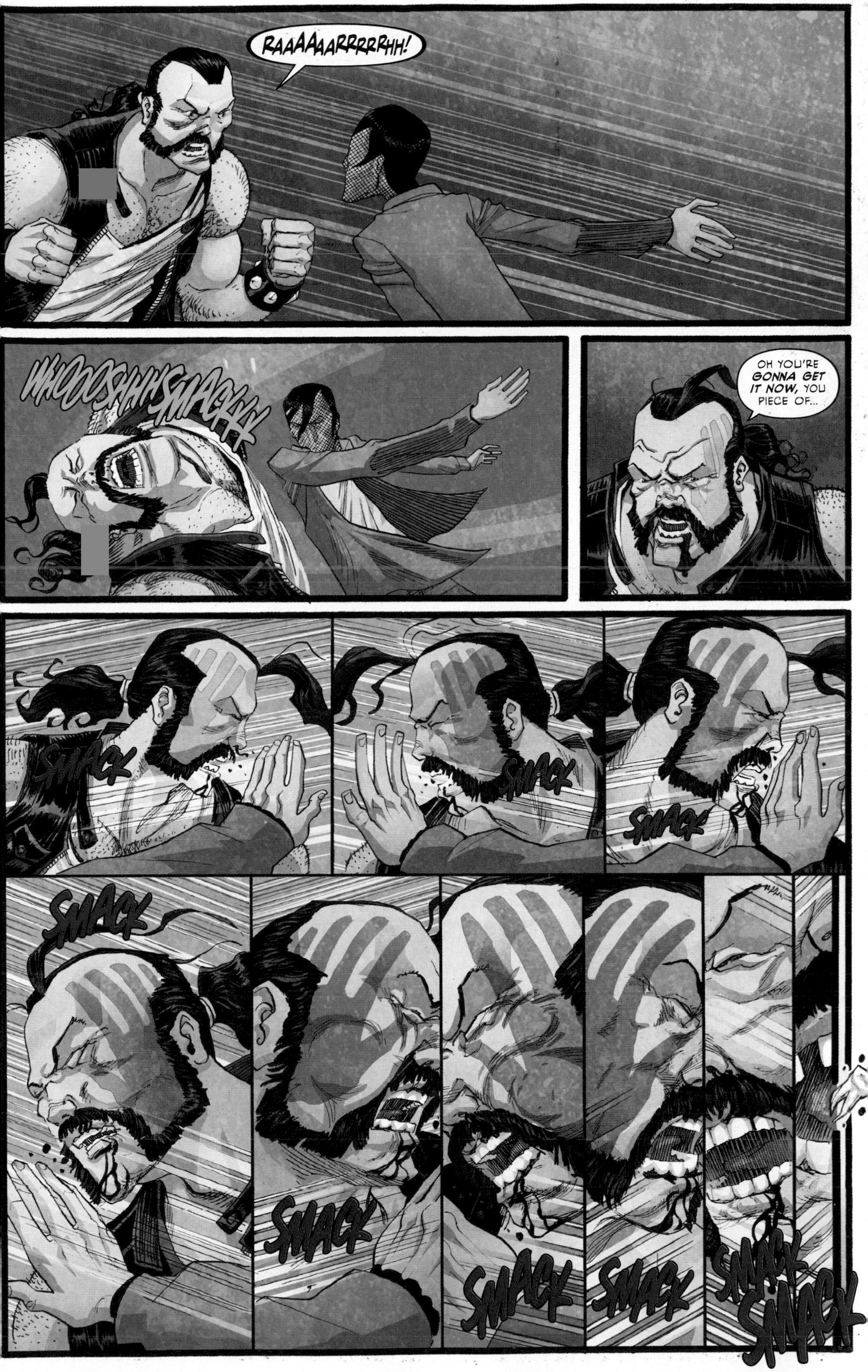
RAAAAAARRRRRHH!
WHOOOSHHHSMACKKK
OH YOU'RE GONNA GET IT NOW, YOU PIECE OF...
SMACK
SMACK
SMACK
SMACK
SMACK
SMACK
SMACK
SMACK
SMACK

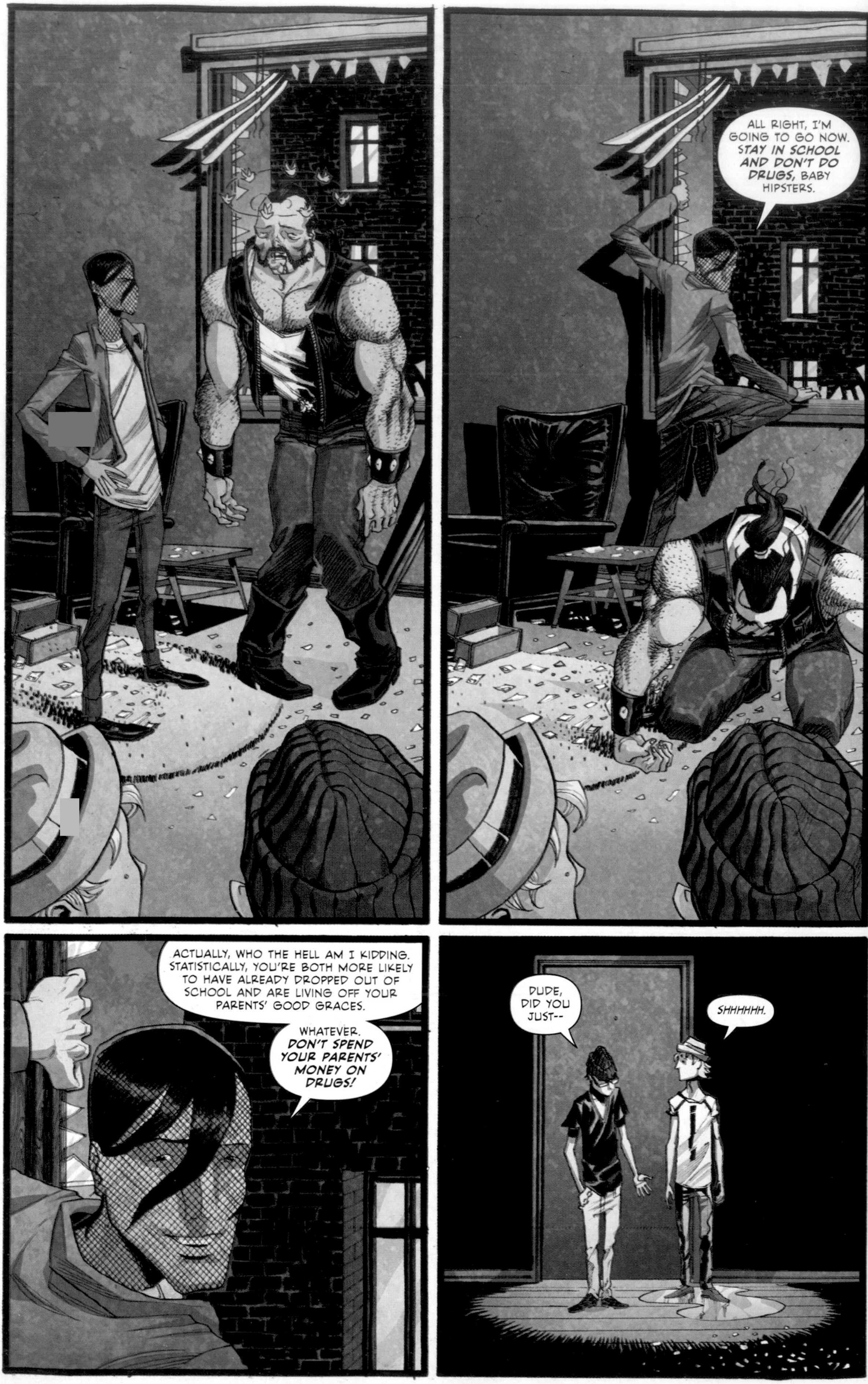
ALL RIGHT, I'M GOING TO GO NOW. **STAY IN SCHOOL AND DON'T DO DRUGS,** BABY HIPSTERS.
ACTUALLY, WHO THE HELL AM I KIDDING. STATISTICALLY, YOU'RE BOTH MORE LIKELY TO HAVE ALREADY DROPPED OUT OF SCHOOL AND ARE LIVING OFF YOUR PARENTS' GOOD GRACES.
WHATEVER. **DON'T SPEND YOUR PARENTS' MONEY ON DRUGS!**
DUDE, DID YOU JUST--
SHHHHHH.

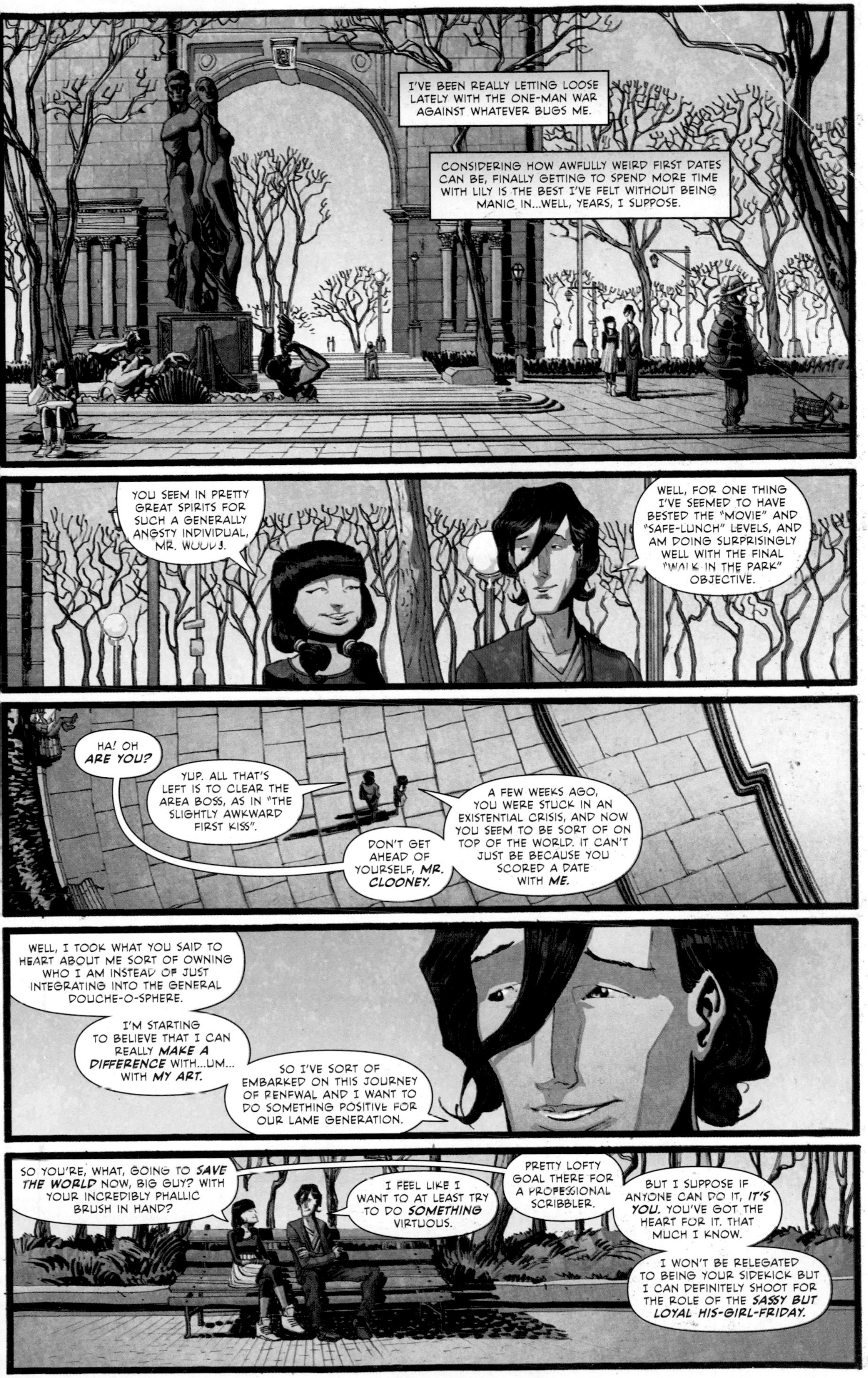
I'VE BEEN REALLY LETTING LOOSE LATELY WITH THE ONE-MAN WAR AGAINST WHATEVER BUGS ME.
CONSIDERING HOW AWFULLY WEIRD FIRST DATES CAN BE, FINALLY GETTING TO SPEND MORE TIME WITH LILY IS THE BEST I'VE FELT WITHOUT BEING MANIC IN...WELL, YEARS, I SUPPOSE.
YOU SEEM IN PRETTY GREAT SPIRITS FOR SUCH A GENERALLY ANGSTY INDIVIDUAL, MR. WOODS.
WELL, FOR ONE THING I'VE SEEMED TO HAVE BESTED THE "MOVIE" AND "SAFE-LUNCH" LEVELS, AND AM DOING SURPRISINGLY WELL WITH THE FINAL "WALK IN THE PARK" OBJECTIVE.
HA! OH *ARE YOU?*
YUP. ALL THAT'S LEFT IS TO CLEAR THE AREA BOSS, AS IN "THE SLIGHTLY AWKWARD FIRST KISS".
DON'T GET AHEAD OF YOURSELF, *MR. CLOONEY.*
A FEW WEEKS AGO, YOU WERE STUCK IN AN EXISTENTIAL CRISIS, AND NOW YOU SEEM TO BE SORT OF ON TOP OF THE WORLD. IT CAN'T JUST BE BECAUSE YOU SCORED A DATE WITH *ME.*
WELL, I TOOK WHAT YOU SAID TO HEART ABOUT ME SORT OF OWNING WHO I AM INSTEAD OF JUST INTEGRATING INTO THE GENERAL DOUCHE-O-SPHERE.
I'M STARTING TO BELIEVE THAT I CAN REALLY *MAKE A DIFFERENCE* WITH...UM... WITH *MY ART.*
SO I'VE SORT OF EMBARKED ON THIS JOURNEY OF RENEWAL AND I WANT TO DO SOMETHING POSITIVE FOR OUR LAME GENERATION.
SO YOU'RE, WHAT, GOING TO *SAVE THE WORLD* NOW, BIG GUY? WITH YOUR INCREDIBLY PHALLIC BRUSH IN HAND?
I FEEL LIKE I WANT TO AT LEAST TRY TO DO *SOMETHING* VIRTUOUS.
PRETTY LOFTY GOAL THERE FOR A PROFESSIONAL SCRIBBLER.
BUT I SUPPOSE IF ANYONE CAN DO IT, *IT'S YOU.* YOU'VE GOT THE HEART FOR IT. THAT MUCH I KNOW.
I WON'T BE RELEGATED TO BEING YOUR SIDEKICK BUT I CAN DEFINITELY SHOOT FOR THE ROLE OF THE *SASSY BUT LOYAL HIS-GIRL-FRIDAY.*

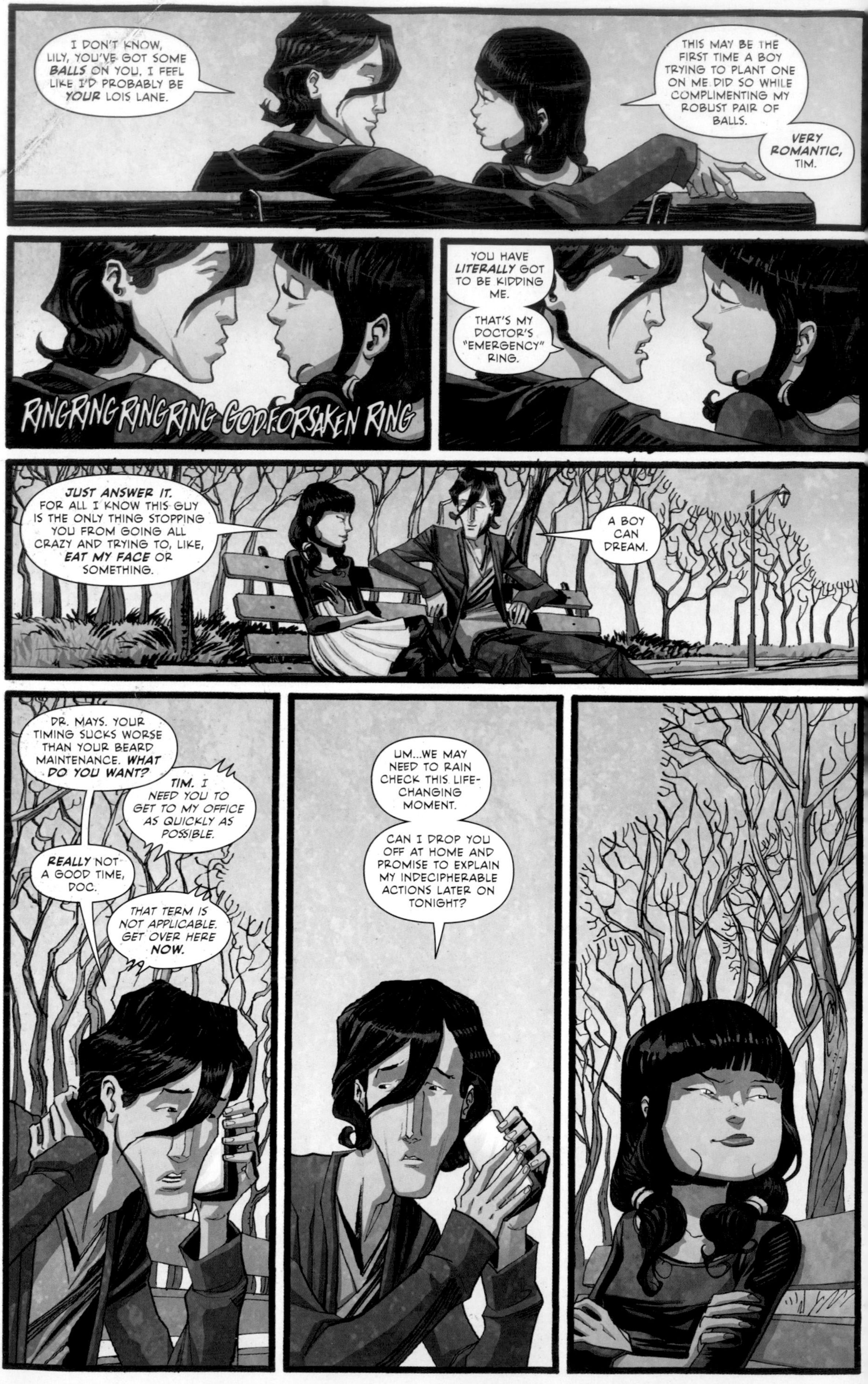

I DON'T KNOW, LILY, YOU'VE GOT SOME BALLS ON YOU. I FEEL LIKE I'D PROBABLY BE YOUR LOIS LANE.
THIS MAY BE THE FIRST TIME A BOY TRYING TO PLANT ONE ON ME DID SO WHILE COMPLIMENTING MY ROBUST PAIR OF BALLS.
VERY ROMANTIC, TIM.
RINGRING RINGRING GODFORSAKEN RING
YOU HAVE LITERALLY GOT TO BE KIDDING ME.
THAT'S MY DOCTOR'S "EMERGENCY" RING.
JUST ANSWER IT. FOR ALL I KNOW THIS GUY IS THE ONLY THING STOPPING YOU FROM GOING ALL CRAZY AND TRYING TO, LIKE, EAT MY FACE OR SOMETHING.
A BOY CAN DREAM.
DR. MAYS. YOUR TIMING SUCKS WORSE THAN YOUR BEARD MAINTENANCE. WHAT DO YOU WANT?
TIM. I NEED YOU TO GET TO MY OFFICE AS QUICKLY AS POSSIBLE.
REALLY NOT A GOOD TIME, DOC.
THAT TERM IS NOT APPLICABLE. GET OVER HERE NOW.
UM...WE MAY NEED TO RAIN CHECK THIS LIFE-CHANGING MOMENT.
CAN I DROP YOU OFF AT HOME AND PROMISE TO EXPLAIN MY INDECIPHERABLE ACTIONS LATER ON TONIGHT?

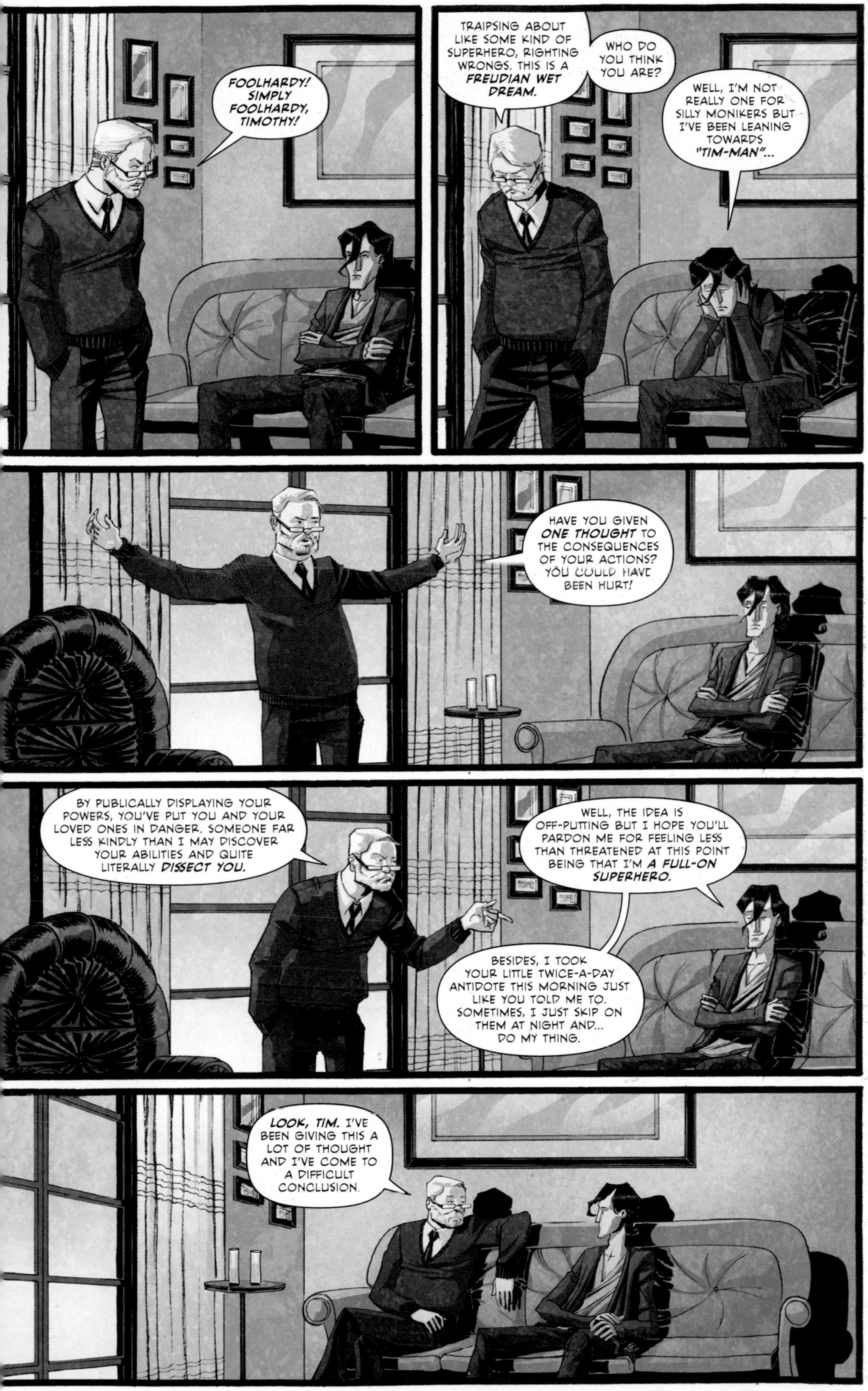
FOOLHARDY! SIMPLY FOOLHARDY, TIMOTHY!
TRAIPSING ABOUT LIKE SOME KIND OF SUPERHERO, RIGHTING WRONGS. THIS IS A FREUDIAN WET DREAM.
WHO DO YOU THINK YOU ARE?
WELL, I'M NOT REALLY ONE FOR SILLY MONIKERS BUT I'VE BEEN LEANING TOWARDS "TIM-MAN"...
HAVE YOU GIVEN ONE THOUGHT TO THE CONSEQUENCES OF YOUR ACTIONS? YOU COULD HAVE BEEN HURT!
BY PUBLICALLY DISPLAYING YOUR POWERS, YOU'VE PUT YOU AND YOUR LOVED ONES IN DANGER. SOMEONE FAR LESS KINDLY THAN I MAY DISCOVER YOUR ABILITIES AND QUITE LITERALLY DISSECT YOU.
WELL, THE IDEA IS OFF-PUTTING BUT I HOPE YOU'LL PARDON ME FOR FEELING LESS THAN THREATENED AT THIS POINT BEING THAT I'M A FULL-ON SUPERHERO.
BESIDES, I TOOK YOUR LITTLE TWICE-A-DAY ANTIDOTE THIS MORNING JUST LIKE YOU TOLD ME TO. SOMETIMES, I JUST SKIP ON THEM AT NIGHT AND... DO MY THING.
LOOK, TIM. I'VE BEEN GIVING THIS A LOT OF THOUGHT AND I'VE COME TO A DIFFICULT CONCLUSION.

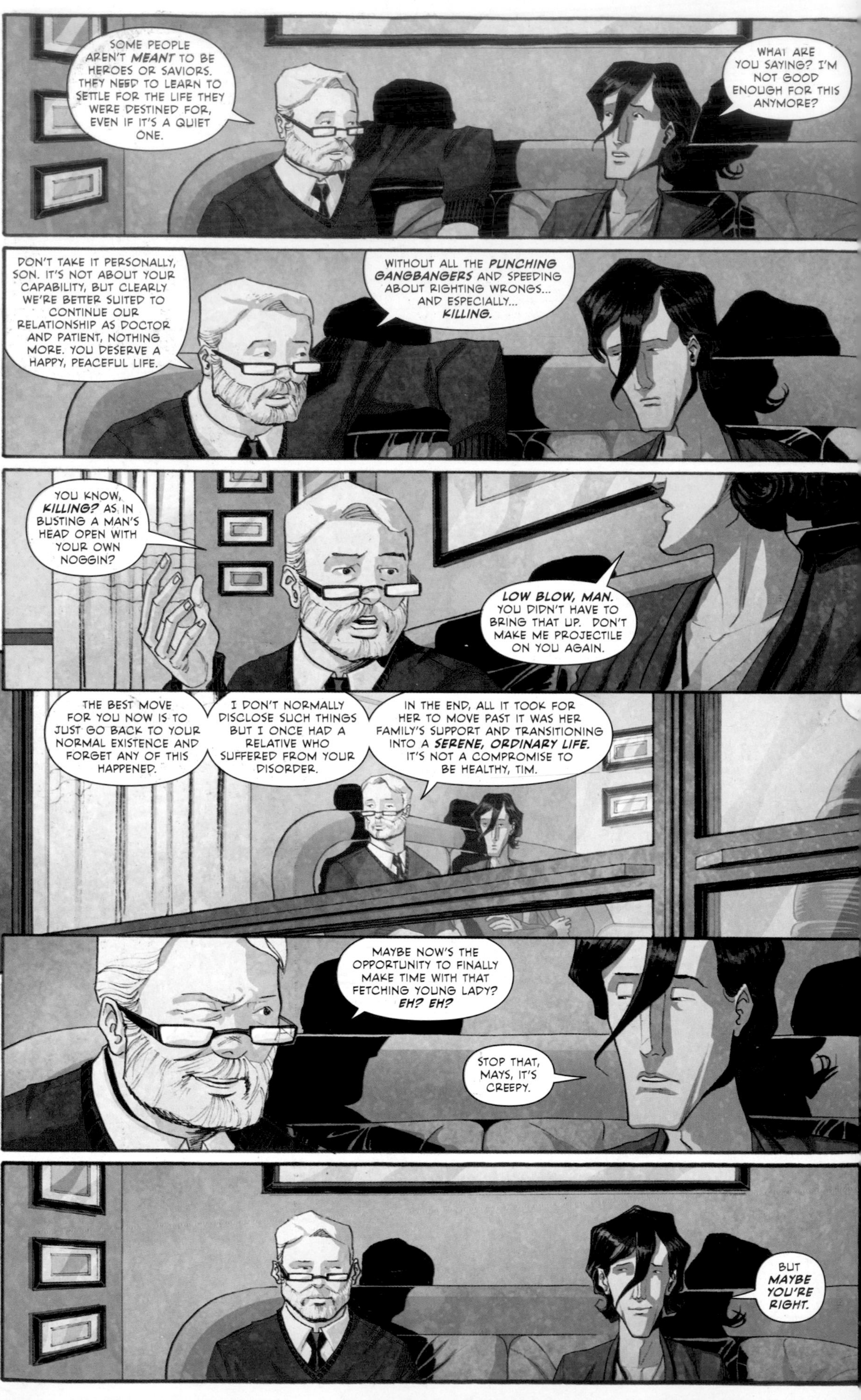

SOME PEOPLE AREN'T MEANT TO BE HEROES OR SAVIORS. THEY NEED TO LEARN TO SETTLE FOR THE LIFE THEY WERE DESTINED FOR, EVEN IF IT'S A QUIET ONE.
WHAT ARE YOU SAYING? I'M NOT GOOD ENOUGH FOR THIS ANYMORE?
DON'T TAKE IT PERSONALLY, SON. IT'S NOT ABOUT YOUR CAPABILITY, BUT CLEARLY WE'RE BETTER SUITED TO CONTINUE OUR RELATIONSHIP AS DOCTOR AND PATIENT, NOTHING MORE. YOU DESERVE A HAPPY, PEACEFUL LIFE.
WITHOUT ALL THE PUNCHING GANGBANGERS AND SPEEDING ABOUT RIGHTING WRONGS... AND ESPECIALLY... KILLING.
YOU KNOW, KILLING? AS IN BUSTING A MAN'S HEAD OPEN WITH YOUR OWN NOGGIN?
LOW BLOW, MAN. YOU DIDN'T HAVE TO BRING THAT UP. DON'T MAKE ME PROJECTILE ON YOU AGAIN.
THE BEST MOVE FOR YOU NOW IS TO JUST GO BACK TO YOUR NORMAL EXISTENCE AND FORGET ANY OF THIS HAPPENED.
I DON'T NORMALLY DISCLOSE SUCH THINGS BUT I ONCE HAD A RELATIVE WHO SUFFERED FROM YOUR DISORDER.
IN THE END, ALL IT TOOK FOR HER TO MOVE PAST IT WAS HER FAMILY'S SUPPORT AND TRANSITIONING INTO A SERENE, ORDINARY LIFE. IT'S NOT A COMPROMISE TO BE HEALTHY, TIM.
MAYBE NOW'S THE OPPORTUNITY TO FINALLY MAKE TIME WITH THAT FETCHING YOUNG LADY? EH? EH?
STOP THAT, MAYS, IT'S CREEPY.
BUT MAYBE YOU'RE RIGHT.

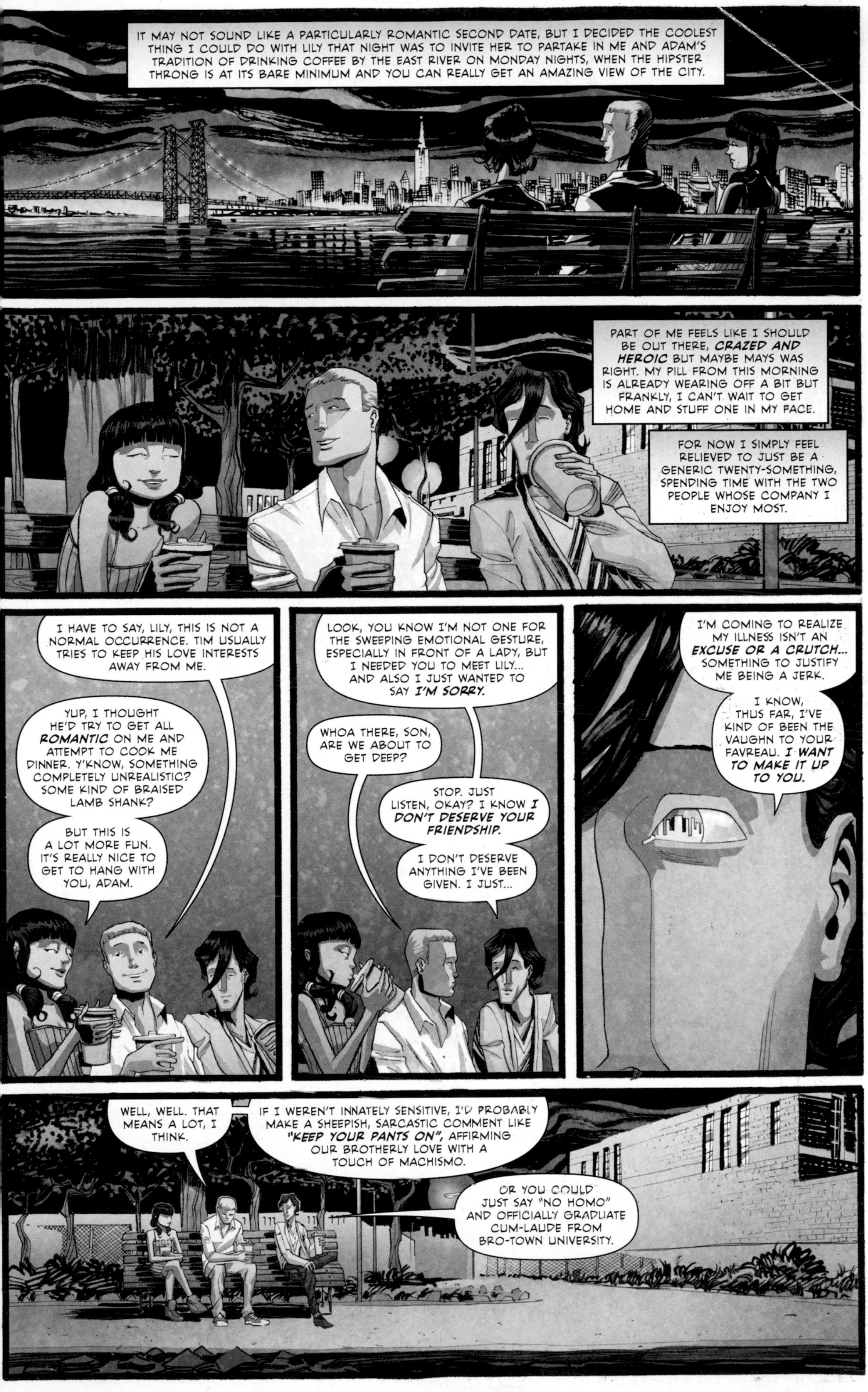

IT MAY NOT SOUND LIKE A PARTICULARLY ROMANTIC SECOND DATE, BUT I DECIDED THE COOLEST THING I COULD DO WITH LILY THAT NIGHT WAS TO INVITE HER TO PARTAKE IN ME AND ADAM'S TRADITION OF DRINKING COFFEE BY THE EAST RIVER ON MONDAY NIGHTS, WHEN THE HIPSTER THRONG IS AT ITS BARE MINIMUM AND YOU CAN REALLY GET AN AMAZING VIEW OF THE CITY.
PART OF ME FEELS LIKE I SHOULD BE OUT THERE, CRAZED AND HEROIC BUT MAYBE MAYS WAS RIGHT. MY PILL FROM THIS MORNING IS ALREADY WEARING OFF A BIT BUT FRANKLY, I CAN'T WAIT TO GET HOME AND STUFF ONE IN MY FACE.
FOR NOW I SIMPLY FEEL RELIEVED TO JUST BE A GENERIC TWENTY-SOMETHING, SPENDING TIME WITH THE TWO PEOPLE WHOSE COMPANY I ENJOY MOST.
I HAVE TO SAY, LILY, THIS IS NOT A NORMAL OCCURRENCE. TIM USUALLY TRIES TO KEEP HIS LOVE INTERESTS AWAY FROM ME.
YUP, I THOUGHT HE'D TRY TO GET ALL ROMANTIC ON ME AND ATTEMPT TO COOK ME DINNER. Y'KNOW, SOMETHING COMPLETELY UNREALISTIC? SOME KIND OF BRAISED LAMB SHANK?
BUT THIS IS A LOT MORE FUN. IT'S REALLY NICE TO GET TO HANG WITH YOU, ADAM.
LOOK, YOU KNOW I'M NOT ONE FOR THE SWEEPING EMOTIONAL GESTURE, ESPECIALLY IN FRONT OF A LADY, BUT I NEEDED YOU TO MEET LILY... AND ALSO I JUST WANTED TO SAY I'M SORRY.
WHOA THERE, SON, ARE WE ABOUT TO GET DEEP?
STOP. JUST LISTEN, OKAY? I KNOW I DON'T DESERVE YOUR FRIENDSHIP.
I DON'T DESERVE ANYTHING I'VE BEEN GIVEN. I JUST...
I'M COMING TO REALIZE MY ILLNESS ISN'T AN EXCUSE OR A CRUTCH... SOMETHING TO JUSTIFY ME BEING A JERK.
I KNOW, THUS FAR, I'VE KIND OF BEEN THE VAUGHN TO YOUR FAVREAU. I WANT TO MAKE IT UP TO YOU.
WELL, WELL. THAT MEANS A LOT, I THINK.
IF I WEREN'T INNATELY SENSITIVE, I'D PROBABLY MAKE A SHEEPISH, SARCASTIC COMMENT LIKE "KEEP YOUR PANTS ON", AFFIRMING OUR BROTHERLY LOVE WITH A TOUCH OF MACHISMO.
OR YOU COULD JUST SAY "NO HOMO" AND OFFICIALLY GRADUATE CUM-LAUDE FROM BRO-TOWN UNIVERSITY.

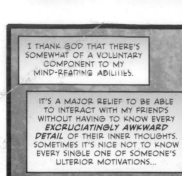

I THANK GOD THAT THERE'S SOMEWHAT OF A VOLUNTARY COMPONENT TO MY MIND-READING ABILITIES.

IT'S A MAJOR RELIEF TO BE ABLE TO INTERACT WITH MY FRIENDS WITHOUT HAVING TO KNOW EVERY *EXCRUCIATINGLY AWKWARD DETAIL* OF THEIR INNER THOUGHTS. SOMETIMES IT'S NICE NOT TO KNOW EVERY SINGLE ONE OF SOMEONE'S ULTERIOR MOTIVATIONS...

HMM. SOMETHING BARELY BEGINS TO NAG ME THAT I CAN'T QUITE PUT MY FINGER ON. SOMETHING ABOUT DOCTOR MAYS...I CAN'T BE SURE BECAUSE I ALWAYS SEEM TO BE FRESHLY PILL'D OUT WHEN WE MEET...

WAS THAT INTENTIONAL? HE PROBABLY HAS ALL KINDS OF *JACKED UP SECRET-AGENT STUFF* IN THAT HEAD OF HIS...

HEY, *A.D.D. BOY*, YOU MIGHT WANNA LISTEN TO THIS!

EH, WHATEVER. PROBABLY HAS SOMETHING TO DO WITH DOCTOR/PATIENT CONFIDENTIALITY, LIKE HE DIDN'T WANT ME TO KNOW WHICH SOCCER MOMS WERE HUMPING THEIR TENNIS INSTRUCTORS. *PARANOID AS ALWAYS.* NEED MY PILLS.

I WAS FILLING LILY IN ON THE *MAN-CRUSH* YOU HAD ON JAMES VAN DER BEEK IN HIGH SCHOOL.

DUDE. *NO.*

TIM DECIDED HE WANTED TO BE A DIRECTOR ONLY BECAUSE DAWSON DID *AND* HE PLAYED JV FOOTBALL BECAUSE OF "VARSITY BLUES."

THIS IS WHY YOU NEVER MEET ANYONE I'M DATING UNTIL LIKE FIVE DATES IN.

IT'S OKAY THAT YOU WORE A *PUKA SHELL CHOKER*, HOMIE; NOBODY HERE'S GOING TO JUDGE YOU.

I WOULDN'T SAY THAT. I'M DEFINITELY JUDGING YOU, TIM.

ANOTHER NAGGING THOUGHT...WHY WOULD MAYS *THROW AWAY HIS OPERATION SO QUICKLY?* ALL THOSE YEARS OF RESEARCH JUST BECAUSE HE'S WORRIED ABOUT ME PLAYING BATMAN?

YOU GUYS *SUCK ASS.*

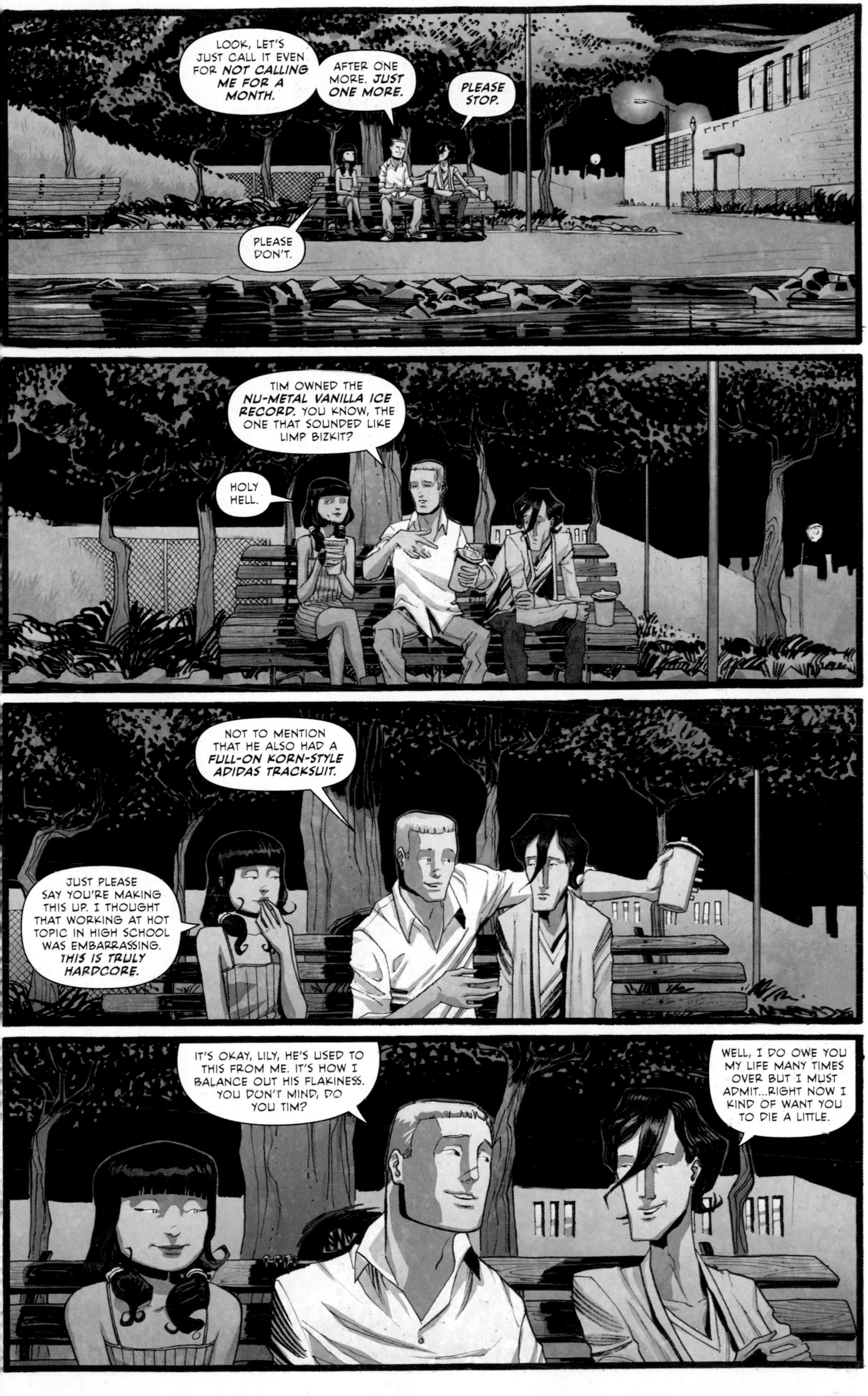
LOOK, LET'S JUST CALL IT EVEN FOR NOT CALLING ME FOR A MONTH.
AFTER ONE MORE. JUST ONE MORE.
PLEASE STOP.
PLEASE DON'T.
TIM OWNED THE NU-METAL VANILLA ICE RECORD. YOU KNOW, THE ONE THAT SOUNDED LIKE LIMP BIZKIT?
HOLY HELL.
NOT TO MENTION THAT HE ALSO HAD A FULL-ON KORN-STYLE ADIDAS TRACKSUIT.
JUST PLEASE SAY YOU'RE MAKING THIS UP. I THOUGHT THAT WORKING AT HOT TOPIC IN HIGH SCHOOL WAS EMBARRASSING. THIS IS TRULY HARDCORE.
IT'S OKAY, LILY, HE'S USED TO THIS FROM ME. IT'S HOW I BALANCE OUT HIS FLAKINESS. YOU DON'T MIND, DO YOU TIM?
WELL, I DO OWE YOU MY LIFE MANY TIMES OVER BUT I MUST ADMIT...RIGHT NOW I KIND OF WANT YOU TO DIE A LITTLE.

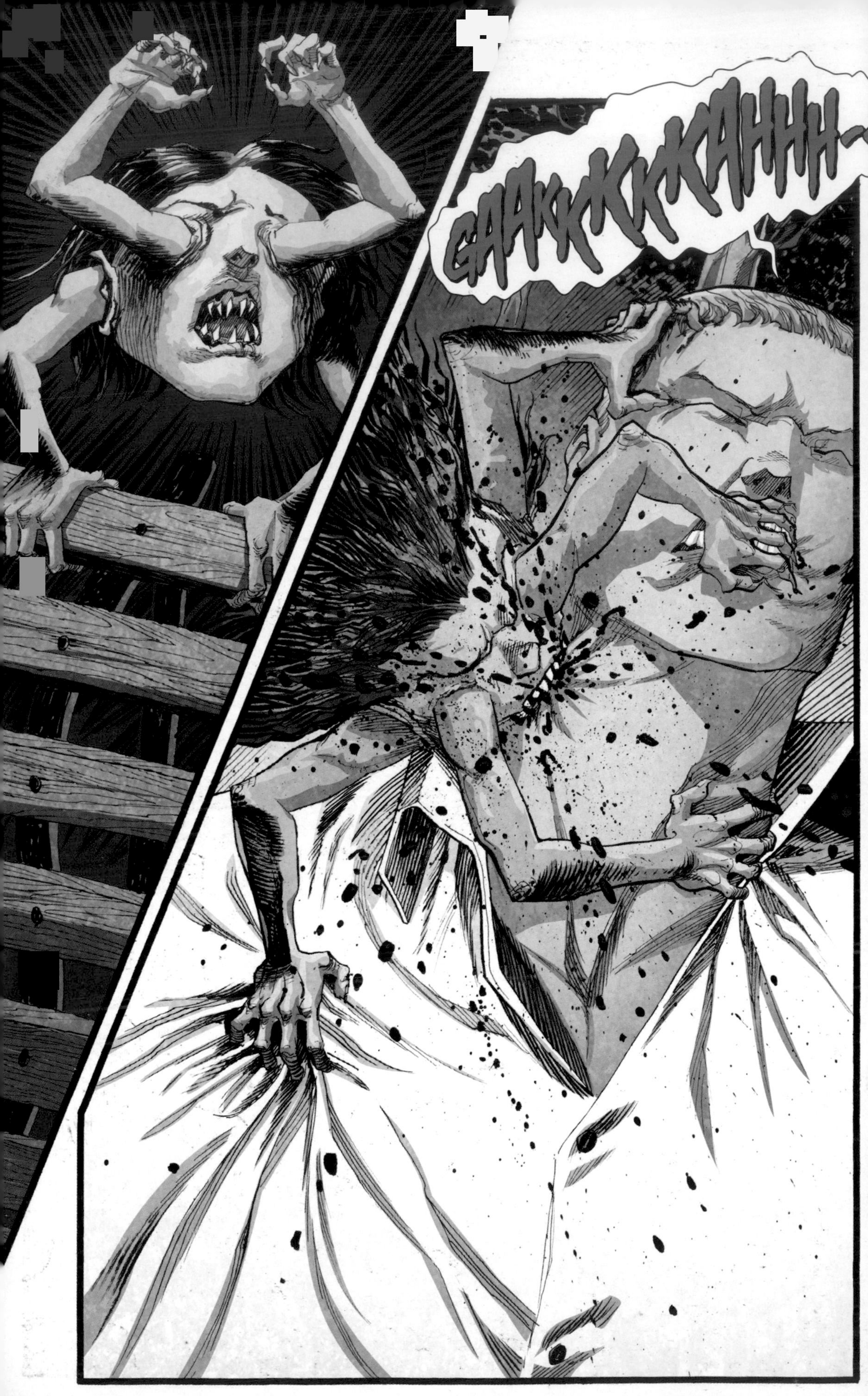
GAAKKKKAHHH--

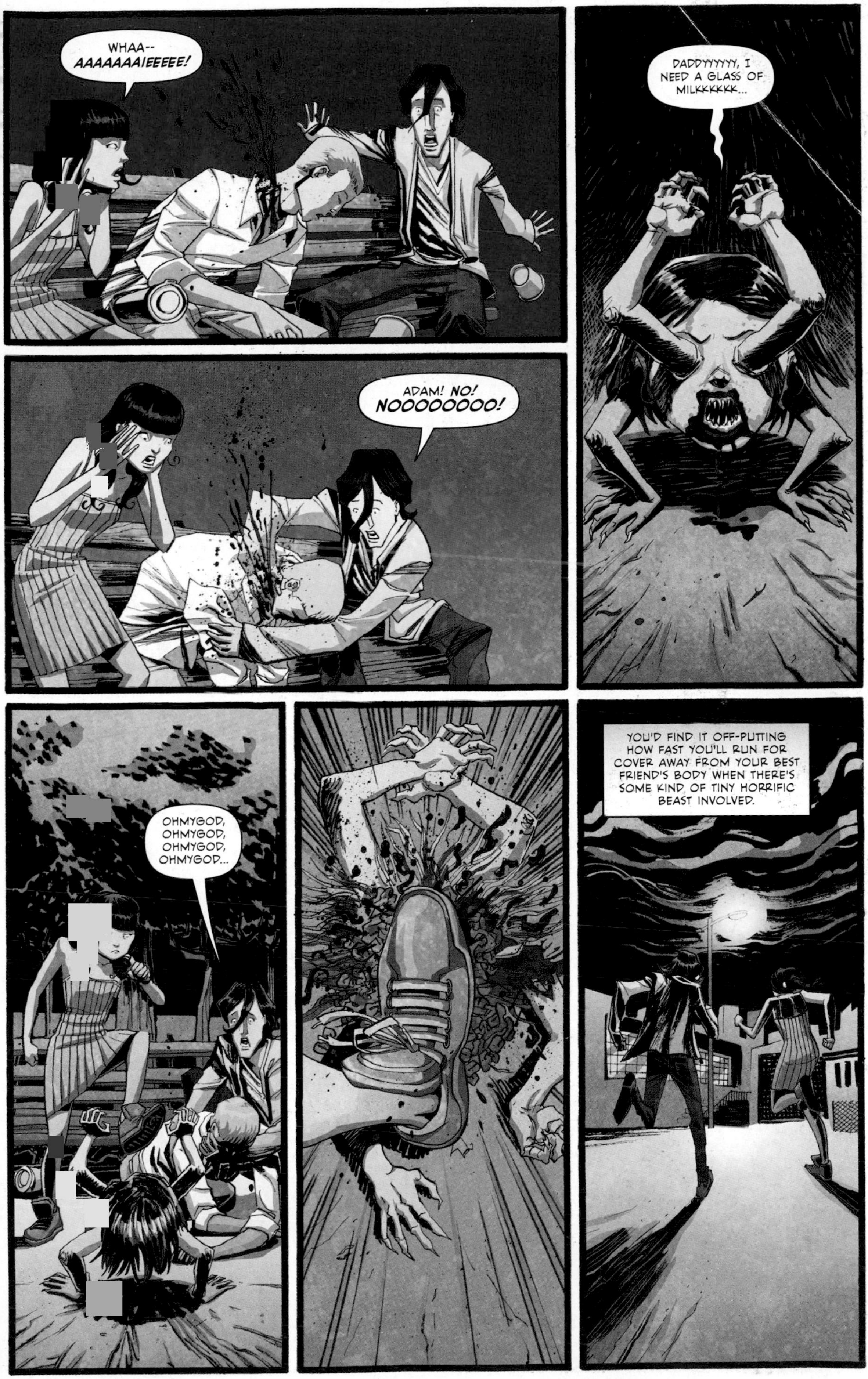
WHAA--
AAAAAAAIEEEEE!
DADDYYYYY, I NEED A GLASS OF MILKKKKKK...
ADAM! NO! NOOOOOOOO!
OHMYGOD, OHMYGOD, OHMYGOD, OHMYGOD...
YOU'D FIND IT OFF-PUTTING HOW FAST YOU'LL RUN FOR COVER AWAY FROM YOUR BEST FRIEND'S BODY WHEN THERE'S SOME KIND OF TINY HORRIFIC BEAST INVOLVED.

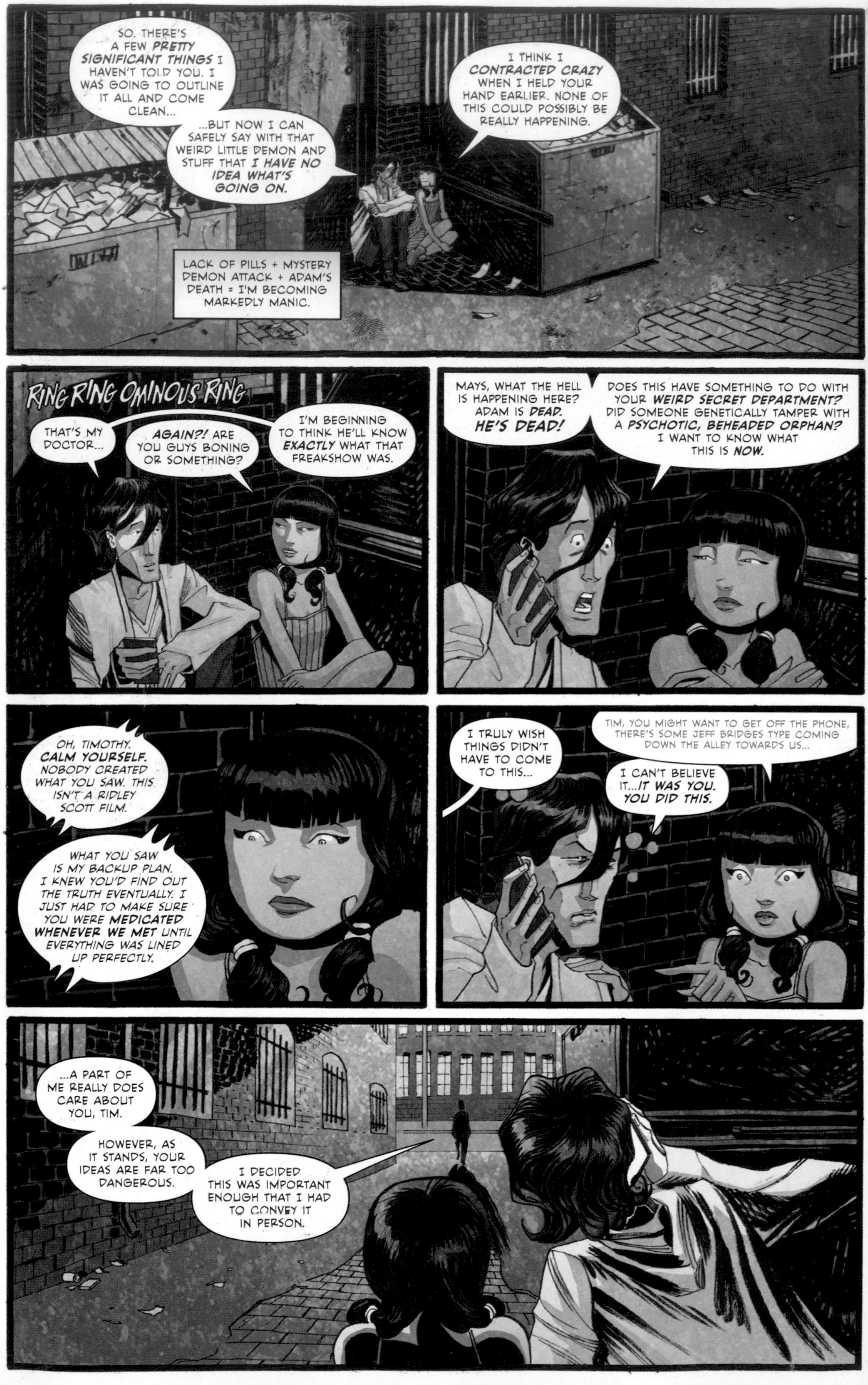
SO. THERE'S A FEW PRETTY SIGNIFICANT THINGS I HAVEN'T TOLD YOU. I WAS GOING TO OUTLINE IT ALL AND COME CLEAN...
...BUT NOW I CAN SAFELY SAY WITH THAT WEIRD LITTLE DEMON AND STUFF THAT I HAVE NO IDEA WHAT'S GOING ON.
I THINK I CONTRACTED CRAZY WHEN I HELD YOUR HAND EARLIER. NONE OF THIS COULD POSSIBLY BE REALLY HAPPENING.
LACK OF PILLS + MYSTERY DEMON ATTACK + ADAM'S DEATH = I'M BECOMING MARKEDLY MANIC.
RING RING OMINOUS RING
THAT'S MY DOCTOR...
AGAIN?! ARE YOU GUYS BONING OR SOMETHING?
I'M BEGINNING TO THINK HE'LL KNOW EXACTLY WHAT THAT FREAKSHOW WAS.
MAYS, WHAT THE HELL IS HAPPENING HERE? ADAM IS DEAD. HE'S DEAD!
DOES THIS HAVE SOMETHING TO DO WITH YOUR WEIRD SECRET DEPARTMENT? DID SOMEONE GENETICALLY TAMPER WITH A PSYCHOTIC, BEHEADED ORPHAN? I WANT TO KNOW WHAT THIS IS NOW.
OH, TIMOTHY. CALM YOURSELF. NOBODY CREATED WHAT YOU SAW. THIS ISN'T A RIDLEY SCOTT FILM.
WHAT YOU SAW IS MY BACKUP PLAN. I KNEW YOU'D FIND OUT THE TRUTH EVENTUALLY. I JUST HAD TO MAKE SURE YOU WERE MEDICATED WHENEVER WE MET UNTIL EVERYTHING WAS LINED UP PERFECTLY.
I TRULY WISH THINGS DIDN'T HAVE TO COME TO THIS...
TIM, YOU MIGHT WANT TO GET OFF THE PHONE, THERE'S SOME JEFF BRIDGES TYPE COMING DOWN THE ALLEY TOWARDS US...
I CAN'T BELIEVE IT...IT WAS YOU. YOU DID THIS.
...A PART OF ME REALLY DOES CARE ABOUT YOU, TIM.
HOWEVER, AS IT STANDS, YOUR IDEAS ARE FAR TOO DANGEROUS.
I DECIDED THIS WAS IMPORTANT ENOUGH THAT I HAD TO CONVEY IT IN PERSON.

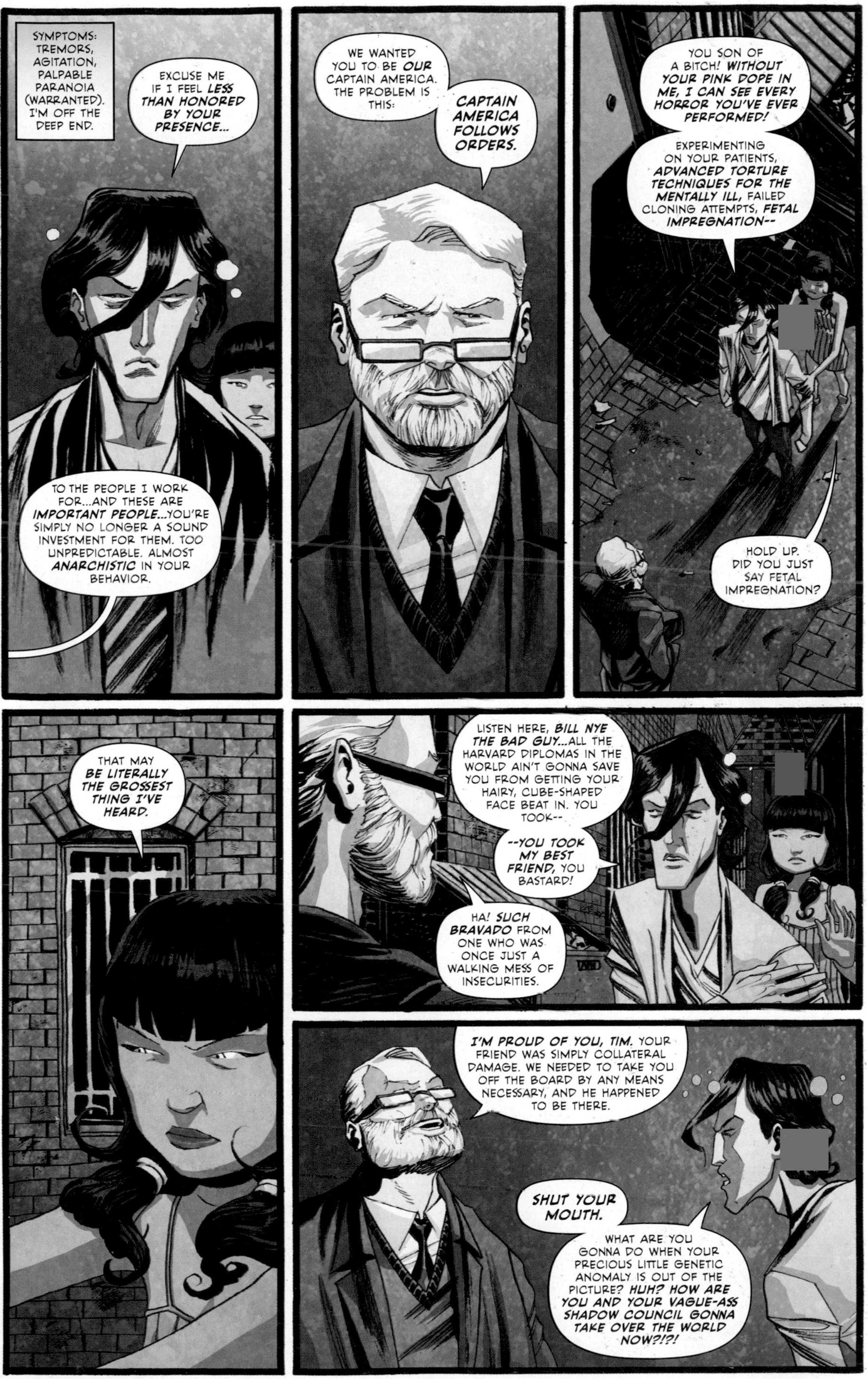
SYMPTOMS: TREMORS, AGITATION, PALPABLE PARANOIA (WARRANTED). I'M OFF THE DEEP END.
EXCUSE ME IF I FEEL LESS THAN HONORED BY YOUR PRESENCE...
TO THE PEOPLE I WORK FOR...AND THESE ARE IMPORTANT PEOPLE...YOU'RE SIMPLY NO LONGER A SOUND INVESTMENT FOR THEM. TOO UNPREDICTABLE. ALMOST ANARCHISTIC IN YOUR BEHAVIOR.
WE WANTED YOU TO BE OUR CAPTAIN AMERICA. THE PROBLEM IS THIS:
CAPTAIN AMERICA FOLLOWS ORDERS.
YOU SON OF A BITCH! WITHOUT YOUR PINK DOPE IN ME, I CAN SEE EVERY HORROR YOU'VE EVER PERFORMED!
EXPERIMENTING ON YOUR PATIENTS, ADVANCED TORTURE TECHNIQUES FOR THE MENTALLY ILL, FAILED CLONING ATTEMPTS, FETAL IMPREGNATION--
HOLD UP. DID YOU JUST SAY FETAL IMPREGNATION?
THAT MAY BE LITERALLY THE GROSSEST THING I'VE HEARD.
LISTEN HERE, BILL NYE THE BAD GUY...ALL THE HARVARD DIPLOMAS IN THE WORLD AIN'T GONNA SAVE YOU FROM GETTING YOUR HAIRY, CUBE-SHAPED FACE BEAT IN. YOU TOOK--
--YOU TOOK MY BEST FRIEND, YOU BASTARD!
HA! SUCH BRAVADO FROM ONE WHO WAS ONCE JUST A WALKING MESS OF INSECURITIES.
I'M PROUD OF YOU, TIM. YOUR FRIEND WAS SIMPLY COLLATERAL DAMAGE. WE NEEDED TO TAKE YOU OFF THE BOARD BY ANY MEANS NECESSARY, AND HE HAPPENED TO BE THERE.
SHUT YOUR MOUTH.
WHAT ARE YOU GONNA DO WHEN YOUR PRECIOUS LITTLE GENETIC ANOMALY IS OUT OF THE PICTURE? HUH? HOW ARE YOU AND YOUR VAGUE-ASS SHADOW COUNCIL GONNA TAKE OVER THE WORLD NOW?!?!

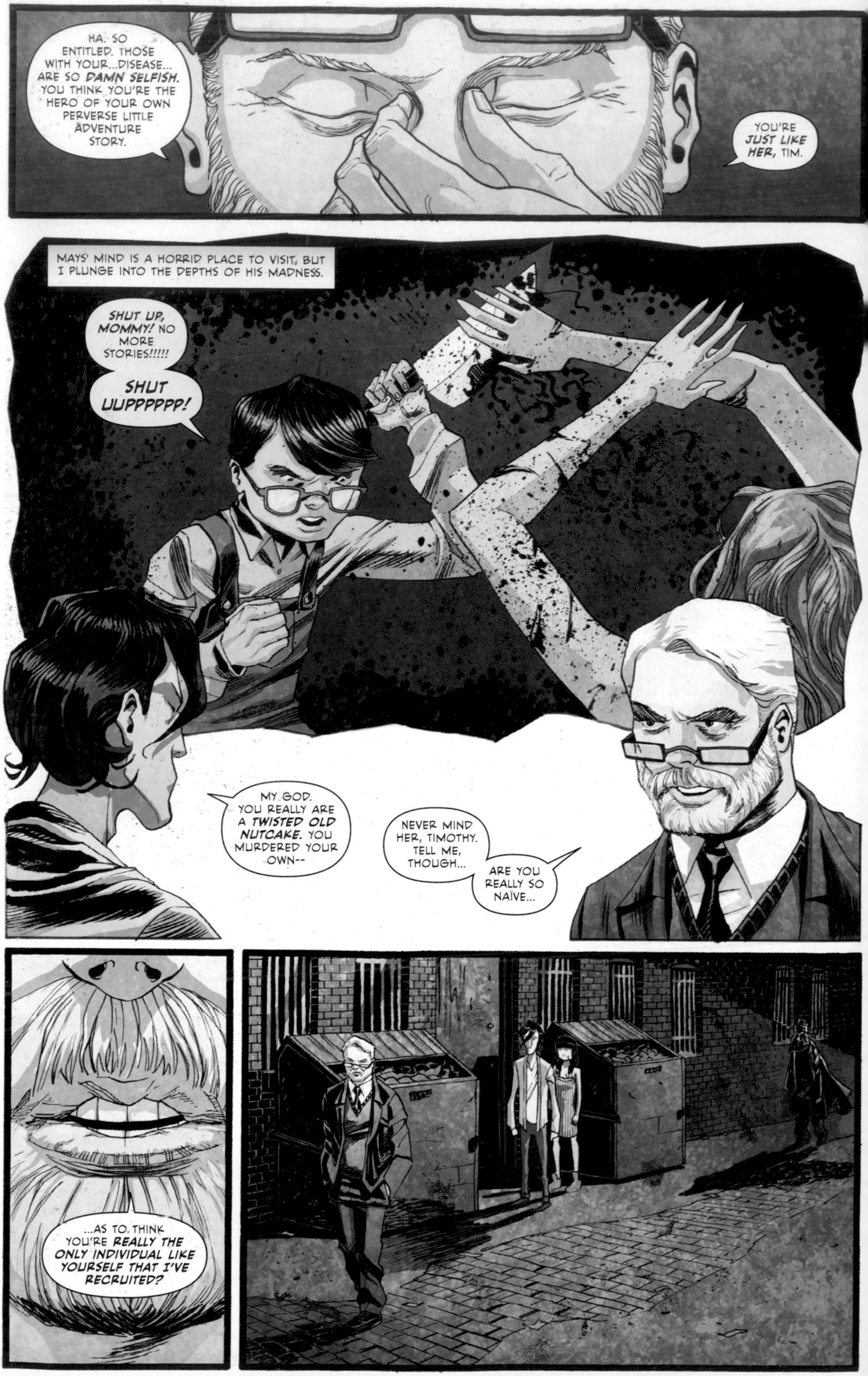
HA. SO ENTITLED. THOSE WITH YOUR...DISEASE... ARE SO DAMN SELFISH. YOU THINK YOU'RE THE HERO OF YOUR OWN PERVERSE LITTLE ADVENTURE STORY.
YOU'RE JUST LIKE HER, TIM.
MAYS' MIND IS A HORRID PLACE TO VISIT, BUT I PLUNGE INTO THE DEPTHS OF HIS MADNESS.
SHUT UP, MOMMY! NO MORE STORIES!!!!!
SHUT UUPPPPPP!
MY GOD. YOU REALLY ARE A TWISTED OLD NUTCAKE. YOU MURDERED YOUR OWN--
NEVER MIND HER, TIMOTHY. TELL ME, THOUGH...
ARE YOU REALLY SO NAÏVE...
...AS TO THINK YOU'RE REALLY THE ONLY INDIVIDUAL LIKE YOURSELF THAT I'VE RECRUITED?

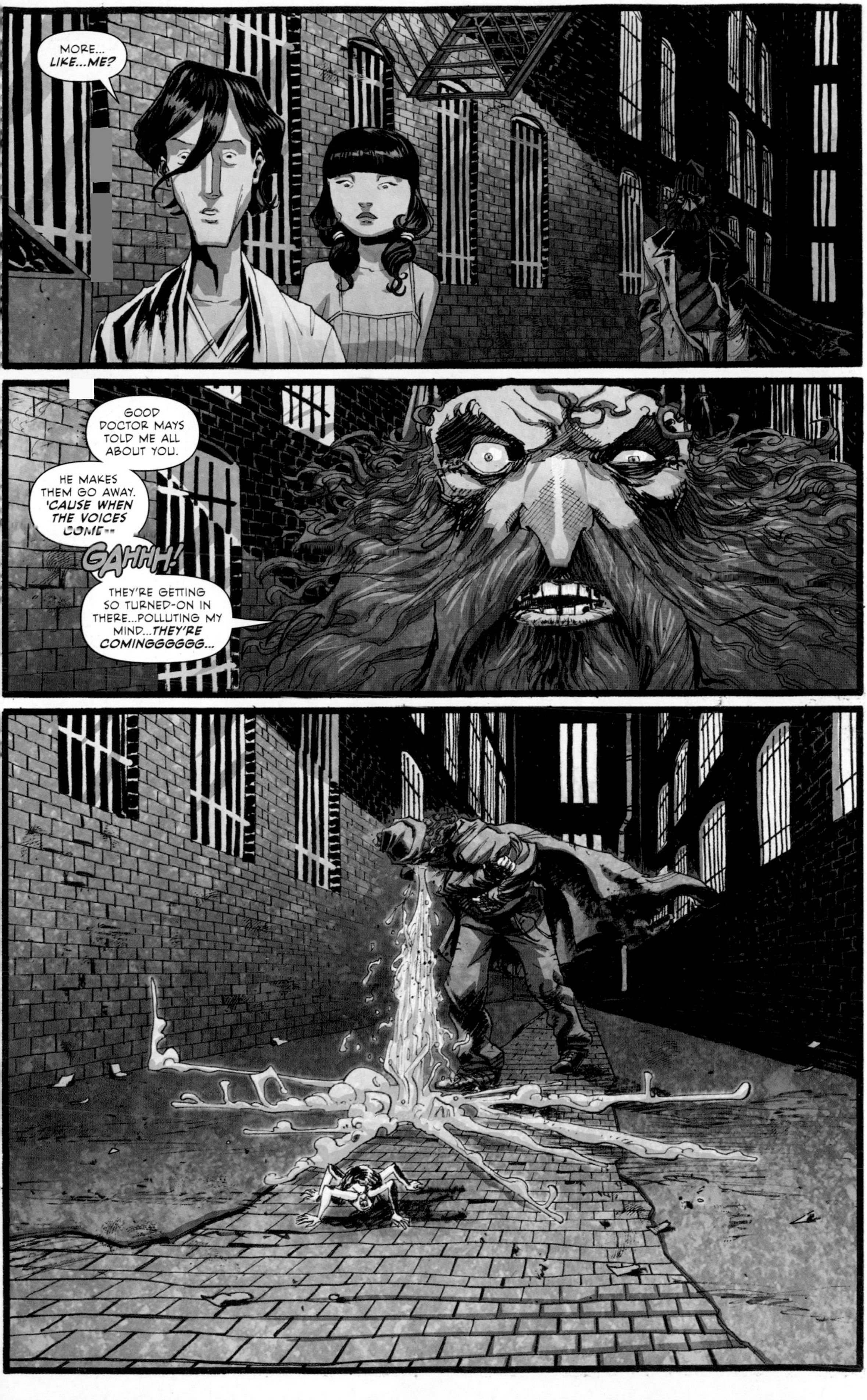
MORE... *LIKE...ME?*
GOOD DOCTOR MAYS TOLD ME ALL ABOUT YOU.
HE MAKES THEM GO AWAY. *'CAUSE WHEN THE VOICES COME--*
GAHHH!
THEY'RE GETTING SO TURNED-ON IN THERE...POLLUTING MY MIND...*THEY'RE COMINGGGGGG...*

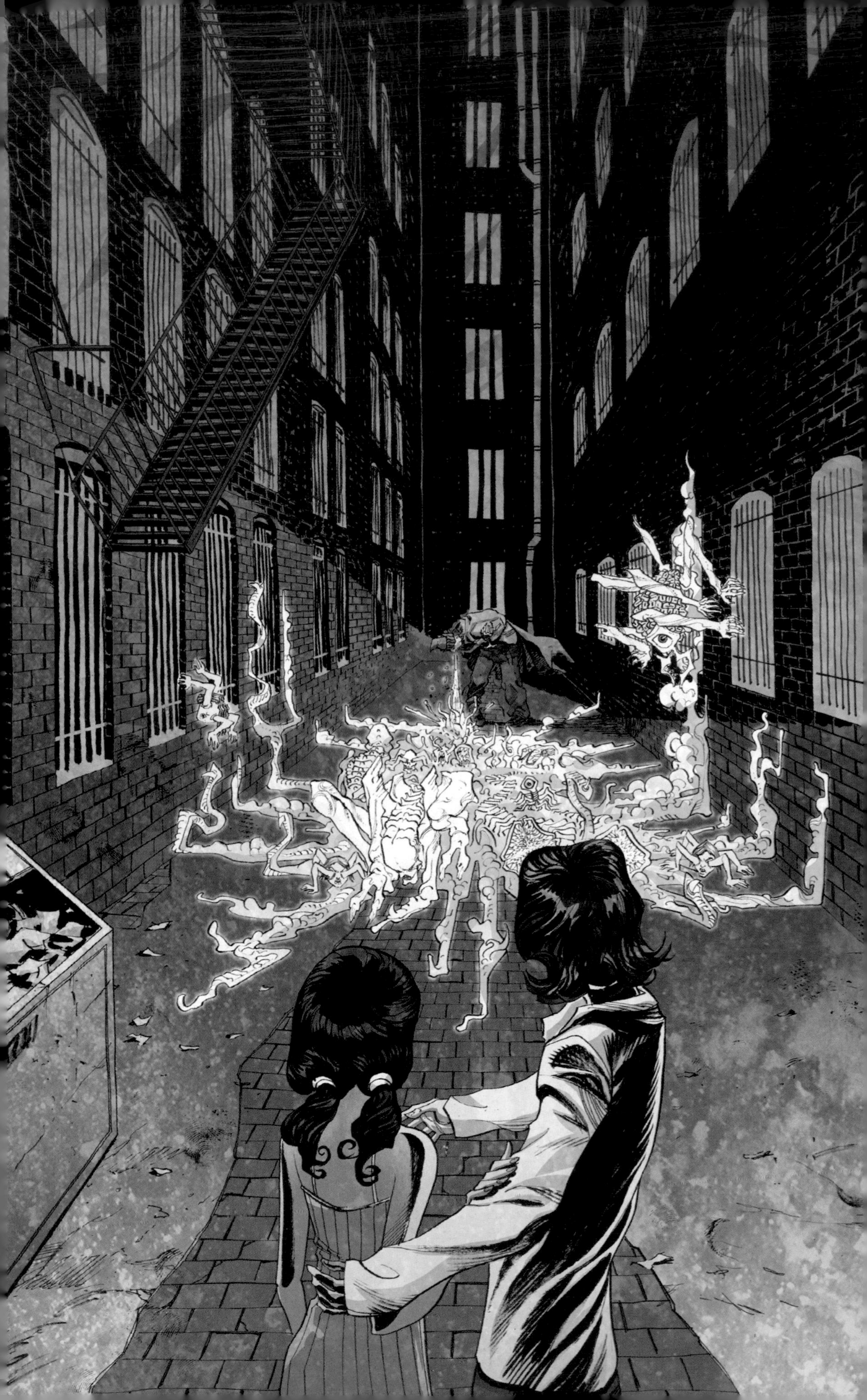

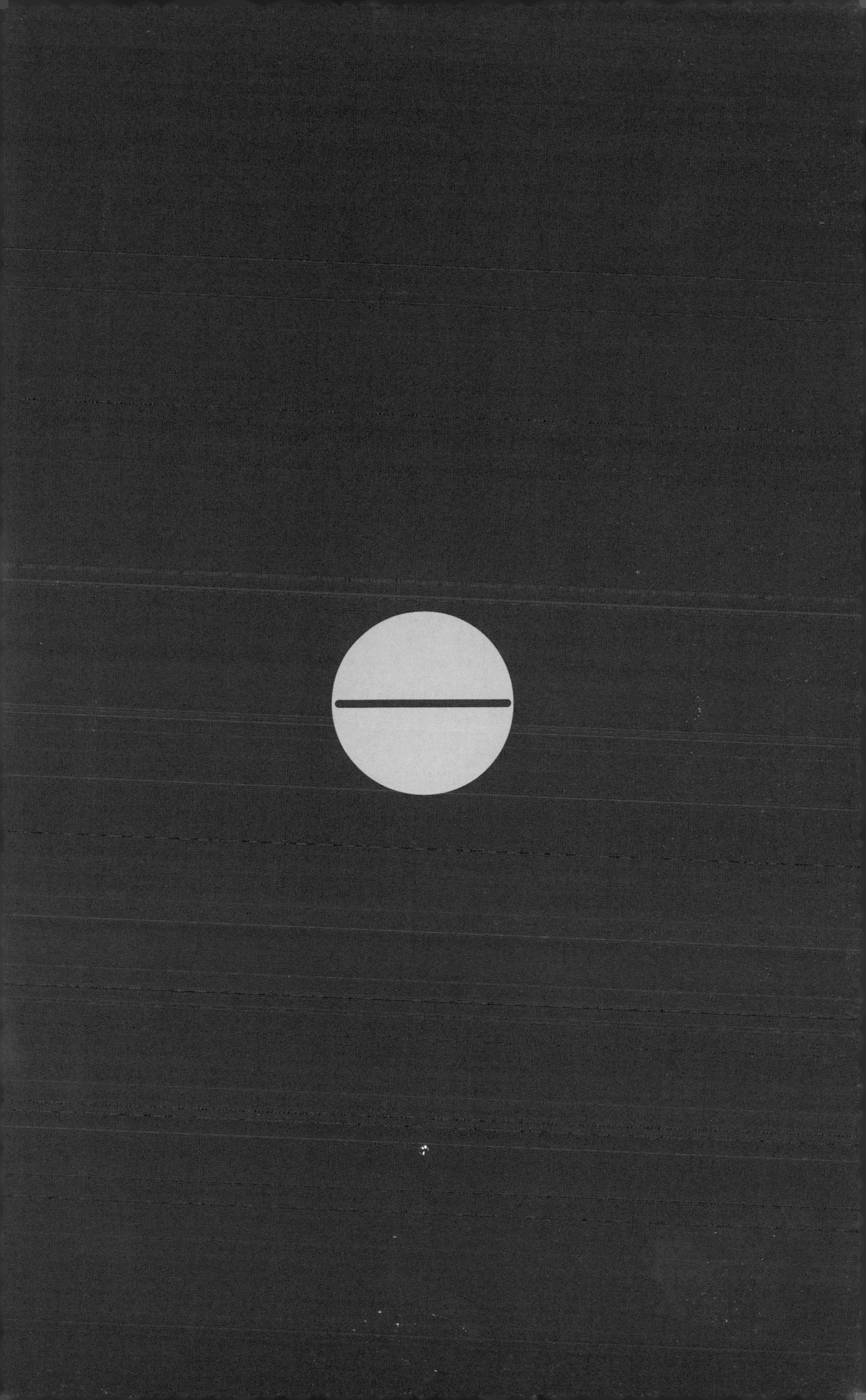

"WHEN THE TRUTH COMES OUT"

THE TRUTH COMES OUT
IT SEEMS THAT I'VE BEEN MANIPULATED
BY SOMETHING GREATER THAN ME
AND EVERYTHING I EVER THOUGHT WAS GOOD INSIDE OF ME

IS ONLY FALSE

THE TRUTH COMES OUT

MY PARENTS ARE MY TORMENTORS
MY LOVE IS MY SERPENT
NOW I THOUGHT I'D REVERSED IT ALL
IT'S COMING BACK AGAIN
ALRIGHT

THE TRUTH COMES OUT

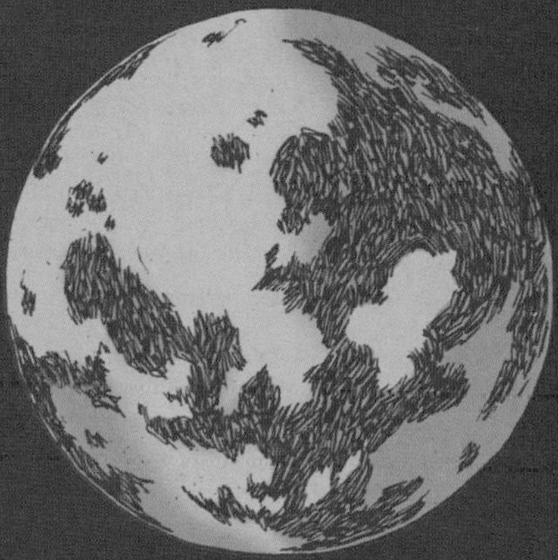

AND I'M GONNA FIGHT BACK

(JUST LIKE MY FAVORITE KNAPSACK SONG)
REVERSE THE ROLES, REVERSE THE ROLES

AND I WON'T ACCEPT THIS

(JUST LIKE MY FAVORITE KNAPSACK SONG)
REVERSE THE ROLES, REVERSE THE ROLES

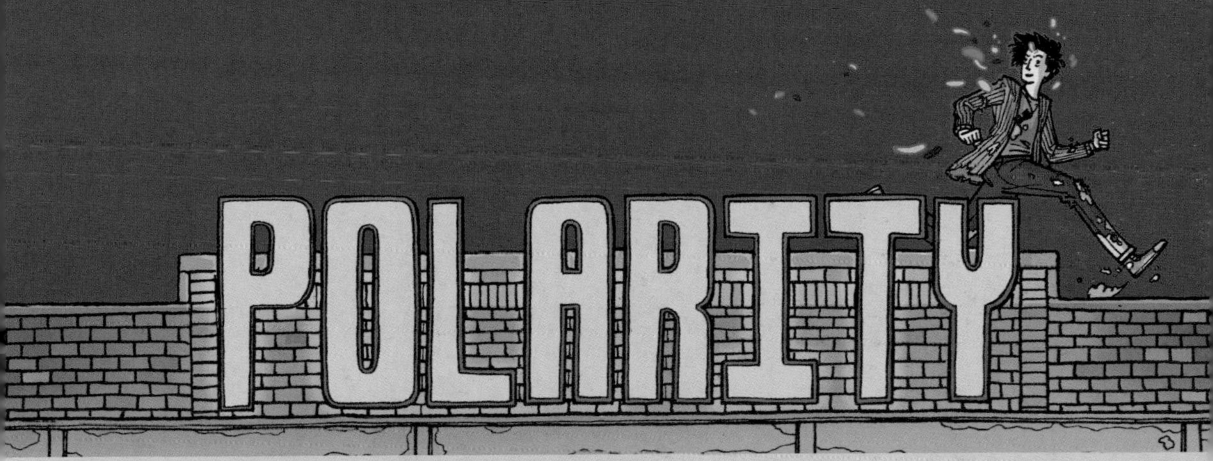
POLARITY

THE TRUTH COMES OUT

"AND SUPERHEROES ALWAYS TELL THE TRUTH, RIGHT?"

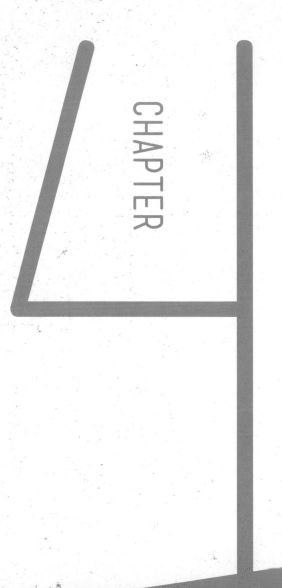

CHAPTER

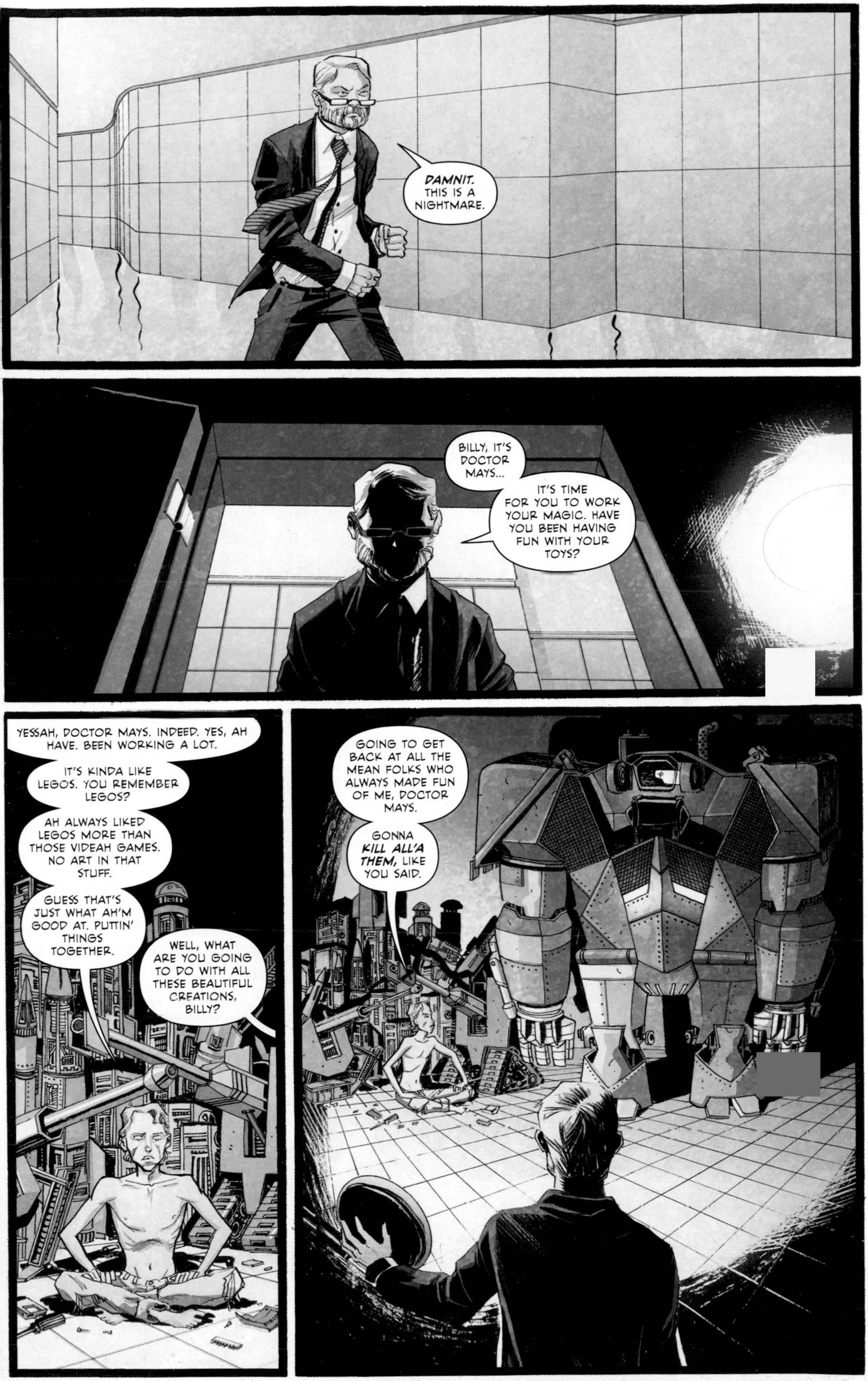

DAMNIT. THIS IS A NIGHTMARE.
BILLY, IT'S DOCTOR MAYS...
IT'S TIME FOR YOU TO WORK YOUR MAGIC. HAVE YOU BEEN HAVING FUN WITH YOUR TOYS?
YESSAH, DOCTOR MAYS. INDEED. YES, AH HAVE. BEEN WORKING A LOT.
IT'S KINDA LIKE LEGOS. YOU REMEMBER LEGOS?
AH ALWAYS LIKED LEGOS MORE THAN THOSE VIDEAH GAMES. NO ART IN THAT STUFF.
GUESS THAT'S JUST WHAT AH'M GOOD AT. PUTTIN' THINGS TOGETHER.
WELL, WHAT ARE YOU GOING TO DO WITH ALL THESE BEAUTIFUL CREATIONS, BILLY?
GOING TO GET BACK AT ALL THE MEAN FOLKS WHO ALWAYS MADE FUN OF ME, DOCTOR MAYS.
GONNA KILL ALL'A THEM, LIKE YOU SAID.

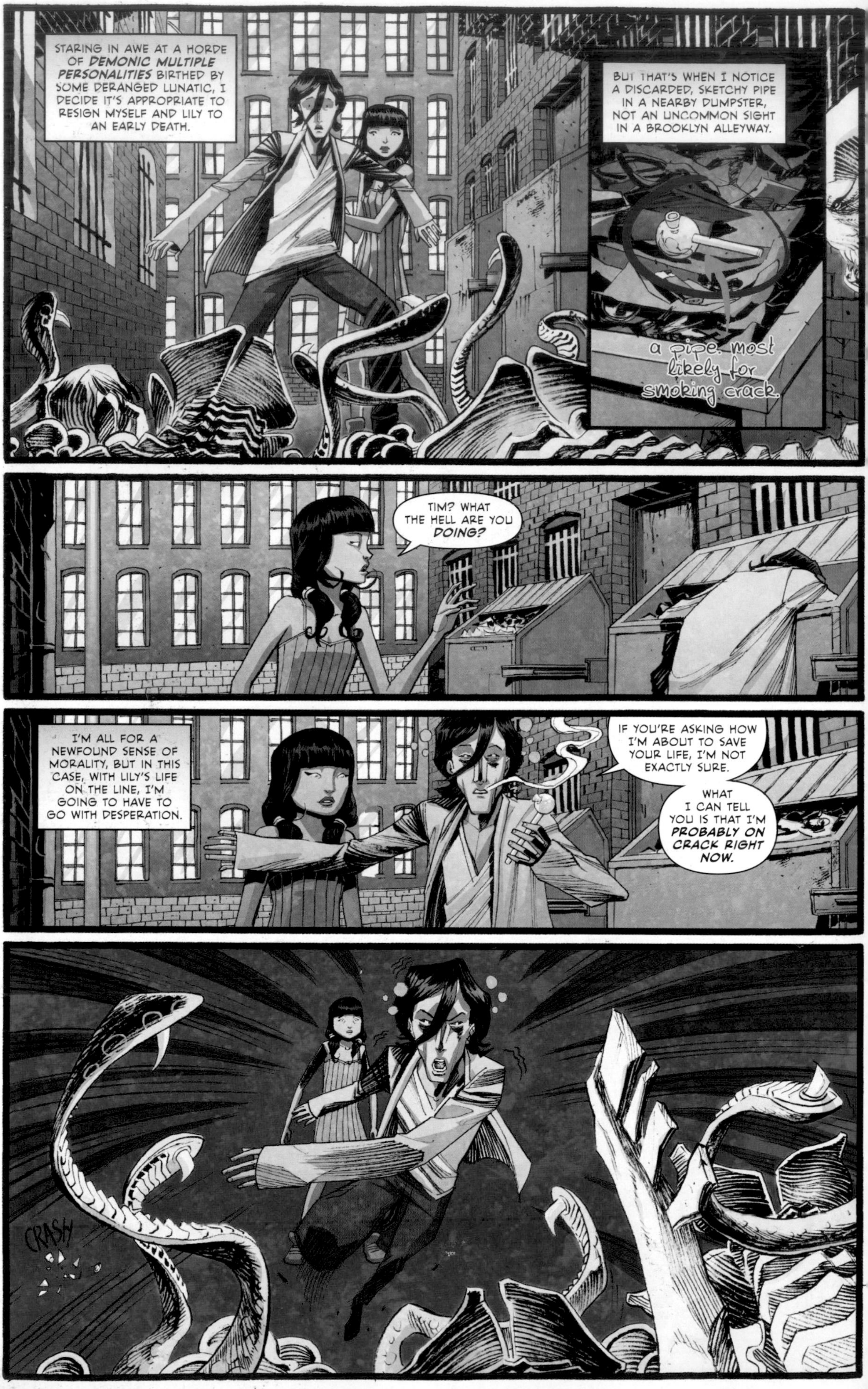
STARING IN AWE AT A HORDE OF DEMONIC MULTIPLE PERSONALITIES BIRTHED BY SOME DERANGED LUNATIC, I DECIDE IT'S APPROPRIATE TO RESIGN MYSELF AND LILY TO AN EARLY DEATH.
BUT THAT'S WHEN I NOTICE A DISCARDED, SKETCHY PIPE IN A NEARBY DUMPSTER, NOT AN UNCOMMON SIGHT IN A BROOKLYN ALLEYWAY.
a pipe. most likely for smoking crack.
TIM? WHAT THE HELL ARE YOU DOING?
I'M ALL FOR A NEWFOUND SENSE OF MORALITY, BUT IN THIS CASE, WITH LILY'S LIFE ON THE LINE, I'M GOING TO HAVE TO GO WITH DESPERATION.
IF YOU'RE ASKING HOW I'M ABOUT TO SAVE YOUR LIFE, I'M NOT EXACTLY SURE.
WHAT I CAN TELL YOU IS THAT I'M PROBABLY ON CRACK RIGHT NOW.
CRASH

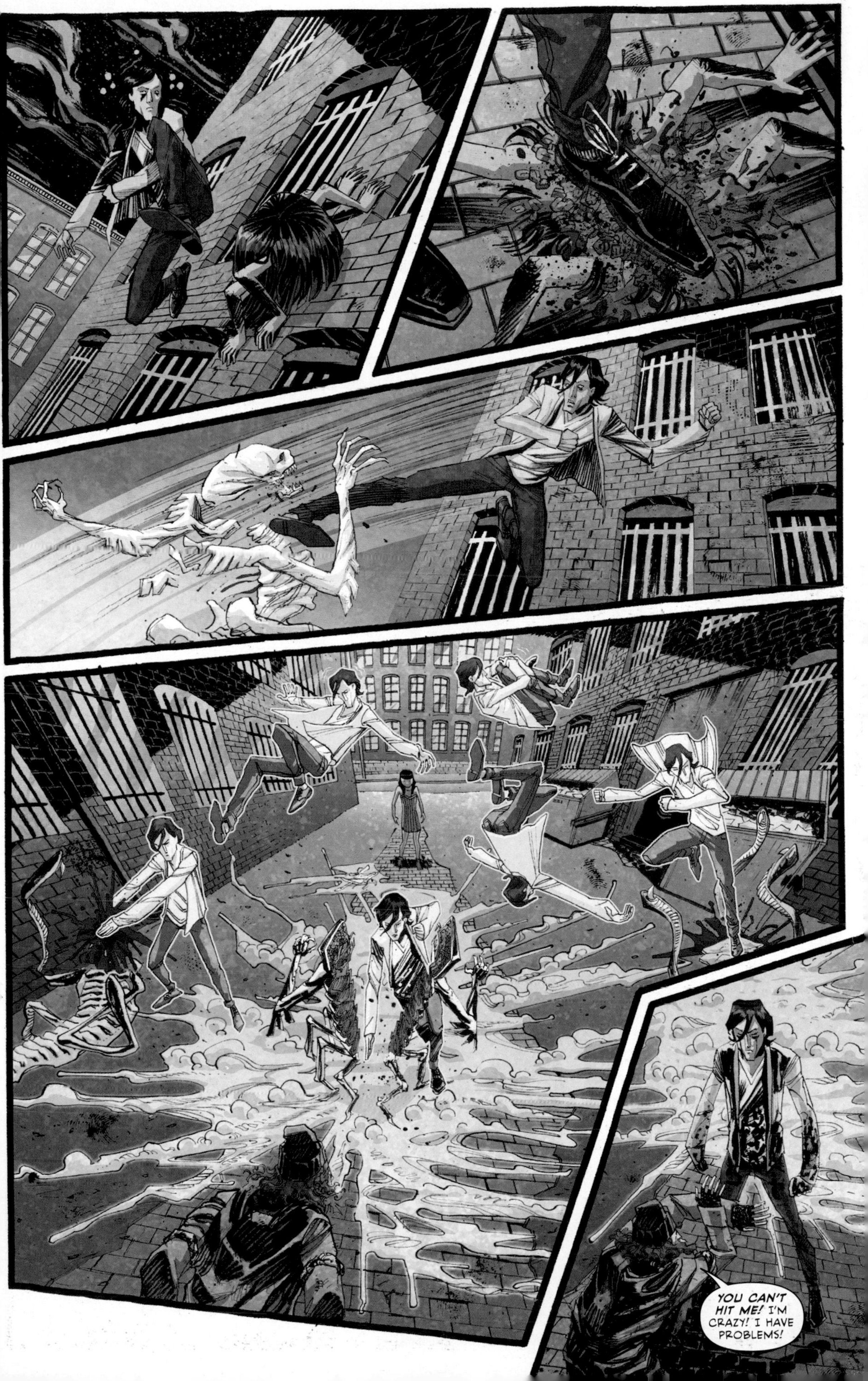
YOU CAN'T HIT ME! I'M CRAZY! I HAVE PROBLEMS!

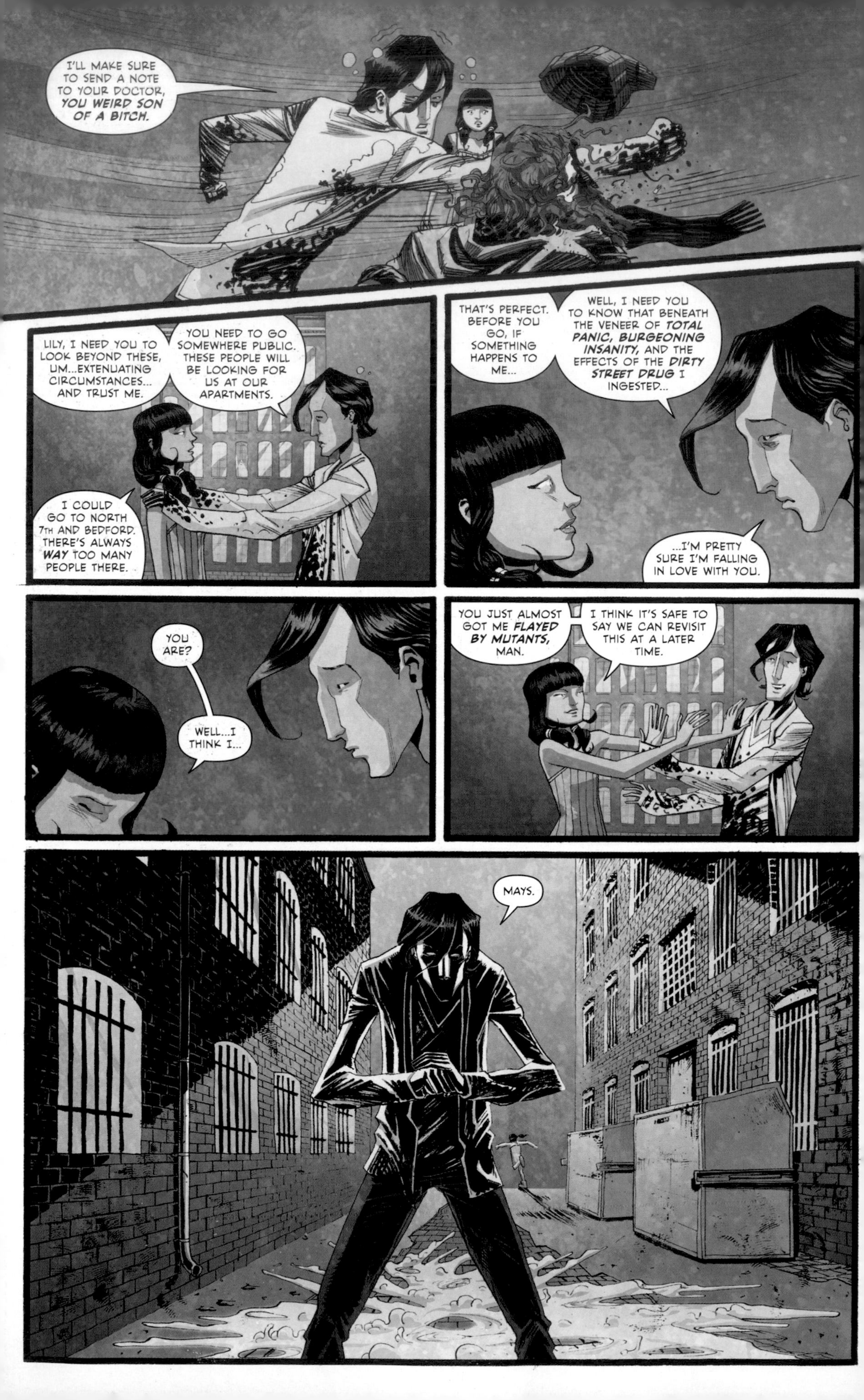
I'LL MAKE SURE TO SEND A NOTE TO YOUR DOCTOR, ***YOU WEIRD SON OF A BITCH.***
LILY, I NEED YOU TO LOOK BEYOND THESE, UM...EXTENUATING CIRCUMSTANCES... AND TRUST ME.
YOU NEED TO GO SOMEWHERE PUBLIC. THESE PEOPLE WILL BE LOOKING FOR US AT OUR APARTMENTS.
I COULD GO TO NORTH 7TH AND BEDFORD. THERE'S ALWAYS ***WAY*** TOO MANY PEOPLE THERE.
THAT'S PERFECT. BEFORE YOU GO, IF SOMETHING HAPPENS TO ME...
WELL, I NEED YOU TO KNOW THAT BENEATH THE VENEER OF ***TOTAL PANIC, BURGEONING INSANITY,*** AND THE EFFECTS OF THE ***DIRTY STREET DRUG*** I INGESTED...
...I'M PRETTY SURE I'M FALLING IN LOVE WITH YOU.
YOU ARE?
WELL...I THINK I...
YOU JUST ALMOST GOT ME ***FLAYED BY MUTANTS,*** MAN.
I THINK IT'S SAFE TO SAY WE CAN REVISIT THIS AT A LATER TIME.
MAYS.

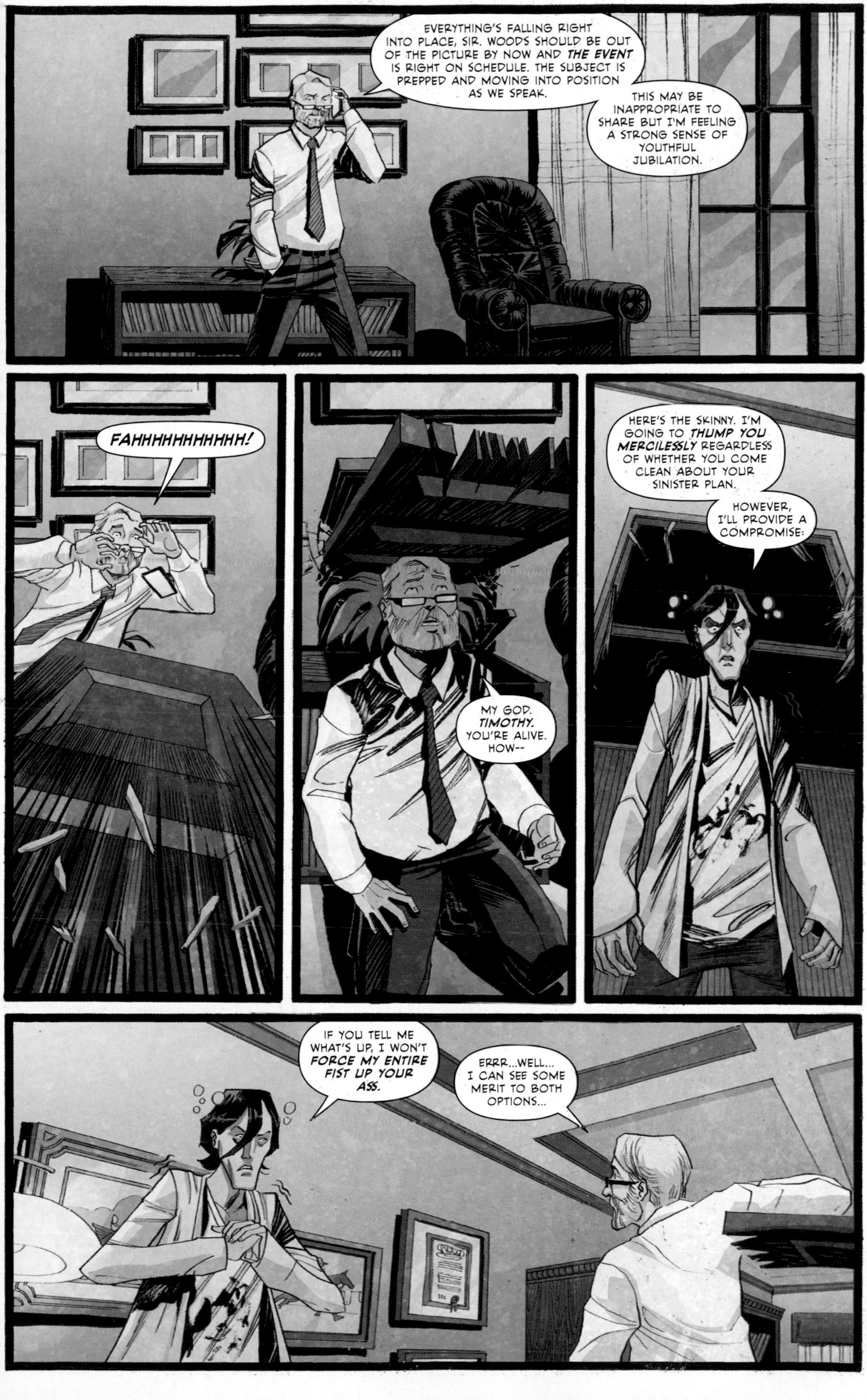
EVERYTHING'S FALLING RIGHT INTO PLACE, SIR. WOODS SHOULD BE OUT OF THE PICTURE BY NOW AND *THE EVENT* IS RIGHT ON SCHEDULE. THE SUBJECT IS PREPPED AND MOVING INTO POSITION AS WE SPEAK.
THIS MAY BE INAPPROPRIATE TO SHARE BUT I'M FEELING A STRONG SENSE OF YOUTHFUL JUBILATION.
FAHHHHHHHHHHH!
MY GOD. *TIMOTHY.* YOU'RE ALIVE. HOW--
HERE'S THE SKINNY. I'M GOING TO *THUMP YOU MERCILESSLY* REGARDLESS OF WHETHER YOU COME CLEAN ABOUT YOUR SINISTER PLAN.
HOWEVER, I'LL PROVIDE A COMPROMISE:
IF YOU TELL ME WHAT'S UP, I WON'T *FORCE MY ENTIRE FIST UP YOUR ASS.*
ERRR...WELL... I CAN SEE SOME MERIT TO BOTH OPTIONS...

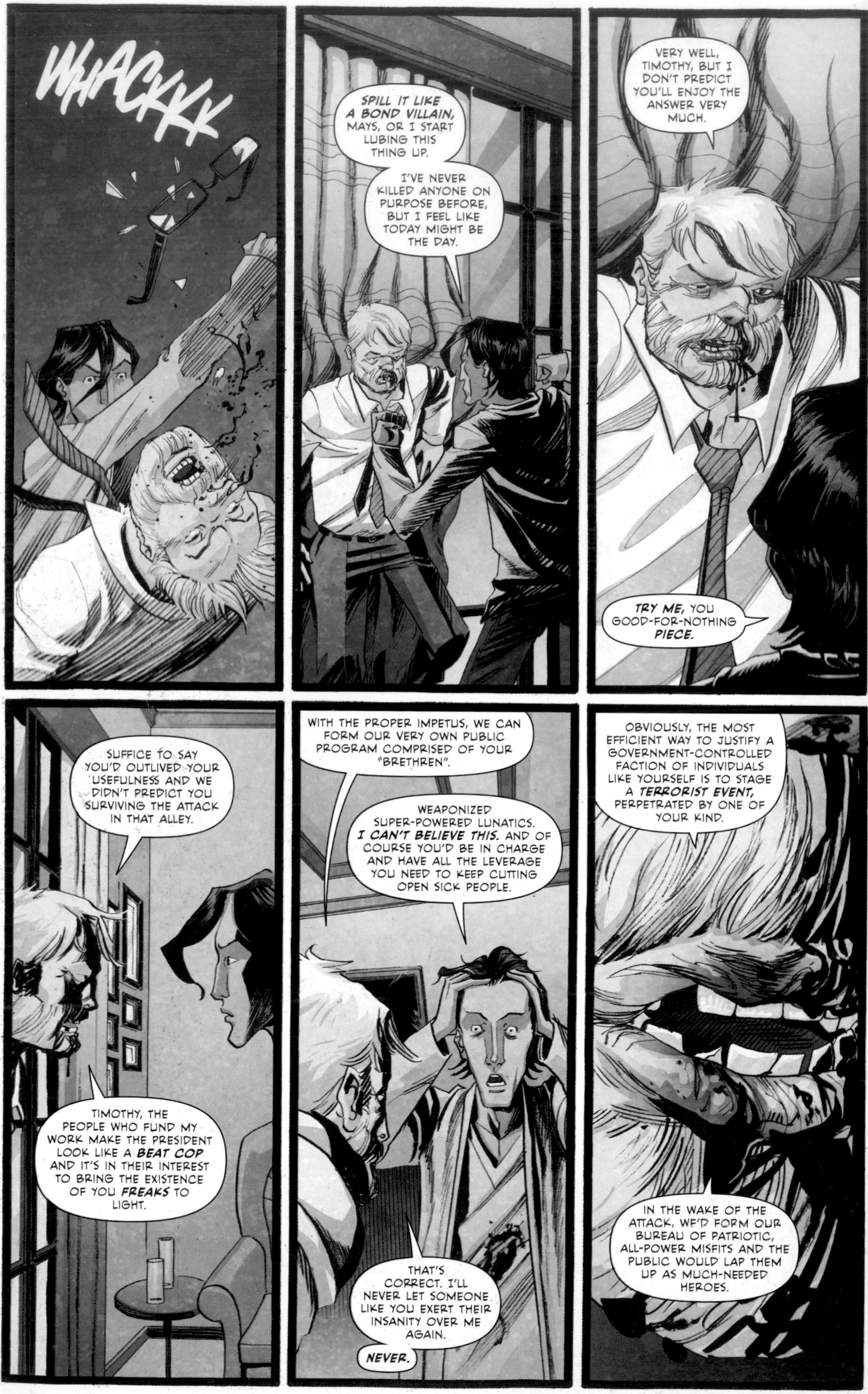
WHACKKK
SPILL IT LIKE A BOND VILLAIN, MAYS, OR I START LUBING THIS THING UP.
I'VE NEVER KILLED ANYONE ON PURPOSE BEFORE, BUT I FEEL LIKE TODAY MIGHT BE THE DAY.
VERY WELL, TIMOTHY, BUT I DON'T PREDICT YOU'LL ENJOY THE ANSWER VERY MUCH.
TRY ME, YOU GOOD-FOR-NOTHING PIECE.
SUFFICE TO SAY YOU'D OUTLIVED YOUR USEFULNESS AND WE DIDN'T PREDICT YOU SURVIVING THE ATTACK IN THAT ALLEY.
TIMOTHY, THE PEOPLE WHO FUND MY WORK MAKE THE PRESIDENT LOOK LIKE A BEAT COP AND IT'S IN THEIR INTEREST TO BRING THE EXISTENCE OF YOU FREAKS TO LIGHT.
WITH THE PROPER IMPETUS, WE CAN FORM OUR VERY OWN PUBLIC PROGRAM COMPRISED OF YOUR "BRETHREN".
WEAPONIZED SUPER-POWERED LUNATICS. I CAN'T BELIEVE THIS. AND OF COURSE YOU'D BE IN CHARGE AND HAVE ALL THE LEVERAGE YOU NEED TO KEEP CUTTING OPEN SICK PEOPLE.
THAT'S CORRECT. I'LL NEVER LET SOMEONE LIKE YOU EXERT THEIR INSANITY OVER ME AGAIN.
NEVER.
OBVIOUSLY, THE MOST EFFICIENT WAY TO JUSTIFY A GOVERNMENT-CONTROLLED FACTION OF INDIVIDUALS LIKE YOURSELF IS TO STAGE A TERRORIST EVENT, PERPETRATED BY ONE OF YOUR KIND.
IN THE WAKE OF THE ATTACK, WE'D FORM OUR BUREAU OF PATRIOTIC, ALL-POWER MISFITS AND THE PUBLIC WOULD LAP THEM UP AS MUCH-NEEDED HEROES.

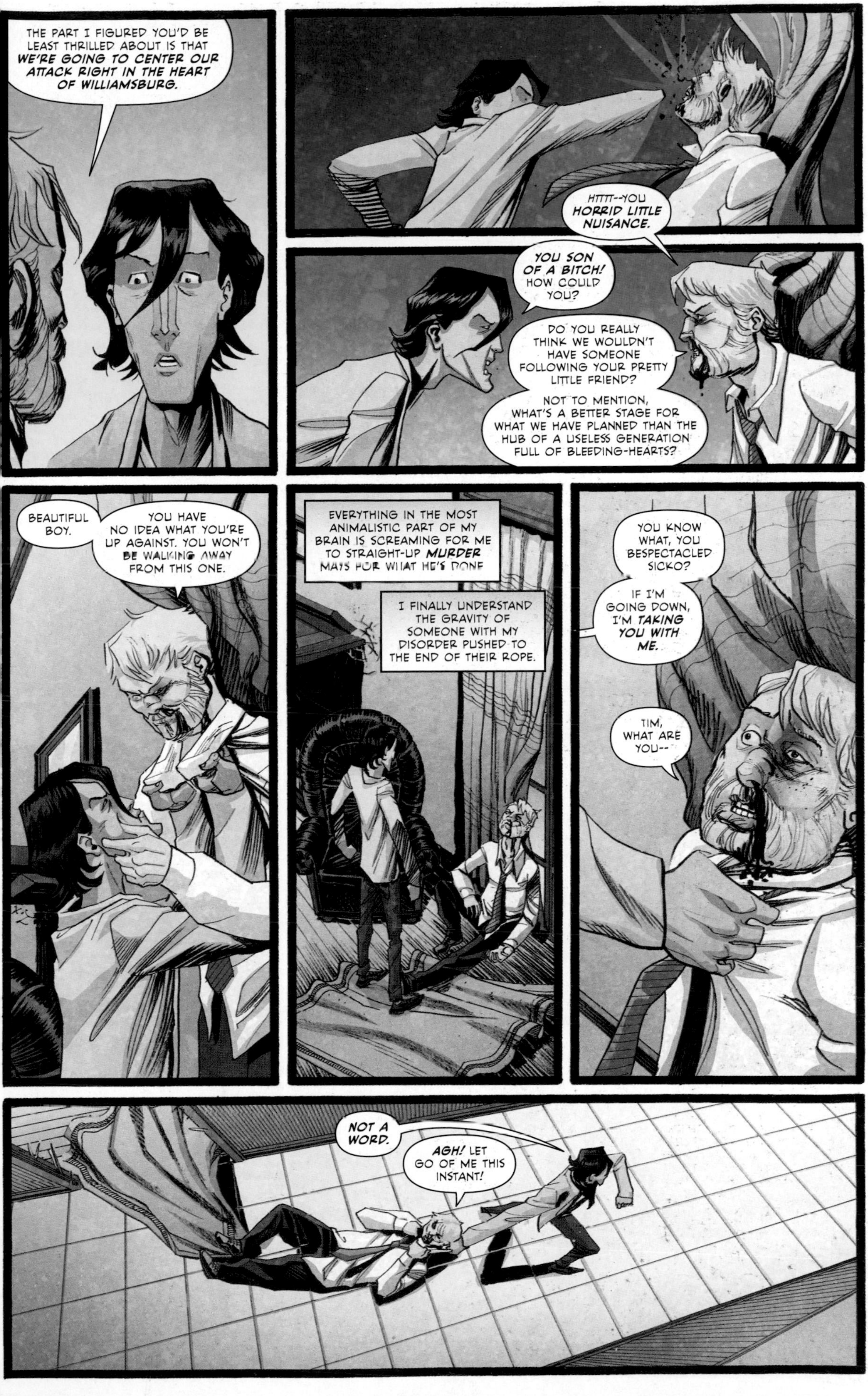
THE PART I FIGURED YOU'D BE LEAST THRILLED ABOUT IS THAT WE'RE GOING TO CENTER OUR ATTACK RIGHT IN THE HEART OF WILLIAMSBURG.
HTTTT--YOU HORRID LITTLE NUISANCE.
YOU SON OF A BITCH! HOW COULD YOU?
DO YOU REALLY THINK WE WOULDN'T HAVE SOMEONE FOLLOWING YOUR PRETTY LITTLE FRIEND?
NOT TO MENTION, WHAT'S A BETTER STAGE FOR WHAT WE HAVE PLANNED THAN THE HUB OF A USELESS GENERATION FULL OF BLEEDING-HEARTS?
BEAUTIFUL BOY.
YOU HAVE NO IDEA WHAT YOU'RE UP AGAINST. YOU WON'T BE WALKING AWAY FROM THIS ONE.
EVERYTHING IN THE MOST ANIMALISTIC PART OF MY BRAIN IS SCREAMING FOR ME TO STRAIGHT-UP MURDER MAYS FOR WHAT HE'S DONE
I FINALLY UNDERSTAND THE GRAVITY OF SOMEONE WITH MY DISORDER PUSHED TO THE END OF THEIR ROPE.
YOU KNOW WHAT, YOU BESPECTACLED SICKO?
IF I'M GOING DOWN, I'M TAKING YOU WITH ME.
TIM, WHAT ARE YOU--
NOT A WORD.
AGH! LET GO OF ME THIS INSTANT!

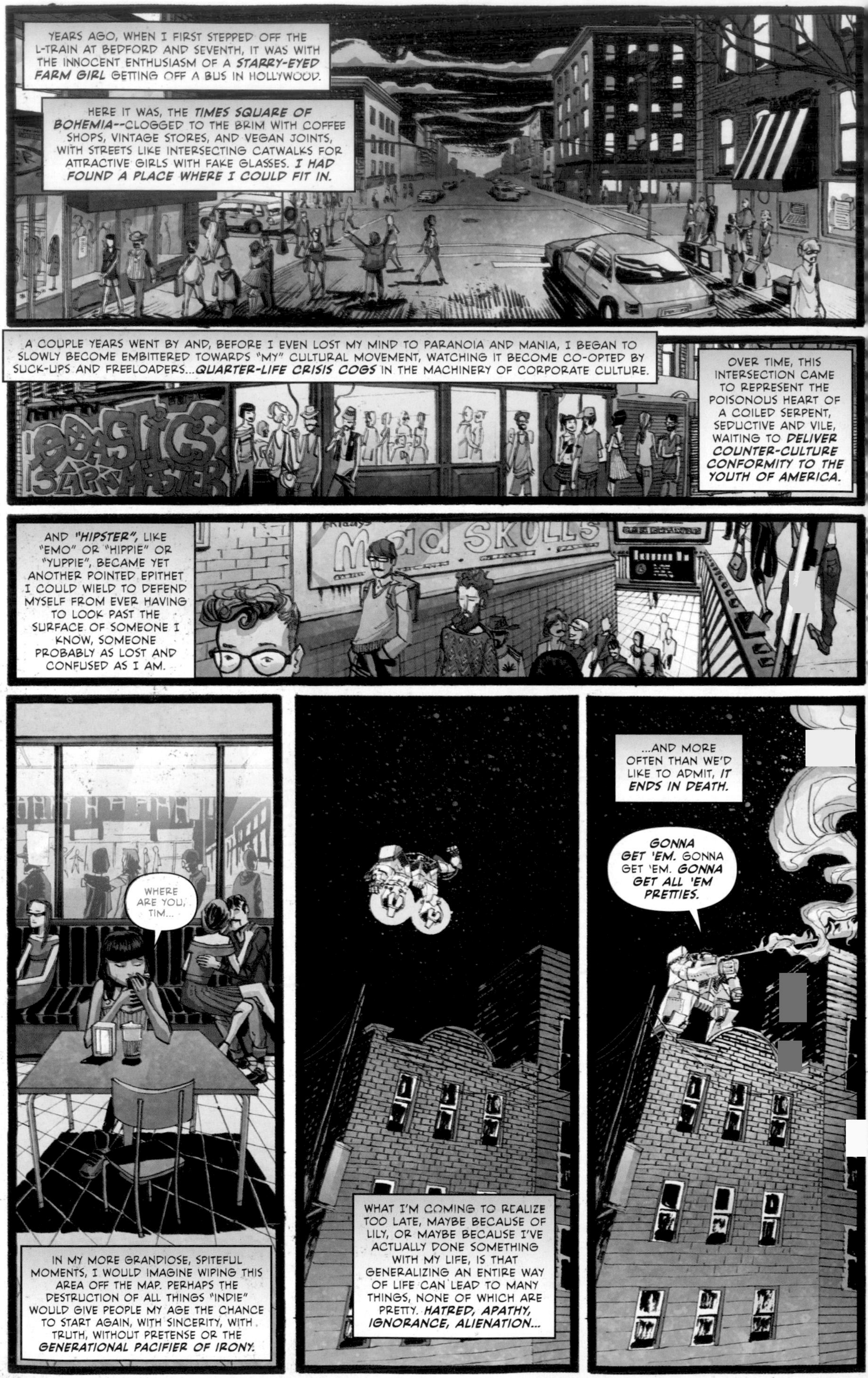
YEARS AGO, WHEN I FIRST STEPPED OFF THE L-TRAIN AT BEDFORD AND SEVENTH, IT WAS WITH THE INNOCENT ENTHUSIASM OF A STARRY-EYED FARM GIRL GETTING OFF A BUS IN HOLLYWOOD.
HERE IT WAS, THE TIMES SQUARE OF BOHEMIA--CLOGGED TO THE BRIM WITH COFFEE SHOPS, VINTAGE STORES, AND VEGAN JOINTS, WITH STREETS LIKE INTERSECTING CATWALKS FOR ATTRACTIVE GIRLS WITH FAKE GLASSES. I HAD FOUND A PLACE WHERE I COULD FIT IN.
A COUPLE YEARS WENT BY AND, BEFORE I EVEN LOST MY MIND TO PARANOIA AND MANIA, I BEGAN TO SLOWLY BECOME EMBITTERED TOWARDS "MY" CULTURAL MOVEMENT, WATCHING IT BECOME CO-OPTED BY SUCK-UPS AND FREELOADERS...QUARTER-LIFE CRISIS COGS IN THE MACHINERY OF CORPORATE CULTURE.
OVER TIME, THIS INTERSECTION CAME TO REPRESENT THE POISONOUS HEART OF A COILED SERPENT, SEDUCTIVE AND VILE, WAITING TO DELIVER COUNTER-CULTURE CONFORMITY TO THE YOUTH OF AMERICA.
AND "HIPSTER", LIKE "EMO" OR "HIPPIE" OR "YUPPIE", BECAME YET ANOTHER POINTED EPITHET I COULD WIELD TO DEFEND MYSELF FROM EVER HAVING TO LOOK PAST THE SURFACE OF SOMEONE I KNOW, SOMEONE PROBABLY AS LOST AND CONFUSED AS I AM.
WHERE ARE YOU, TIM...
IN MY MORE GRANDIOSE, SPITEFUL MOMENTS, I WOULD IMAGINE WIPING THIS AREA OFF THE MAP. PERHAPS THE DESTRUCTION OF ALL THINGS "INDIE" WOULD GIVE PEOPLE MY AGE THE CHANCE TO START AGAIN, WITH SINCERITY, WITH TRUTH, WITHOUT PRETENSE OR THE GENERATIONAL PACIFIER OF IRONY.
WHAT I'M COMING TO REALIZE TOO LATE, MAYBE BECAUSE OF LILY, OR MAYBE BECAUSE I'VE ACTUALLY DONE SOMETHING WITH MY LIFE, IS THAT GENERALIZING AN ENTIRE WAY OF LIFE CAN LEAD TO MANY THINGS, NONE OF WHICH ARE PRETTY. HATRED, APATHY, IGNORANCE, ALIENATION...
...AND MORE OFTEN THAN WE'D LIKE TO ADMIT, IT ENDS IN DEATH.
GONNA GET 'EM. GONNA GET 'EM. GONNA GET ALL 'EM PRETTIES.

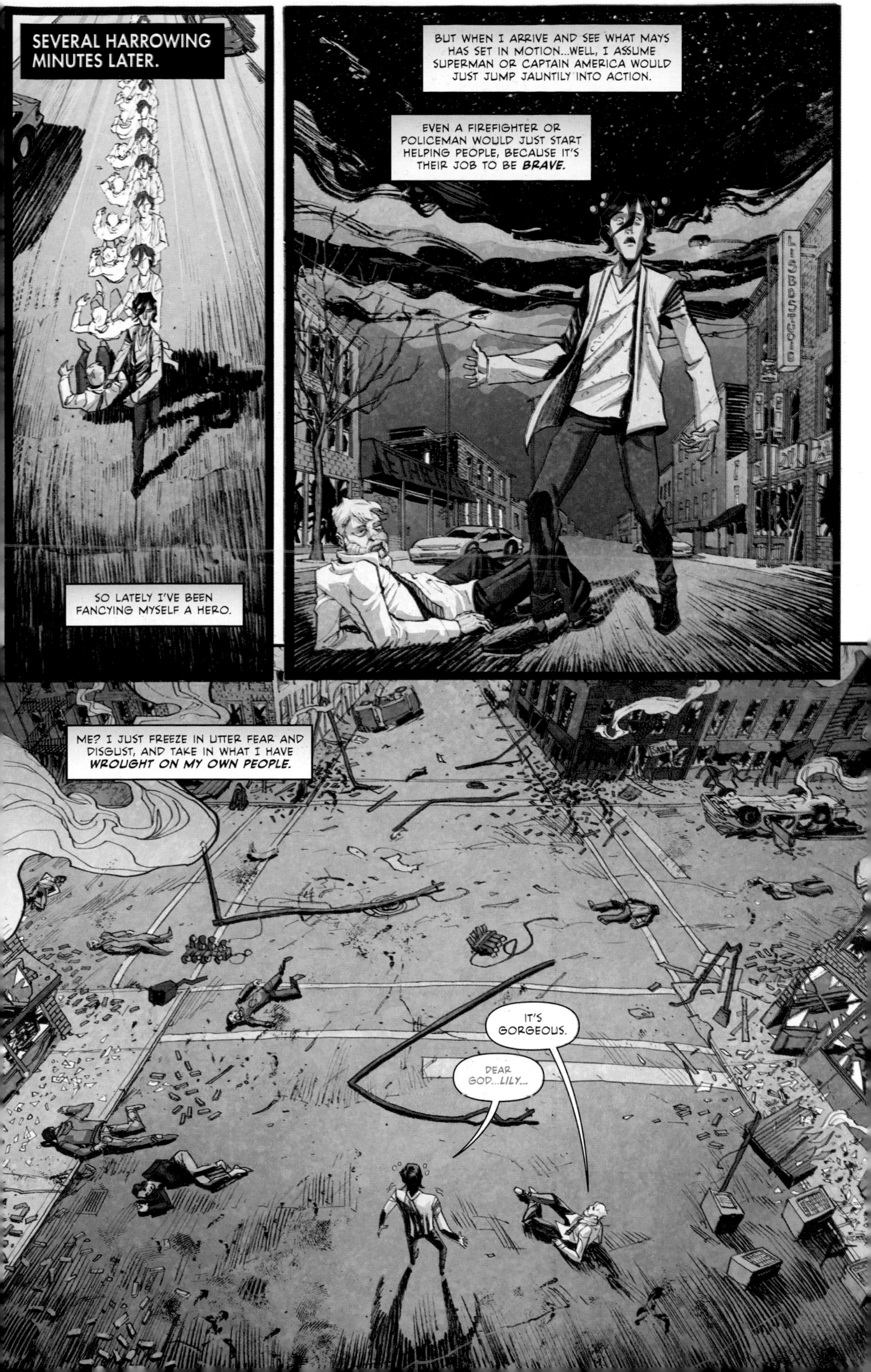
SEVERAL HARROWING MINUTES LATER.
SO LATELY I'VE BEEN FANCYING MYSELF A HERO.
BUT WHEN I ARRIVE AND SEE WHAT MAYS HAS SET IN MOTION...WELL, I ASSUME SUPERMAN OR CAPTAIN AMERICA WOULD JUST JUMP JAUNTILY INTO ACTION.
EVEN A FIREFIGHTER OR POLICEMAN WOULD JUST START HELPING PEOPLE, BECAUSE IT'S THEIR JOB TO BE ***BRAVE.***
ME? I JUST FREEZE IN UTTER FEAR AND DISGUST, AND TAKE IN WHAT I HAVE ***WROUGHT ON MY OWN PEOPLE.***
IT'S GORGEOUS.
DEAR GOD...*LILY...*

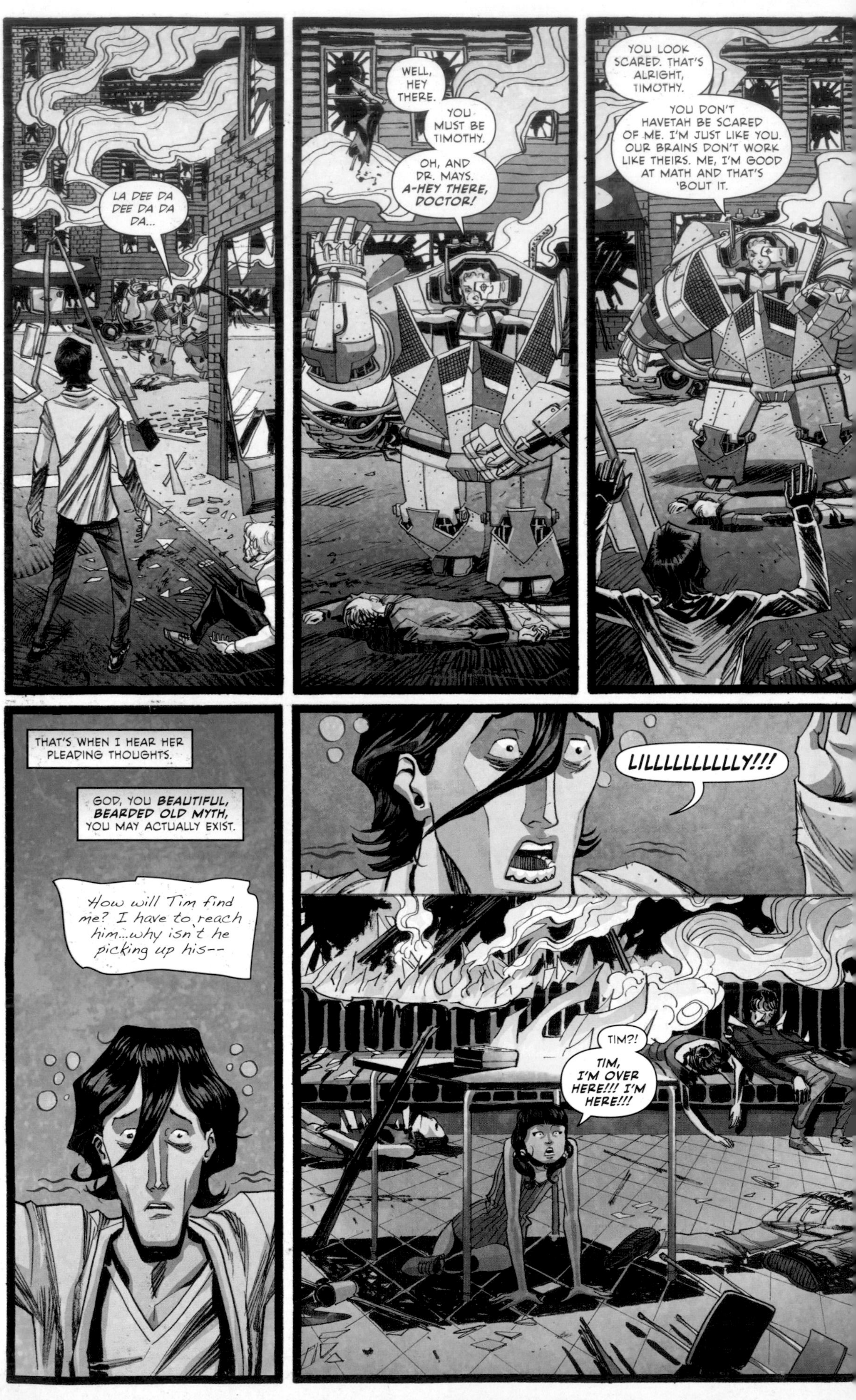

LA DEE DA DEE DA DA DA...
WELL, HEY THERE.
YOU MUST BE TIMOTHY.
OH, AND DR. MAYS. A-HEY THERE, DOCTOR!
YOU LOOK SCARED. THAT'S ALRIGHT, TIMOTHY.
YOU DON'T HAVETAH BE SCARED OF ME. I'M JUST LIKE YOU. OUR BRAINS DON'T WORK LIKE THEIRS. ME, I'M GOOD AT MATH AND THAT'S 'BOUT IT.
THAT'S WHEN I HEAR HER PLEADING THOUGHTS.
GOD, YOU BEAUTIFUL, BEARDED OLD MYTH, YOU MAY ACTUALLY EXIST.
How will Tim find me? I have to reach him...why isn't he picking up his--
LILLLLLLLLLLY!!!
TIM?!
TIM, I'M OVER HERE!!! I'M HERE!!!

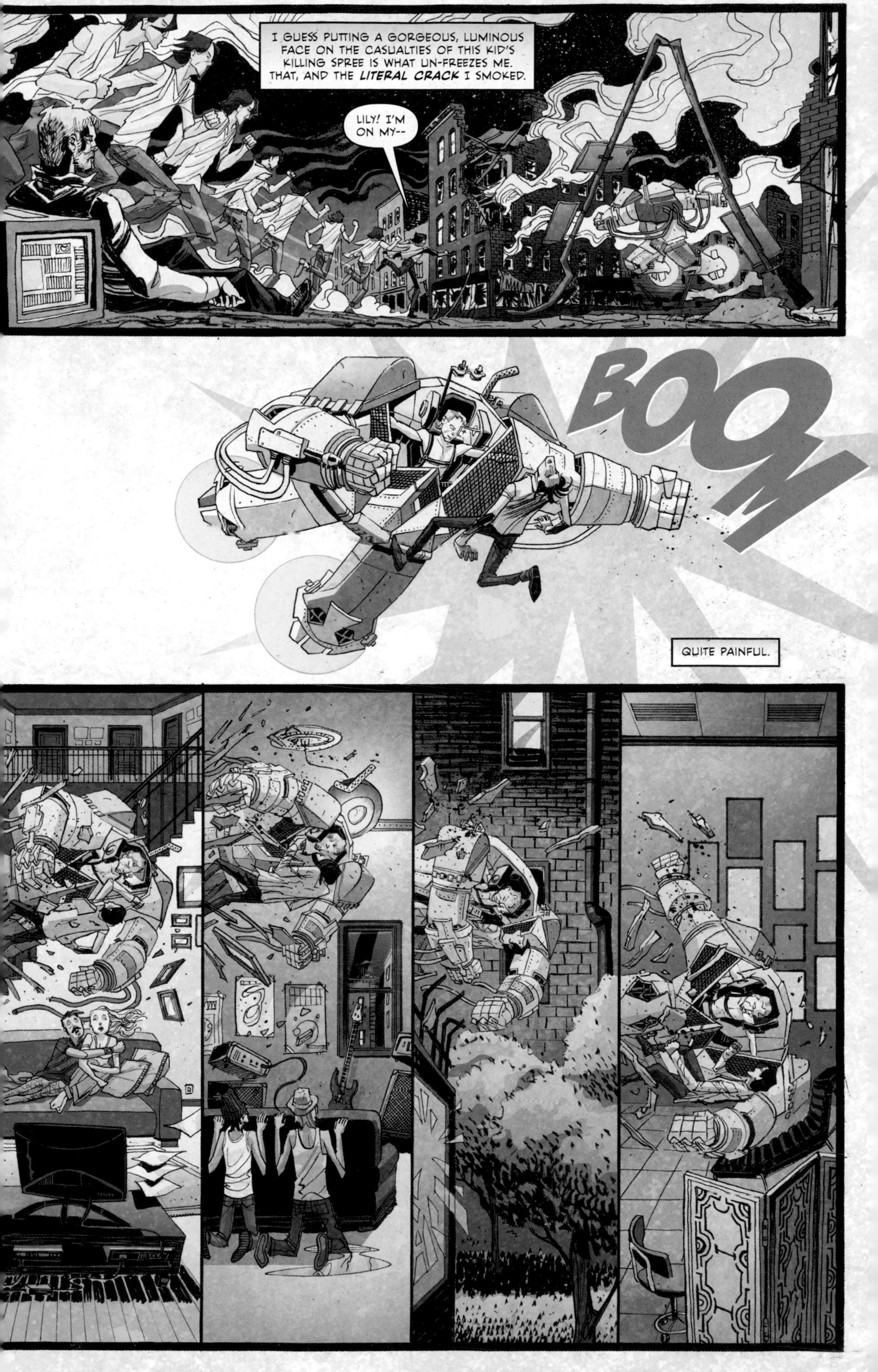
I GUESS PUTTING A GORGEOUS, LUMINOUS FACE ON THE CASUALTIES OF THIS KID'S KILLING SPREE IS WHAT UN-FREEZES ME. THAT, AND THE *LITERAL CRACK* I SMOKED.
LILY! I'M ON MY--
BOOM
QUITE PAINFUL.

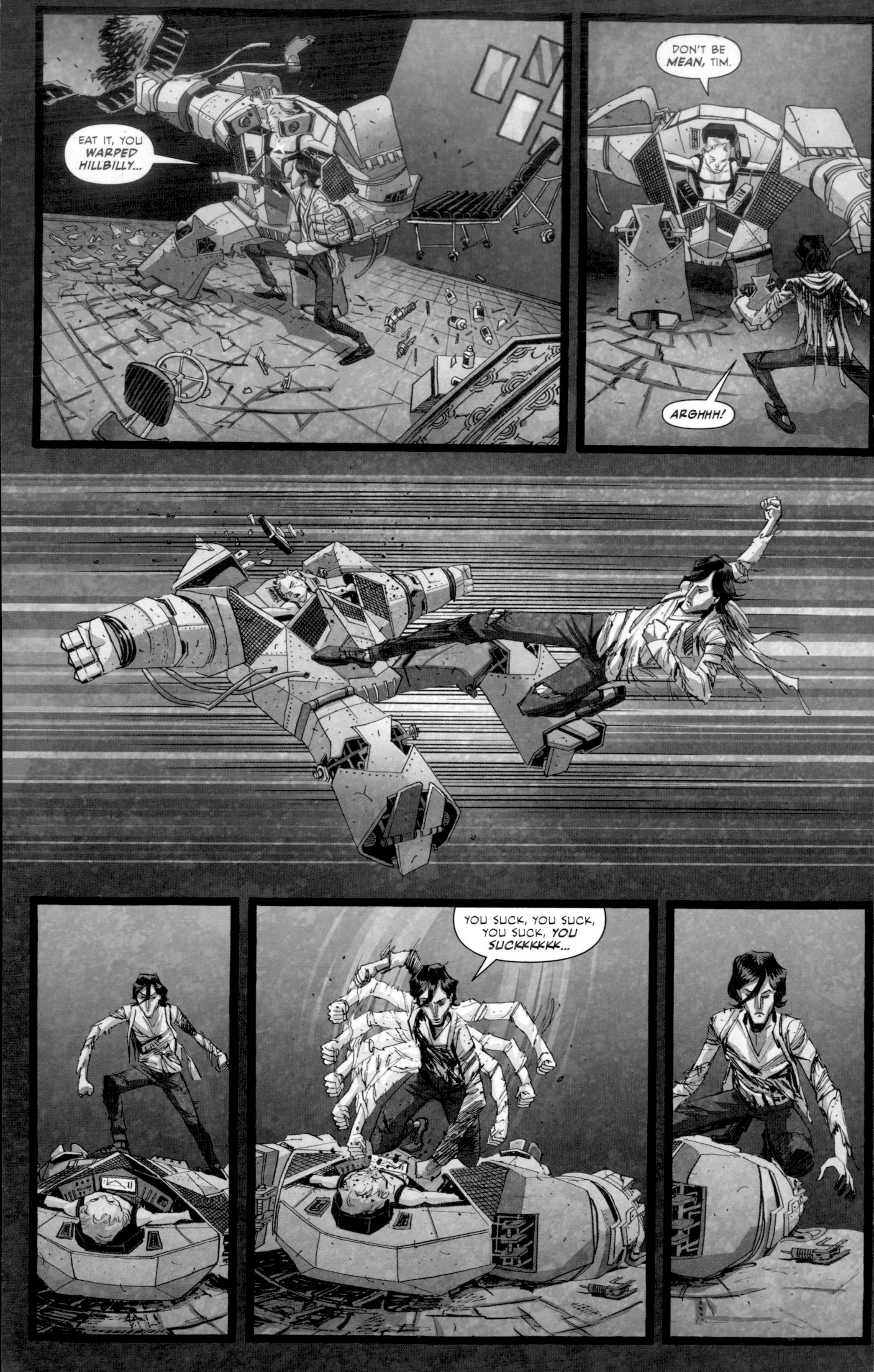
EAT IT, YOU WARPED HILLBILLY...
DON'T BE MEAN, TIM.
ARGHHH!
YOU SUCK, YOU SUCK, YOU SUCK, YOU SUCKKKKKK...

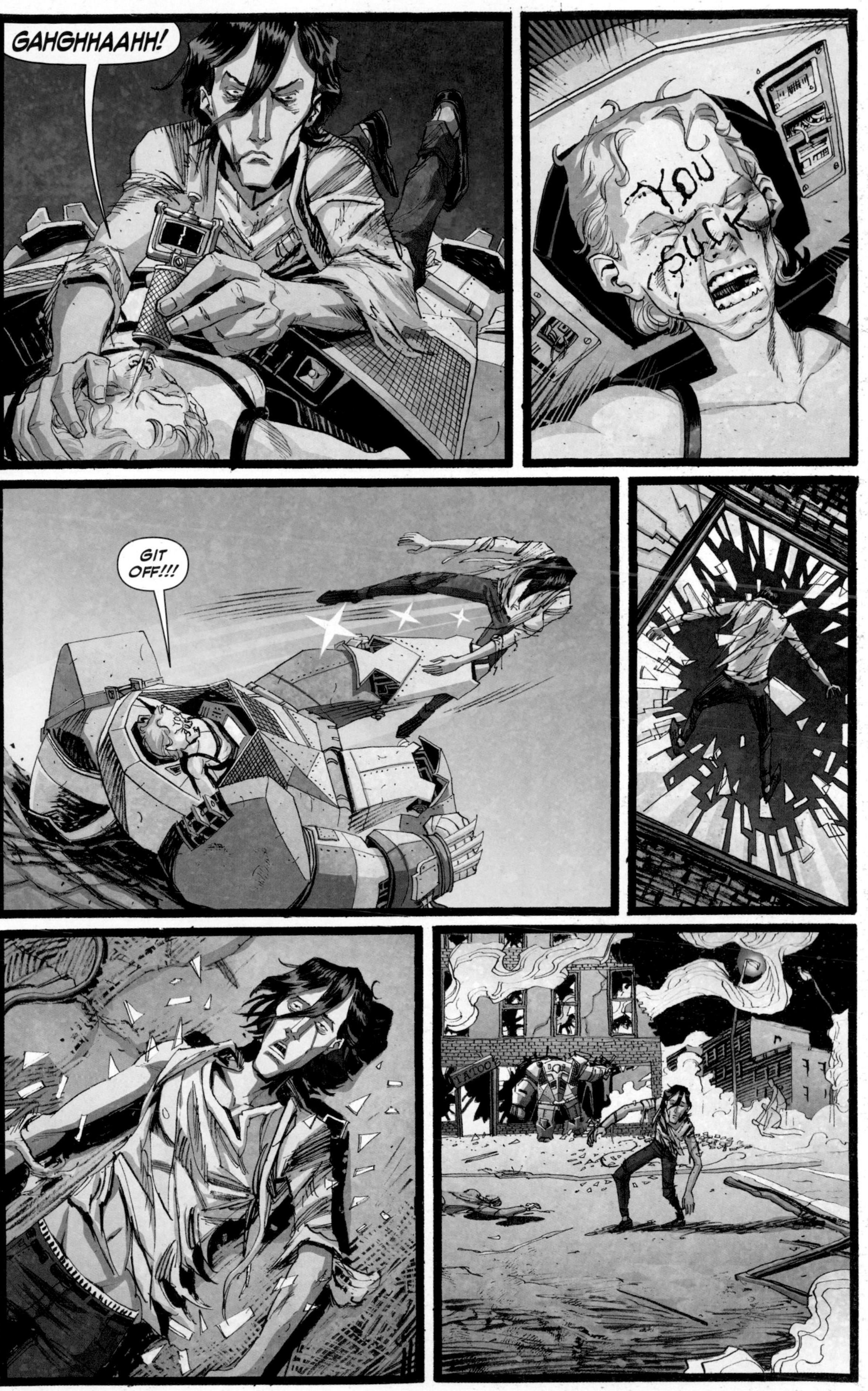
GAGHHAAHH!
YOU SUCK
GIT OFF!!!
TATOO

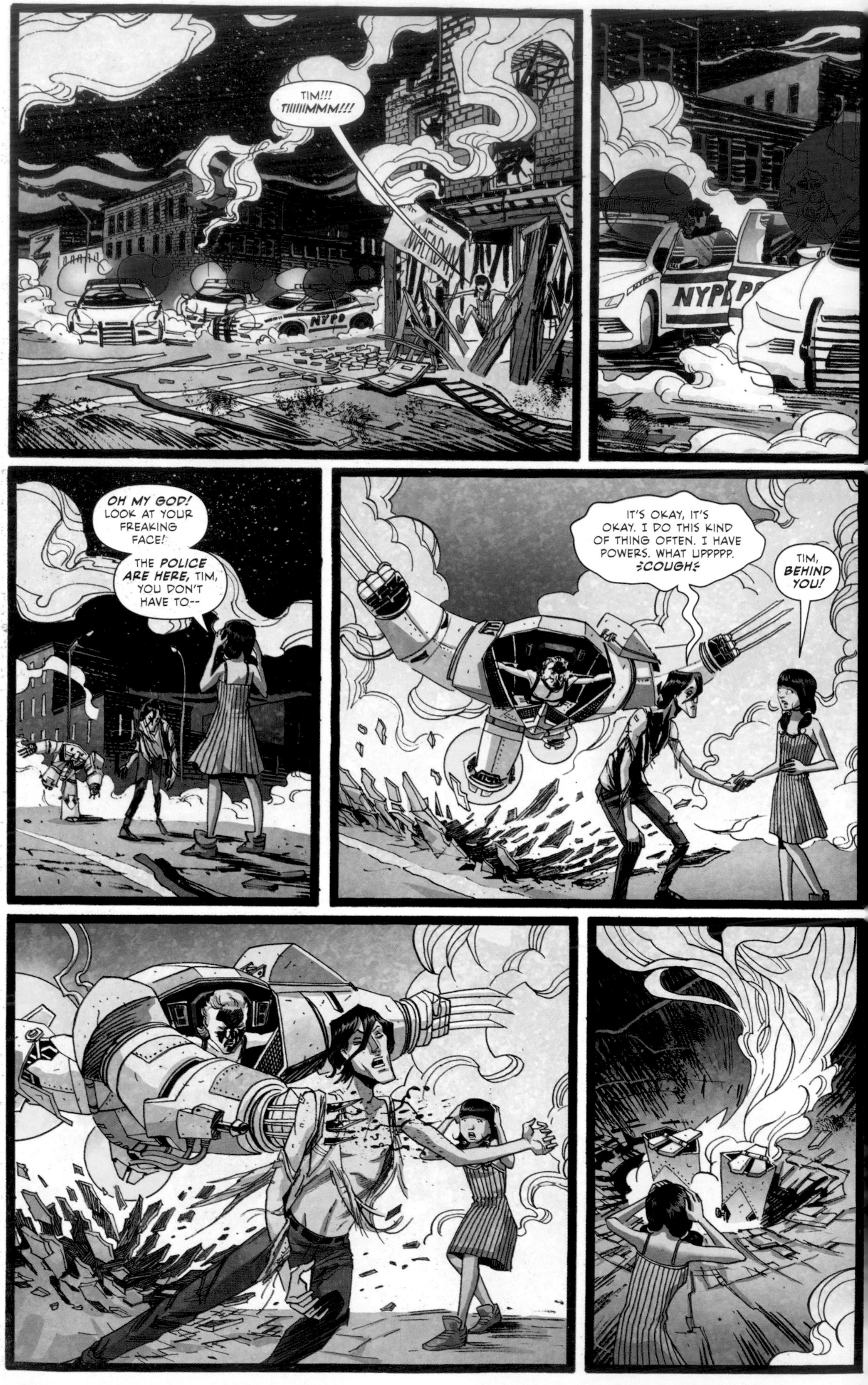

TIM!!! TIIIIIMMM!!!
OH MY GOD! LOOK AT YOUR FREAKING FACE!
THE POLICE ARE HERE, TIM, YOU DON'T HAVE TO--
IT'S OKAY, IT'S OKAY. I DO THIS KIND OF THING OFTEN. I HAVE POWERS. WHAT UPPPPP. COUGH
TIM, BEHIND YOU!

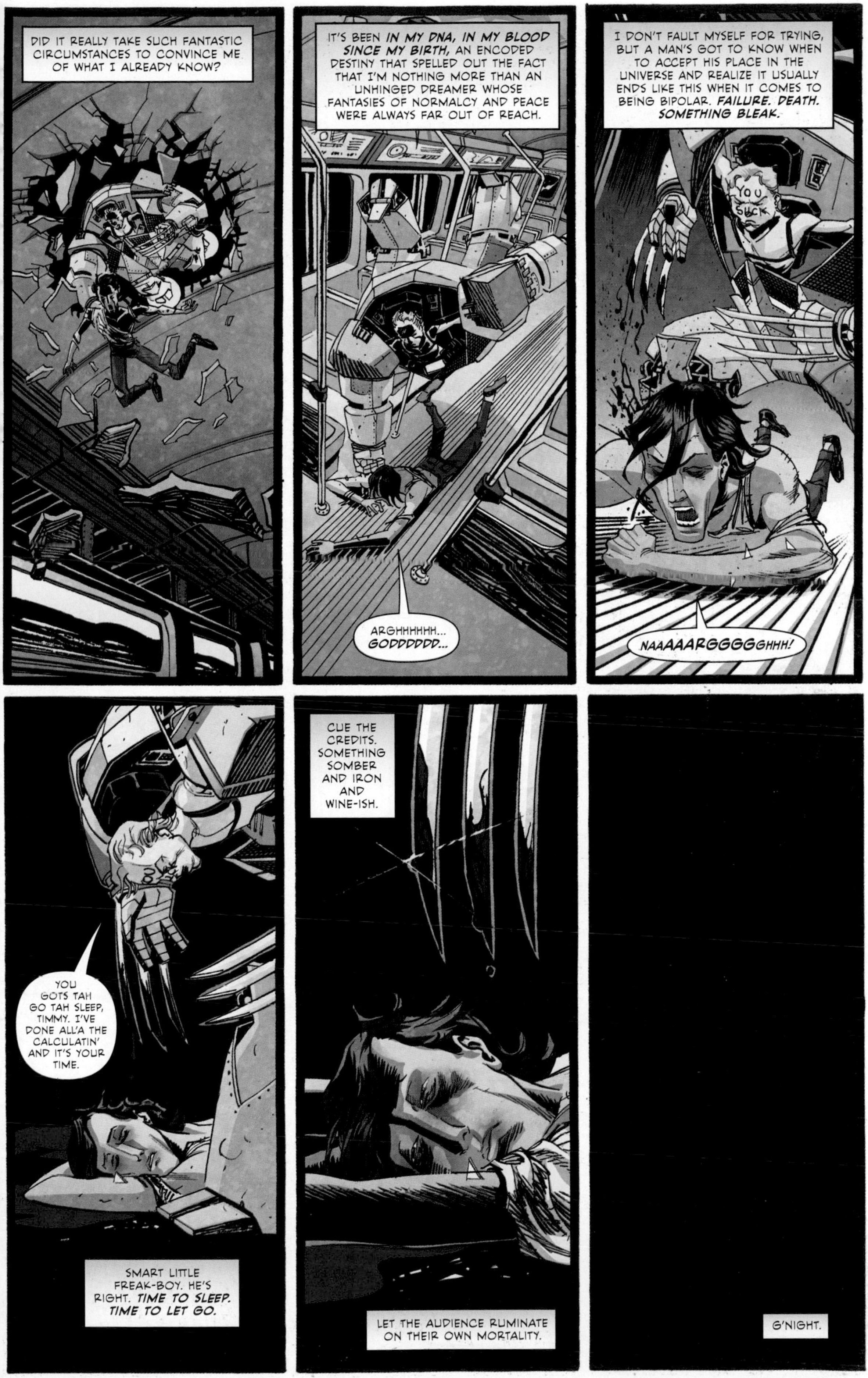
DID IT REALLY TAKE SUCH FANTASTIC CIRCUMSTANCES TO CONVINCE ME OF WHAT I ALREADY KNOW?
IT'S BEEN IN MY DNA, IN MY BLOOD SINCE MY BIRTH, AN ENCODED DESTINY THAT SPELLED OUT THE FACT THAT I'M NOTHING MORE THAN AN UNHINGED DREAMER WHOSE FANTASIES OF NORMALCY AND PEACE WERE ALWAYS FAR OUT OF REACH.
ARGHHHHHH... GODDDDDD...
I DON'T FAULT MYSELF FOR TRYING, BUT A MAN'S GOT TO KNOW WHEN TO ACCEPT HIS PLACE IN THE UNIVERSE AND REALIZE IT USUALLY ENDS LIKE THIS WHEN IT COMES TO BEING BIPOLAR. FAILURE. DEATH. SOMETHING BLEAK.
YOU SUCK
NAAAAARGGGGGHHH!
YOU GOTS TAH GO TAH SLEEP, TIMMY. I'VE DONE ALL'A THE CALCULATIN' AND IT'S YOUR TIME.
SMART LITTLE FREAK-BOY. HE'S RIGHT. TIME TO SLEEP. TIME TO LET GO.
CUE THE CREDITS. SOMETHING SOMBER AND IRON AND WINE-ISH.
LET THE AUDIENCE RUMINATE ON THEIR OWN MORTALITY.
G'NIGHT.

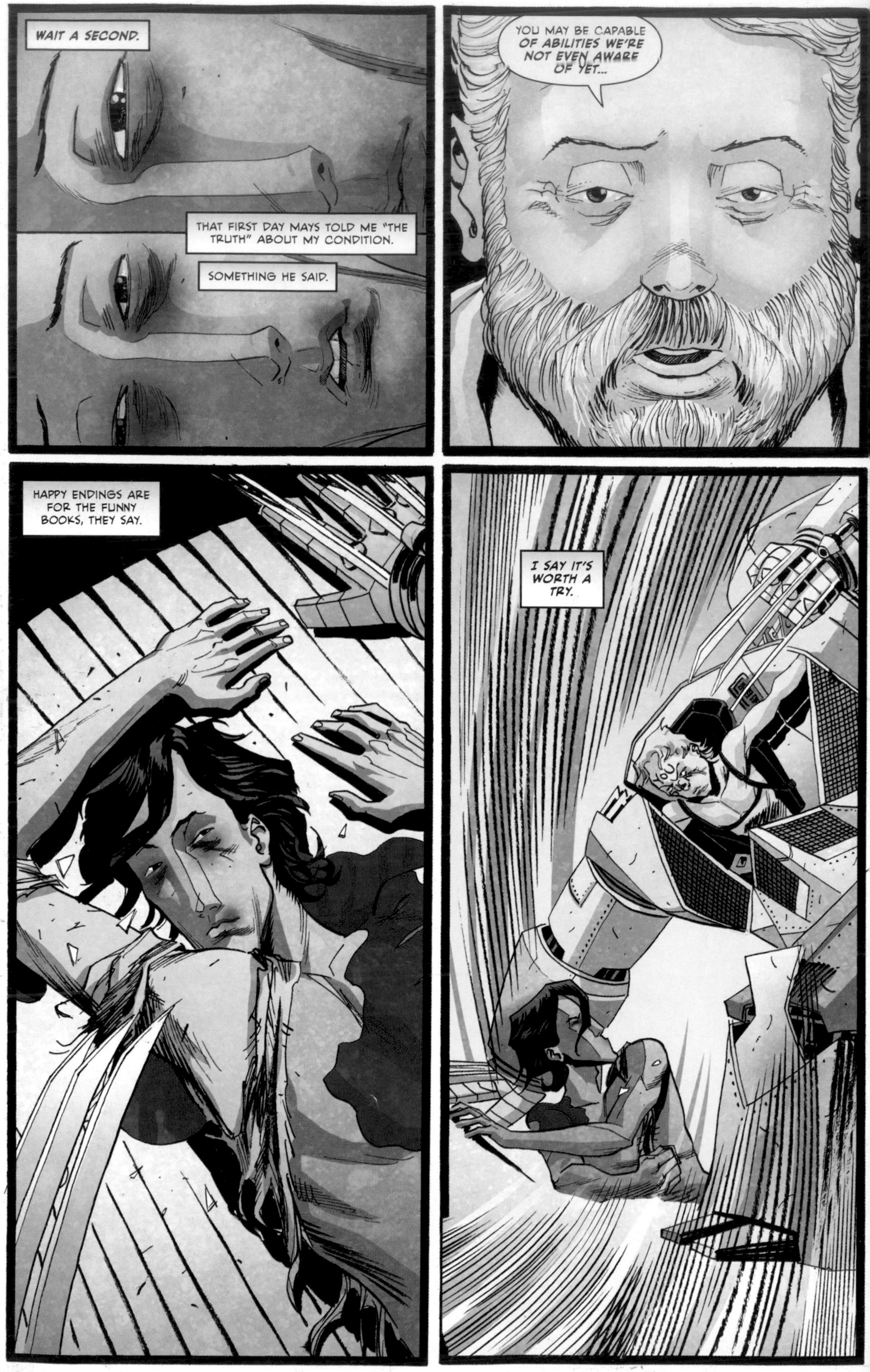
WAIT A SECOND.
THAT FIRST DAY MAYS TOLD ME "THE TRUTH" ABOUT MY CONDITION.
SOMETHING HE SAID.
YOU MAY BE CAPABLE OF ABILITIES WE'RE NOT EVEN AWARE OF YET...
HAPPY ENDINGS ARE FOR THE FUNNY BOOKS, THEY SAY.
I SAY IT'S WORTH A TRY.

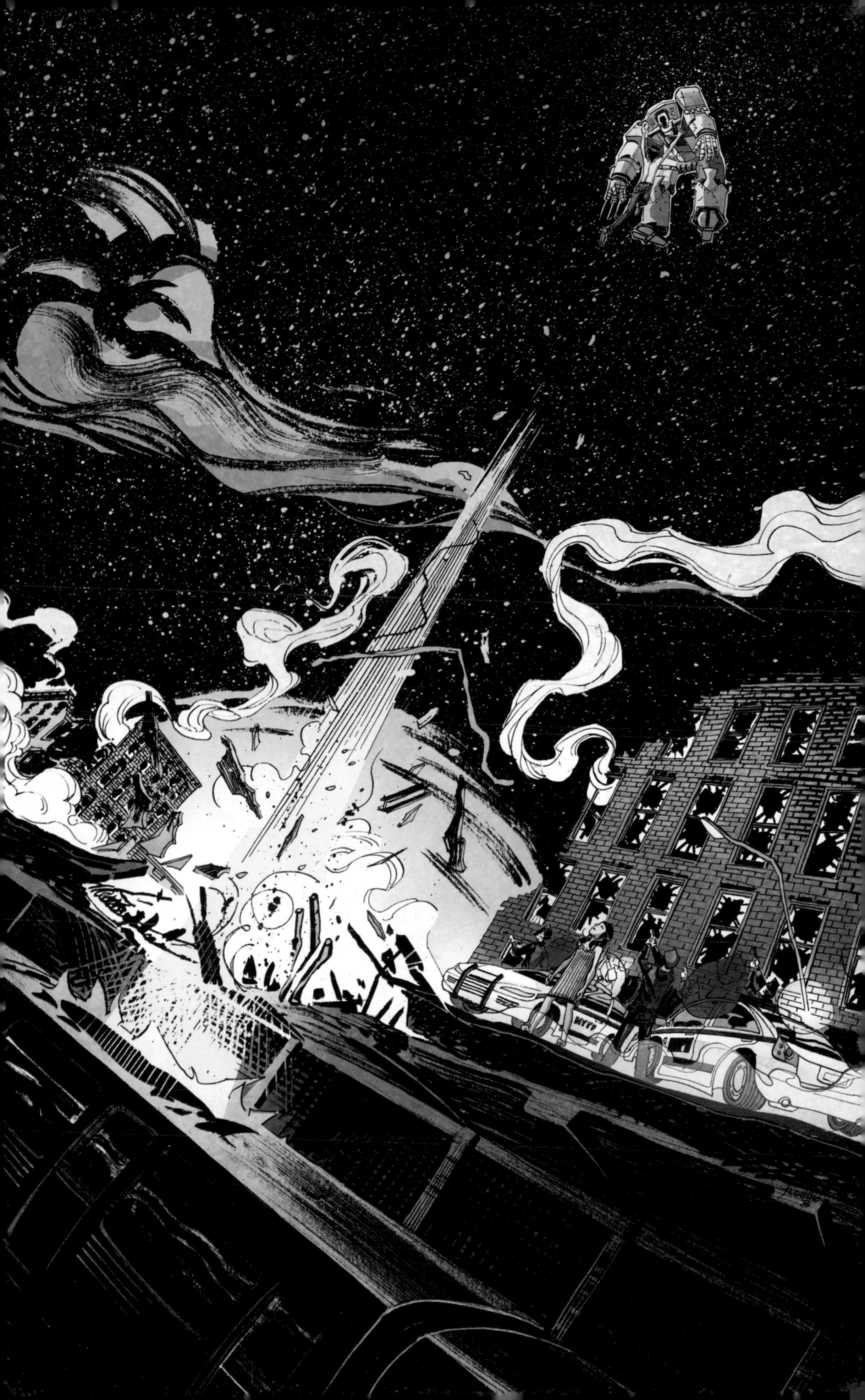

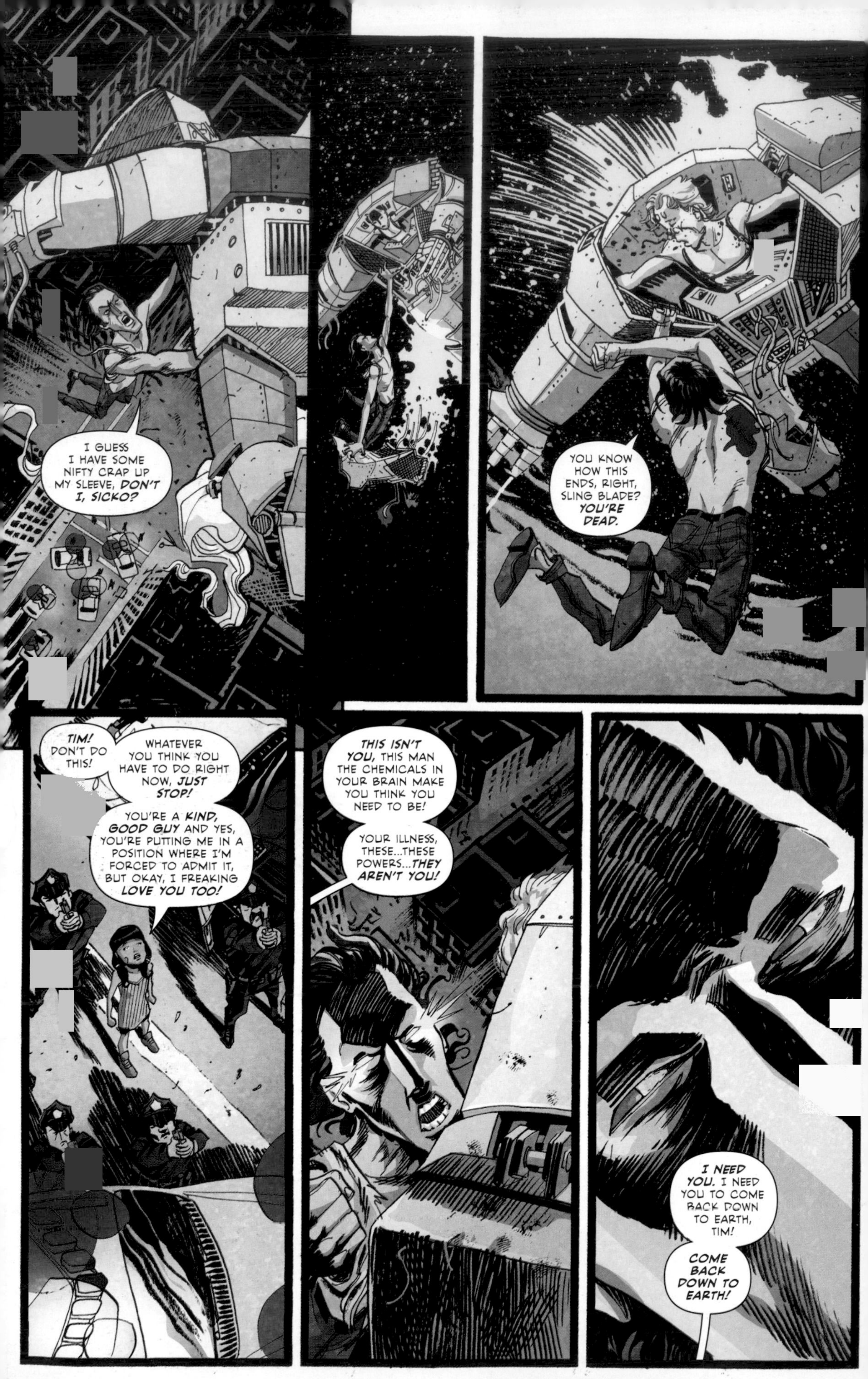
I GUESS I HAVE SOME NIFTY CRAP UP MY SLEEVE, DON'T I, SICKO?
YOU KNOW HOW THIS ENDS, RIGHT, SLING BLADE? YOU'RE DEAD.
TIM! DON'T DO THIS!
WHATEVER YOU THINK YOU HAVE TO DO RIGHT NOW, JUST STOP!
YOU'RE A KIND, GOOD GUY AND YES, YOU'RE PUTTING ME IN A POSITION WHERE I'M FORCED TO ADMIT IT, BUT OKAY, I FREAKING LOVE YOU TOO!
THIS ISN'T YOU, THIS MAN THE CHEMICALS IN YOUR BRAIN MAKE YOU THINK YOU NEED TO BE!
YOUR ILLNESS, THESE...THESE POWERS...THEY AREN'T YOU!
I NEED YOU. I NEED YOU TO COME BACK DOWN TO EARTH, TIM!
COME BACK DOWN TO EARTH!

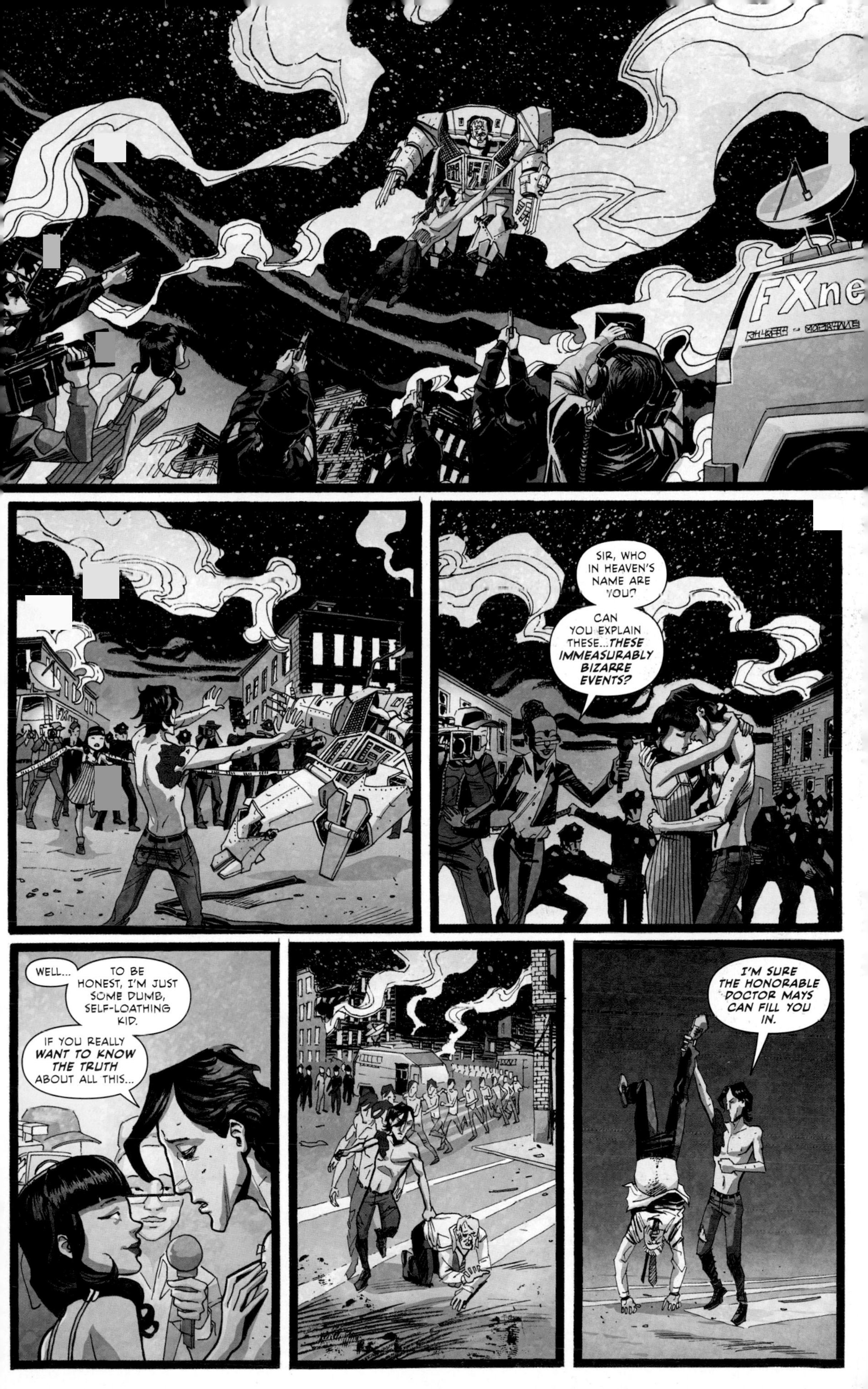
FXne
SIR, WHO IN HEAVEN'S NAME ARE YOU?
CAN YOU EXPLAIN THESE...THESE IMMEASURABLY BIZARRE EVENTS?
WELL... TO BE HONEST, I'M JUST SOME DUMB, SELF-LOATHING KID.
IF YOU REALLY WANT TO KNOW THE TRUTH ABOUT ALL THIS...
I'M SURE THE HONORABLE DOCTOR MAYS CAN FILL YOU IN.

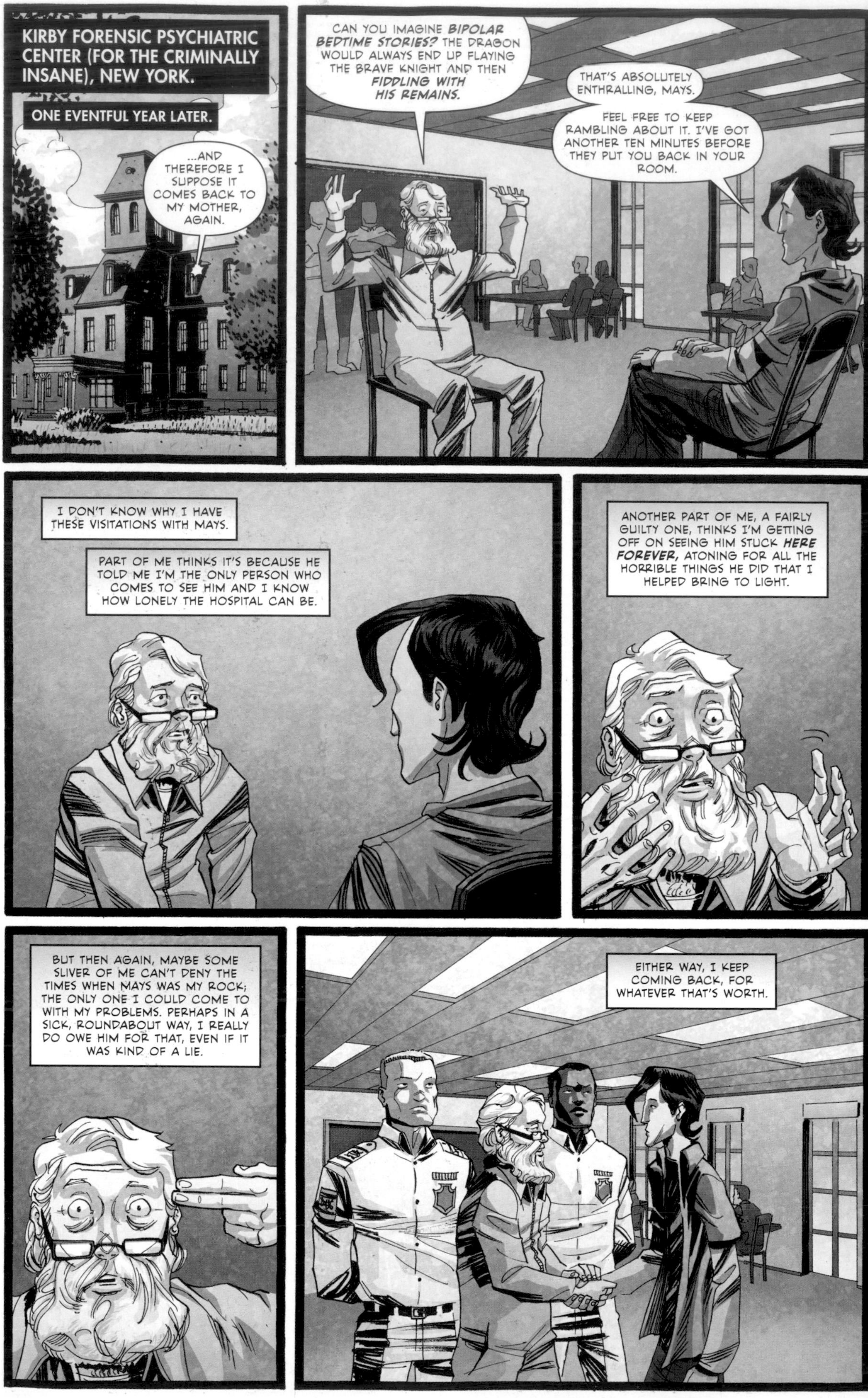
KIRBY FORENSIC PSYCHIATRIC CENTER (FOR THE CRIMINALLY INSANE), NEW YORK.
ONE EVENTFUL YEAR LATER.
...AND THEREFORE I SUPPOSE IT COMES BACK TO MY MOTHER, AGAIN.
CAN YOU IMAGINE BIPOLAR BEDTIME STORIES? THE DRAGON WOULD ALWAYS END UP FLAYING THE BRAVE KNIGHT AND THEN FIDDLING WITH HIS REMAINS.
THAT'S ABSOLUTELY ENTHRALLING, MAYS.
FEEL FREE TO KEEP RAMBLING ABOUT IT. I'VE GOT ANOTHER TEN MINUTES BEFORE THEY PUT YOU BACK IN YOUR ROOM.
I DON'T KNOW WHY I HAVE THESE VISITATIONS WITH MAYS.
PART OF ME THINKS IT'S BECAUSE HE TOLD ME I'M THE ONLY PERSON WHO COMES TO SEE HIM AND I KNOW HOW LONELY THE HOSPITAL CAN BE.
ANOTHER PART OF ME, A FAIRLY GUILTY ONE, THINKS I'M GETTING OFF ON SEEING HIM STUCK HERE FOREVER, ATONING FOR ALL THE HORRIBLE THINGS HE DID THAT I HELPED BRING TO LIGHT.
BUT THEN AGAIN, MAYBE SOME SLIVER OF ME CAN'T DENY THE TIMES WHEN MAYS WAS MY ROCK; THE ONLY ONE I COULD COME TO WITH MY PROBLEMS. PERHAPS IN A SICK, ROUNDABOUT WAY, I REALLY DO OWE HIM FOR THAT, EVEN IF IT WAS KIND OF A LIE.
EITHER WAY, I KEEP COMING BACK, FOR WHATEVER THAT'S WORTH.

SO IT SEEMS I'M BACK AT THE START OF THINGS: MEDICATED AND MUNDANE.

ONE OF THE PERKS OF BECOMING A NATIONAL HERO IS *MAKING ENOUGH MONEY OFF OPRAH-ESQUE EXCLUSIVES* THAT I CAN AFFORD CABS NOW. GREAT WAY TO AVOID BOTH THE SOCIAL ANXIETY AND ENCOURAGED SCRUTINY I NOW RECEIVE ON THE SUBWAY.

ANYONE AS SELF-DESTRUCTIVE AS I AM NEEDS TO ACCEPT THAT THE DOOMED ROMANCE OF ADDICTION WILL ALWAYS BE ABSENT FROM YOUR LIFE. IT WILL ALWAYS BE *YOUR FIRST, TAINTED LOVE.*

BUT WHEN YOU FILL THAT HOLE WITH SOMETHING, OR IN MY CASE SOMEONE, WITH REAL SUBSTANCE...YOU BEGIN TO MISS IT LESS AND LESS.

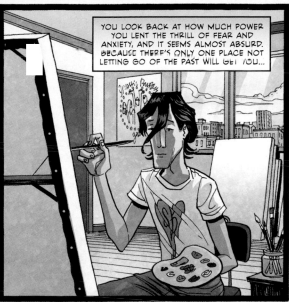

YOU LOOK BACK AT HOW MUCH POWER YOU LENT THE THRILL OF FEAR AND ANXIETY, AND IT SEEMS ALMOST ABSURD. BECAUSE THERE'S ONLY ONE PLACE NOT LETTING GO OF THE PAST WILL GET YOU...

ALONE. *VERY, VERY ALONE.*

SOME WOULD FIND IT PATHETIC THAT WHEN MY POWERS WERE "OUTED" I CHOSE TO REMAIN AN *OBSCURE, JITTERY ARTIST,* FIRMING MY PLACE IN A CULTURE I ENDLESSLY LAMPOON, INSTEAD OF BECOMING "MANIC-MAN" PROFESSIONALLY.

MAYBE I FEEL AT HOME HERE WITH ALL THESE "NORMAL" PEOPLE MY AGE, THE ONES I MAKE FUN OF, THE ONES WHO STARE BACK AT ME LIKE A FUNHOUSE MIRROR AND MAKE ME QUESTION MY OWN VALIDITY.

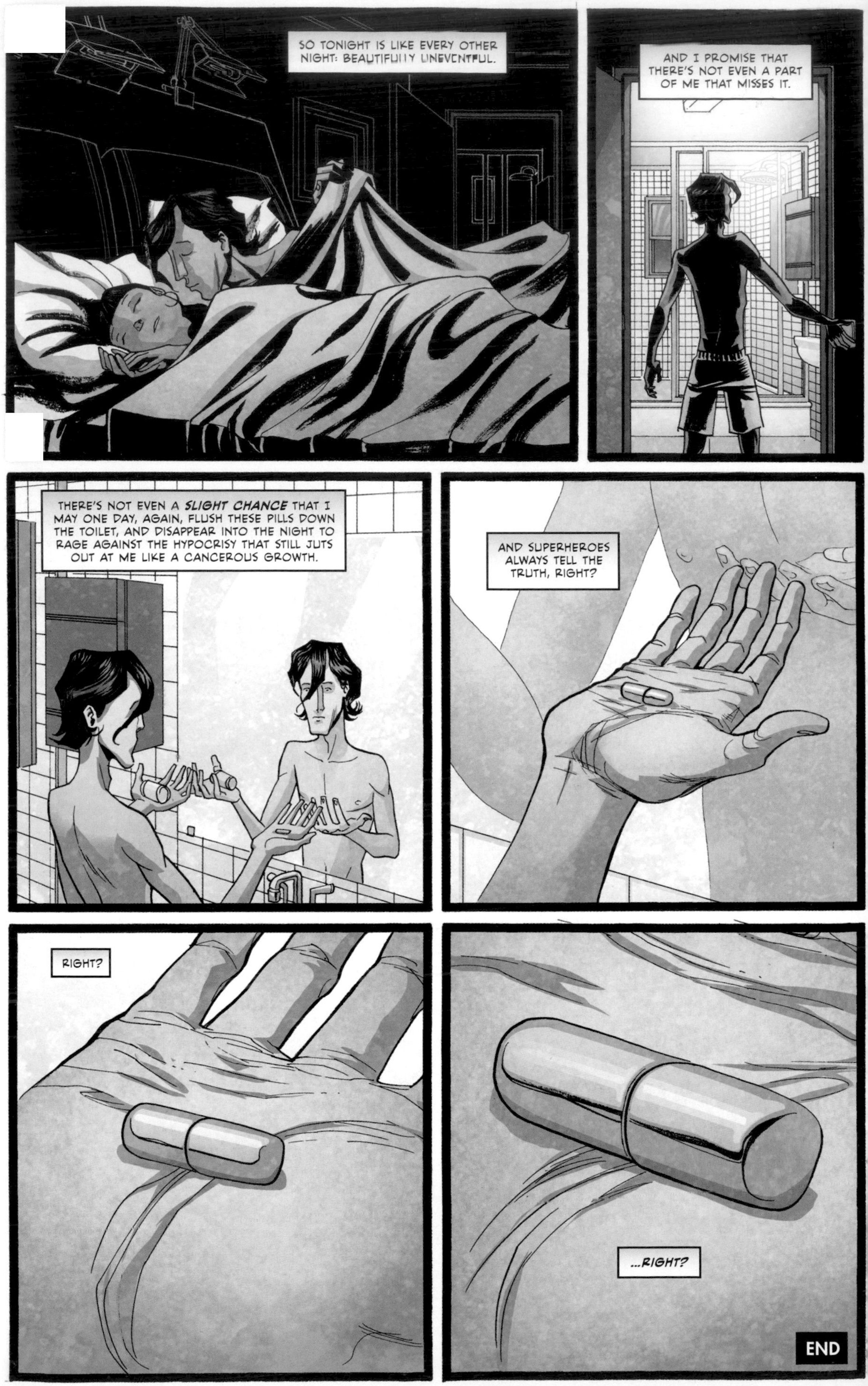
SO TONIGHT IS LIKE EVERY OTHER NIGHT: BEAUTIFULLY UNEVENTFUL.
AND I PROMISE THAT THERE'S NOT EVEN A PART OF ME THAT MISSES IT.
THERE'S NOT EVEN A *SLIGHT CHANCE* THAT I MAY ONE DAY, AGAIN, FLUSH THESE PILLS DOWN THE TOILET, AND DISAPPEAR INTO THE NIGHT TO RAGE AGAINST THE HYPOCRISY THAT STILL JUTS OUT AT ME LIKE A CANCEROUS GROWTH.
AND SUPERHEROES ALWAYS TELL THE TRUTH, RIGHT?
RIGHT?
...RIGHT?
END

"ENGORGED"

LAST NIGHT I SANK BENEATH THE STREET
ENGORGED WITH MY SWELLING DEFEAT
THEY SAID I WAS THE ONE TO BEAT
BUT I WAS WEAK

I WANT YOU TO KNOW
THAT IF I DIE I WANT YOU TO KNOW
THAT IF I DIE I'M WITH YOU

THESE PANELS HOLD MY WILTING FORM
THE FAKEST FLESH I WAS ADORNED IN
A NEW LIFE HAS BEEN REBORN
BECAUSE OF YOU

MONSTERS
ALL THE MAD SCIENTISTS CAN'T GET THROUGH,
GET THROUGH TO ME WITH YOU
NO THEY WON'T

AND NOW IT'S QUIET
I THINK THAT WE'VE SURVIVED
YOU AND ME, GIRL
AND THE CHASM BEHIND MY EYES

I'LL REINVENT EVERYTHING I EVER WAS
THIS IS OVER, IT IS OVER
IT IS OVER
...IS IT?

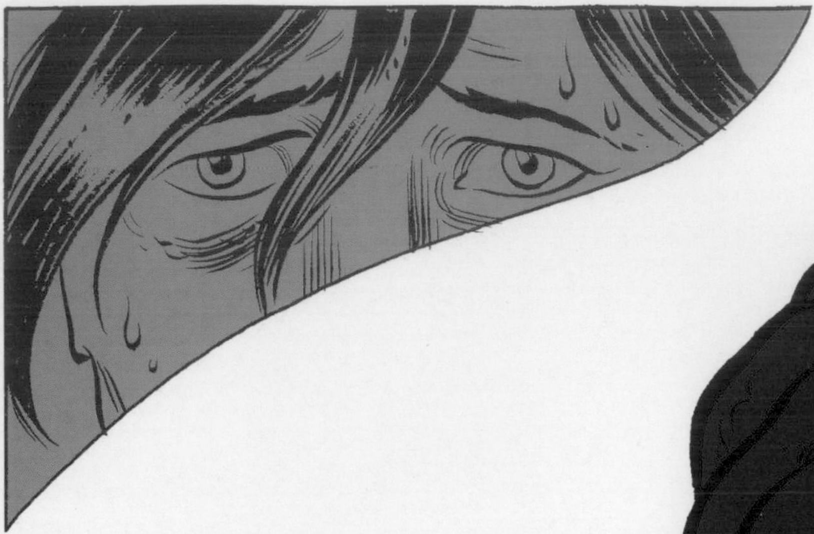

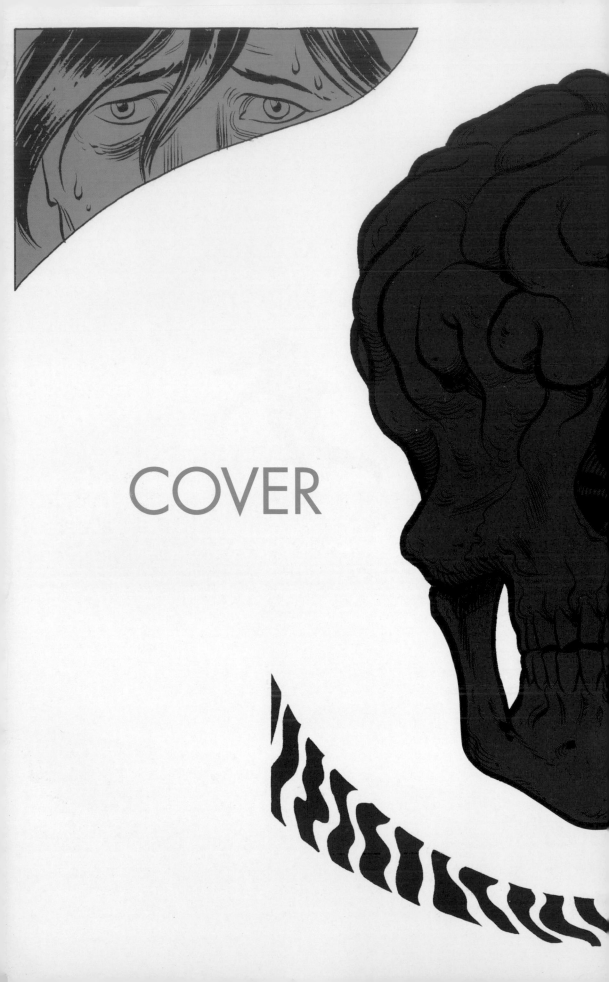

COVER

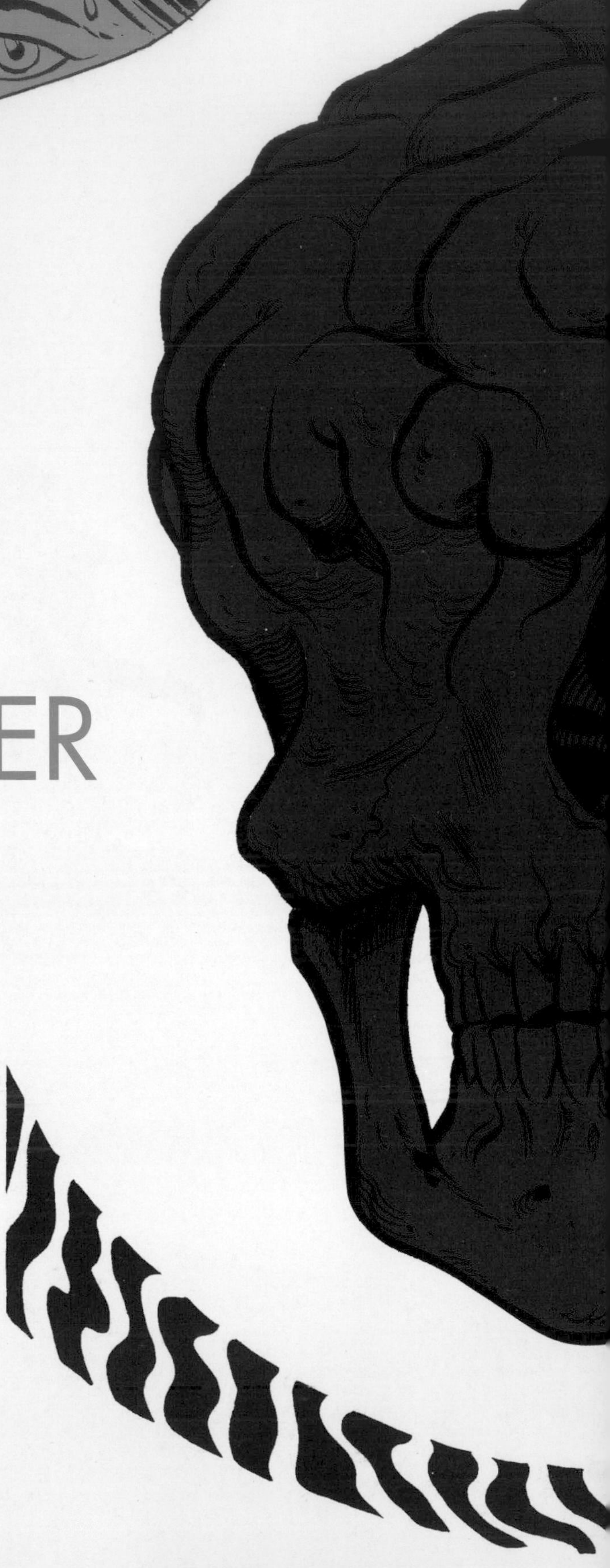

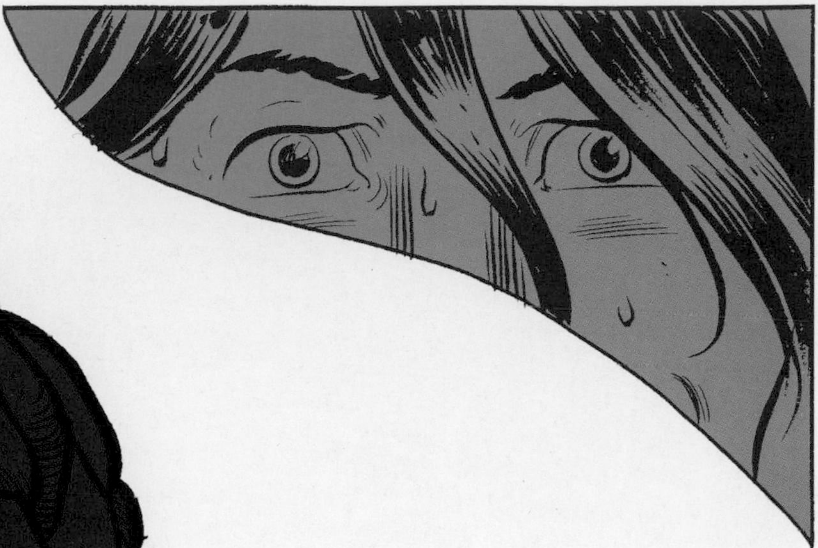

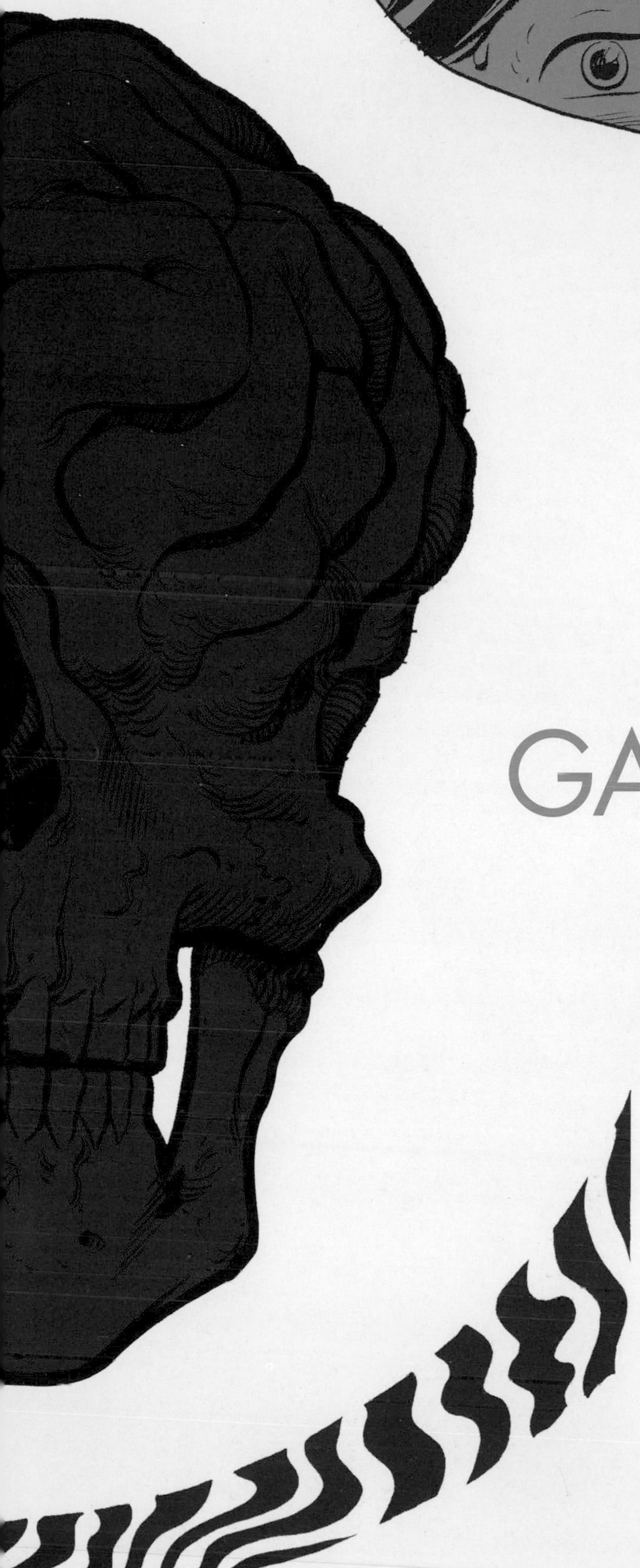

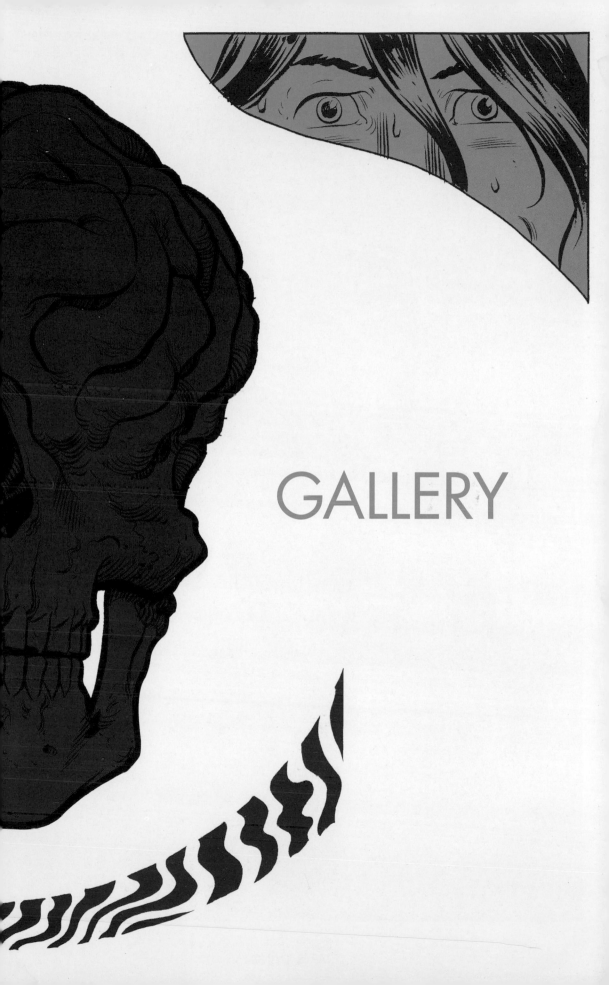

GALLERY

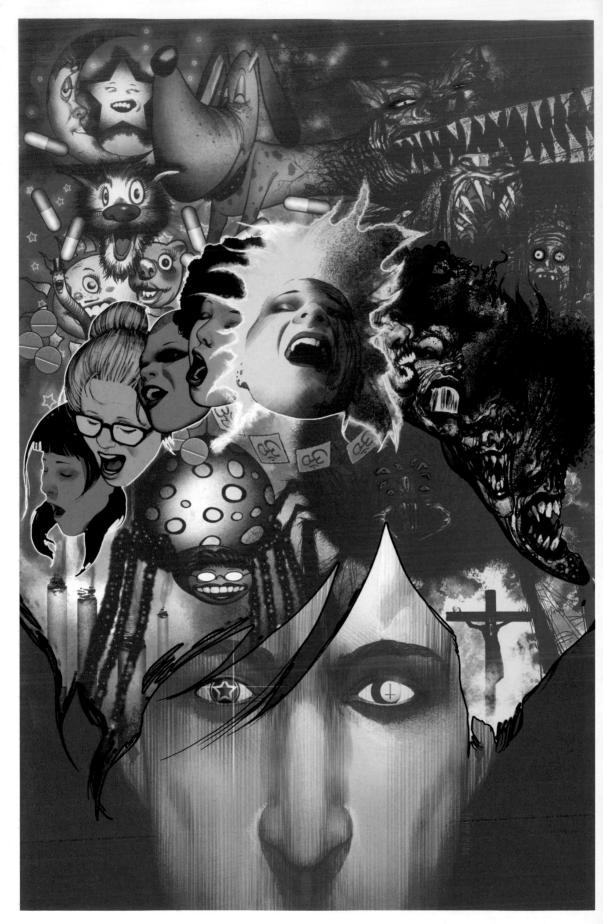

ISSUE ONE
FRAZER IRVING

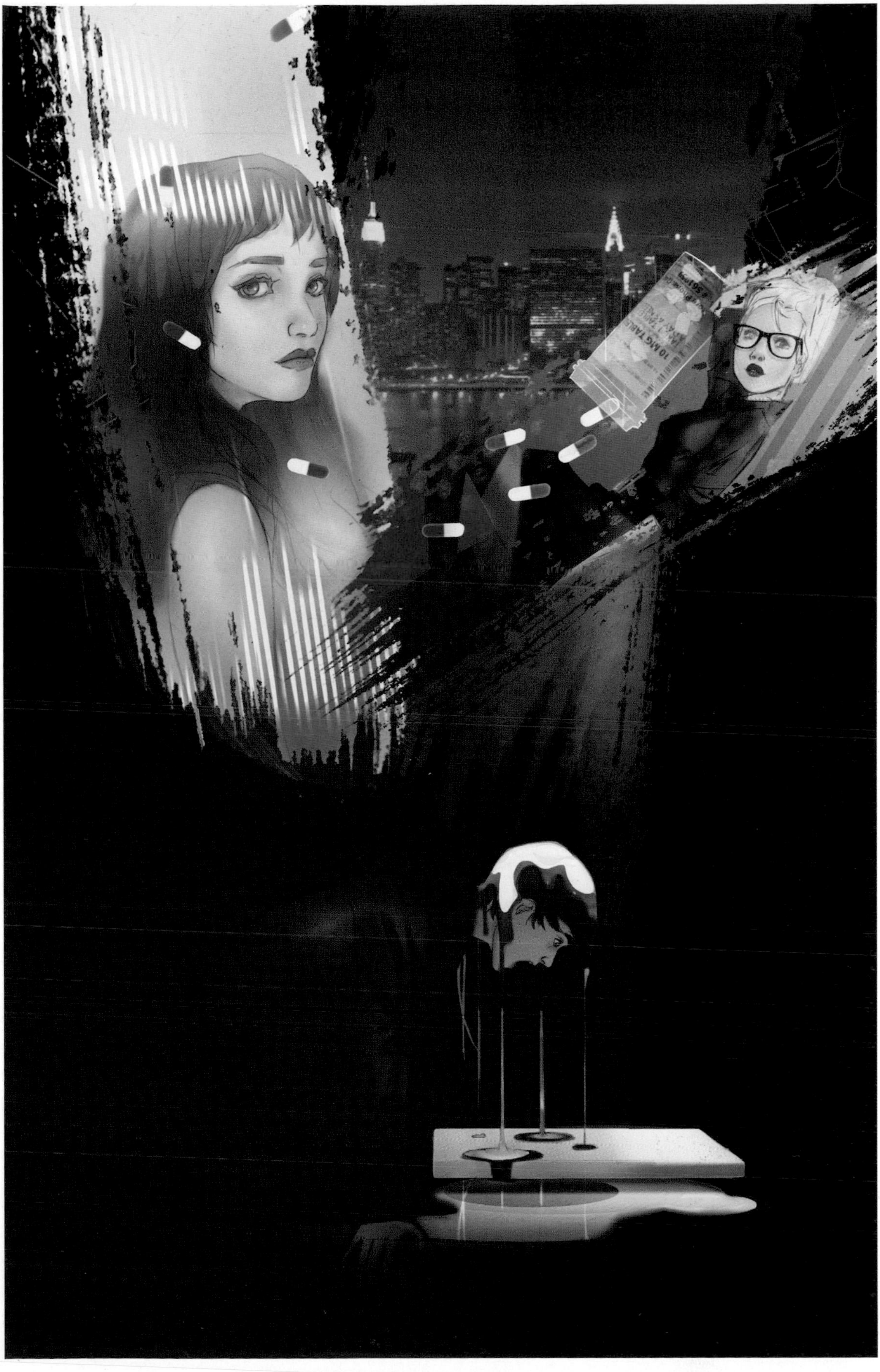

ISSUE ONE
W. SCOTT FORBES

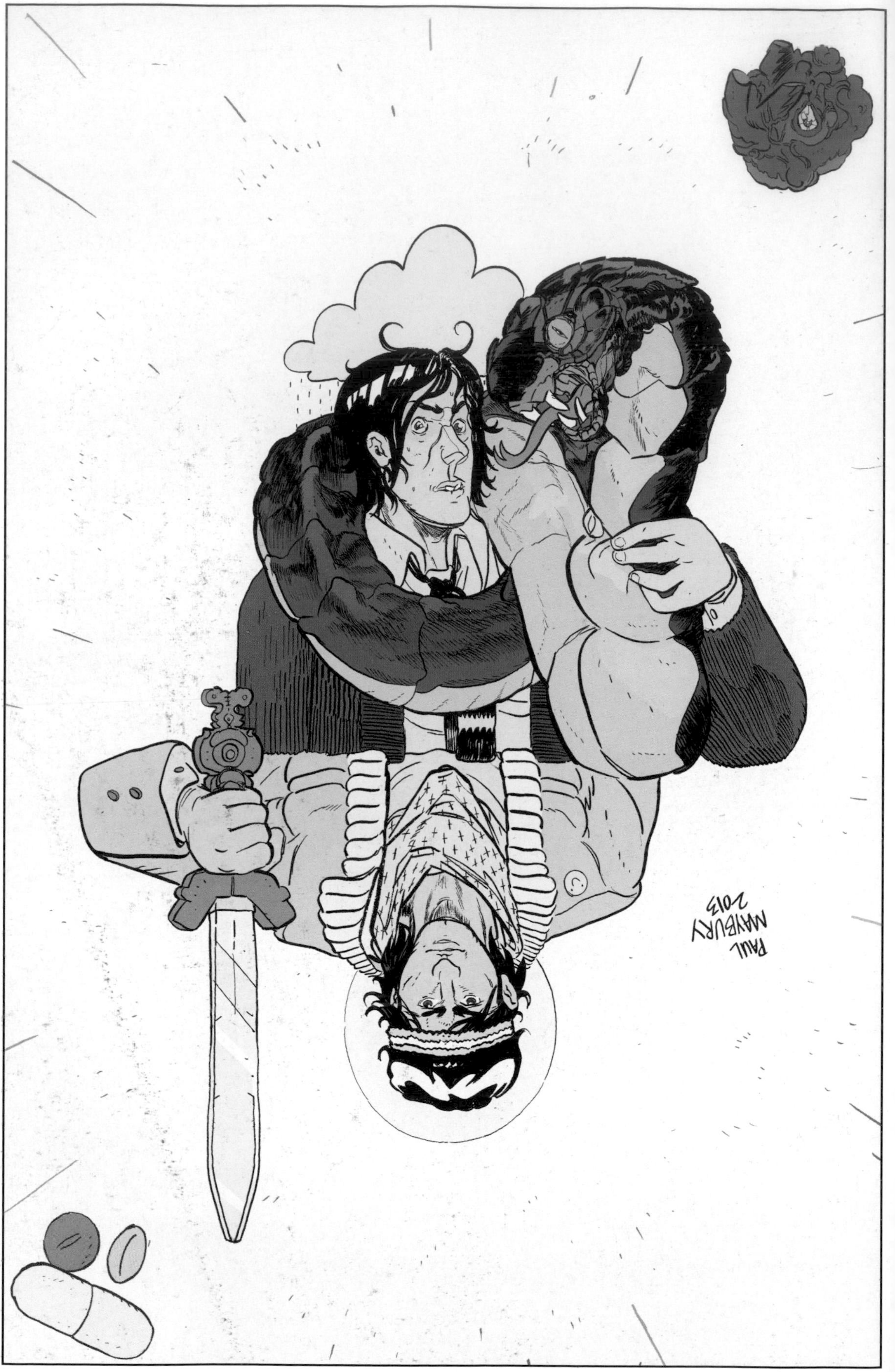
PAUL MAYBURY 2013

ISSUE ONE
PAUL MAYBURY

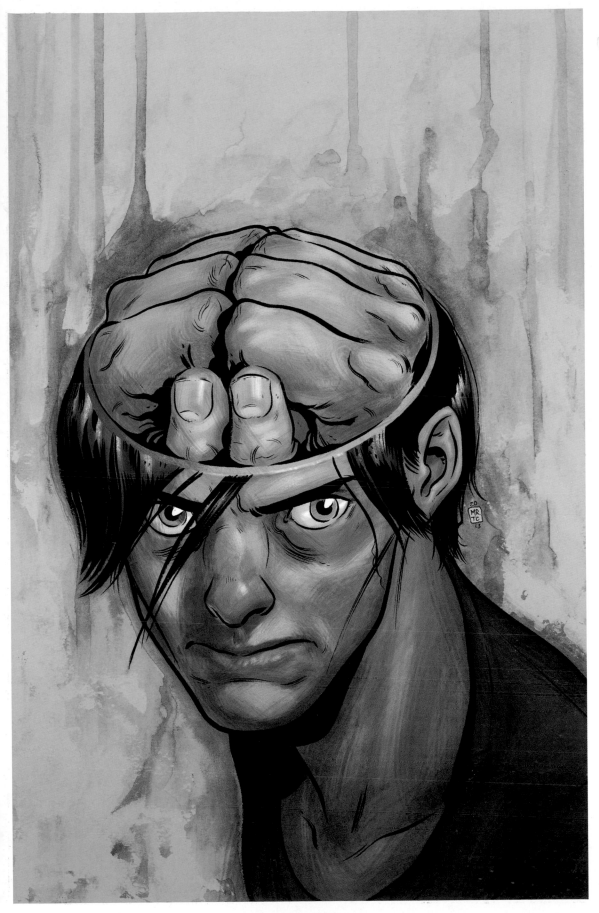

ISSUE TWO
TYLER CROOK

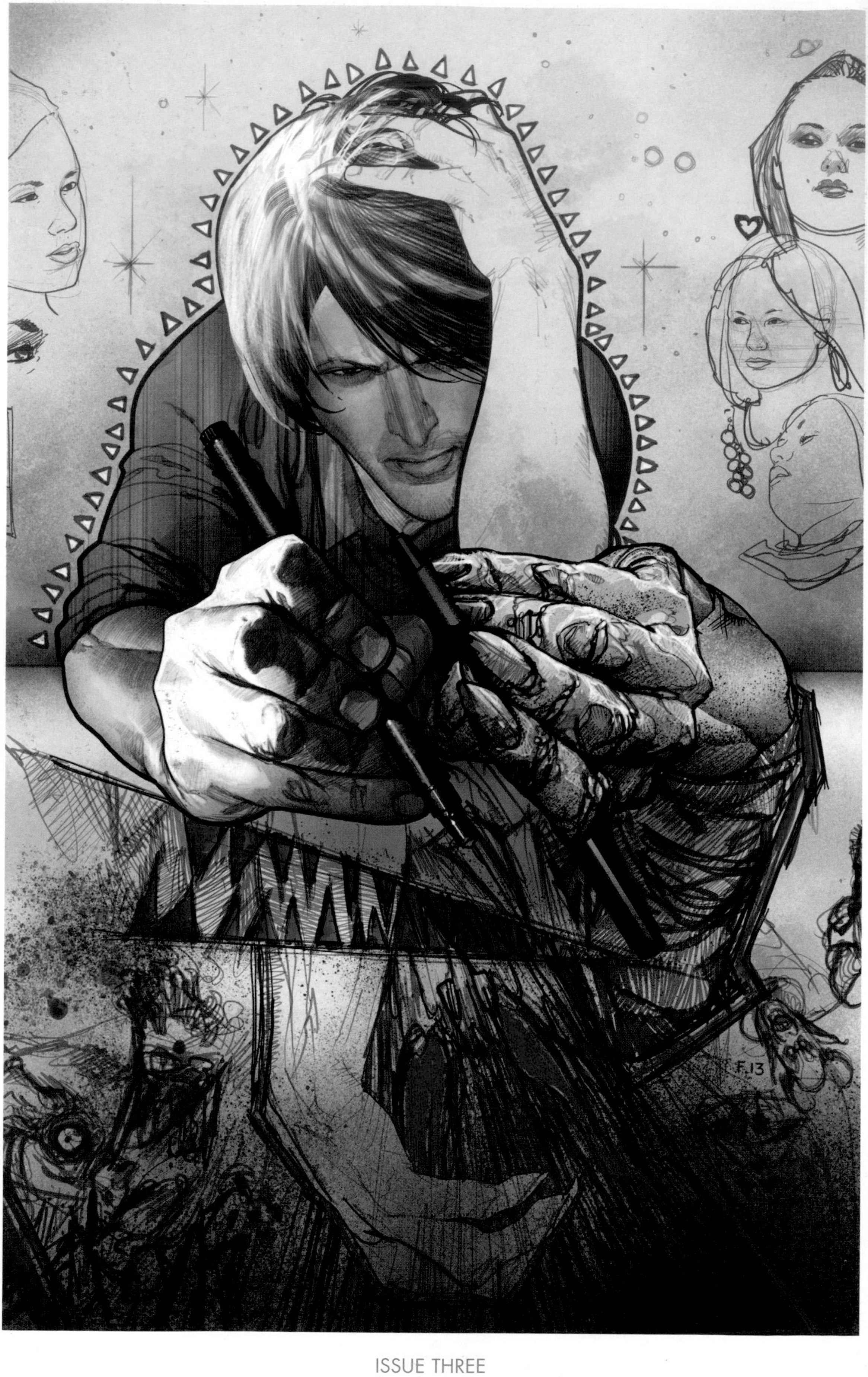
F.13

ISSUE THREE
FRAZER IRVING

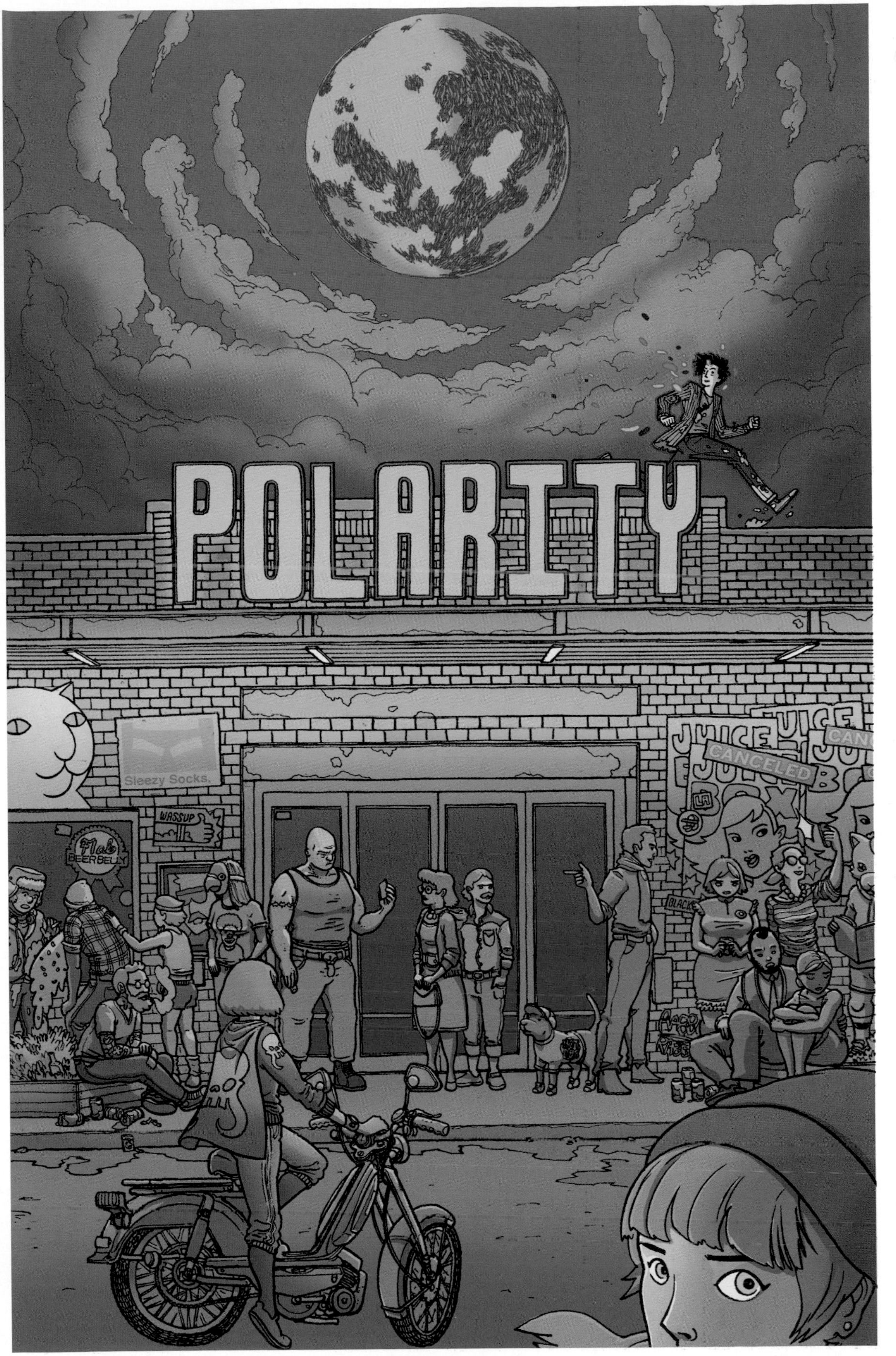
POLARITY
Sleezy Socks.
WASSUP
BEER BELLY
JUICE
JUICE BOX
CANCELED
CANC

ISSUE THREE
ULISES FARINAS

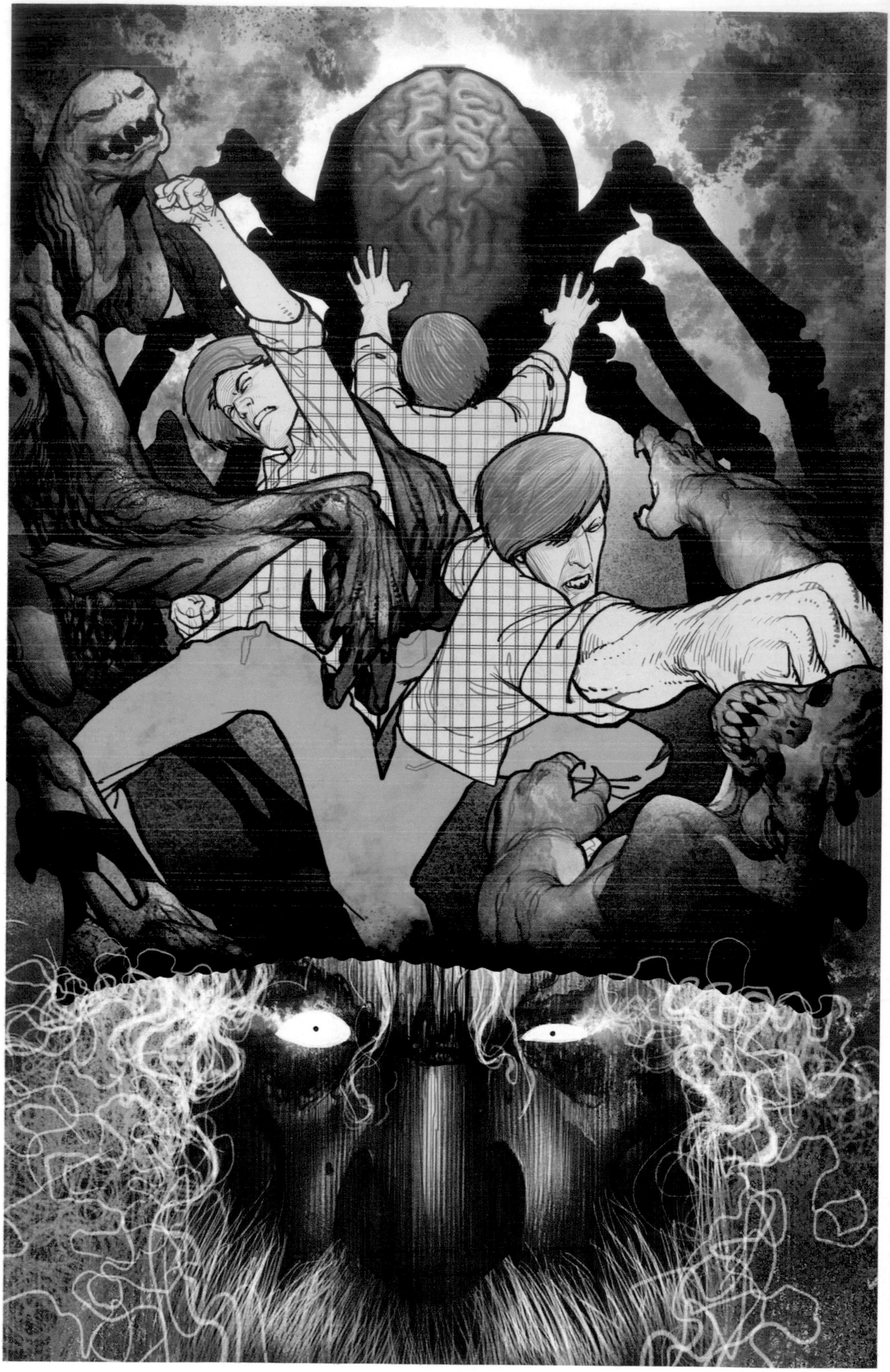

ISSUE FOUR
FRAZER IRVING

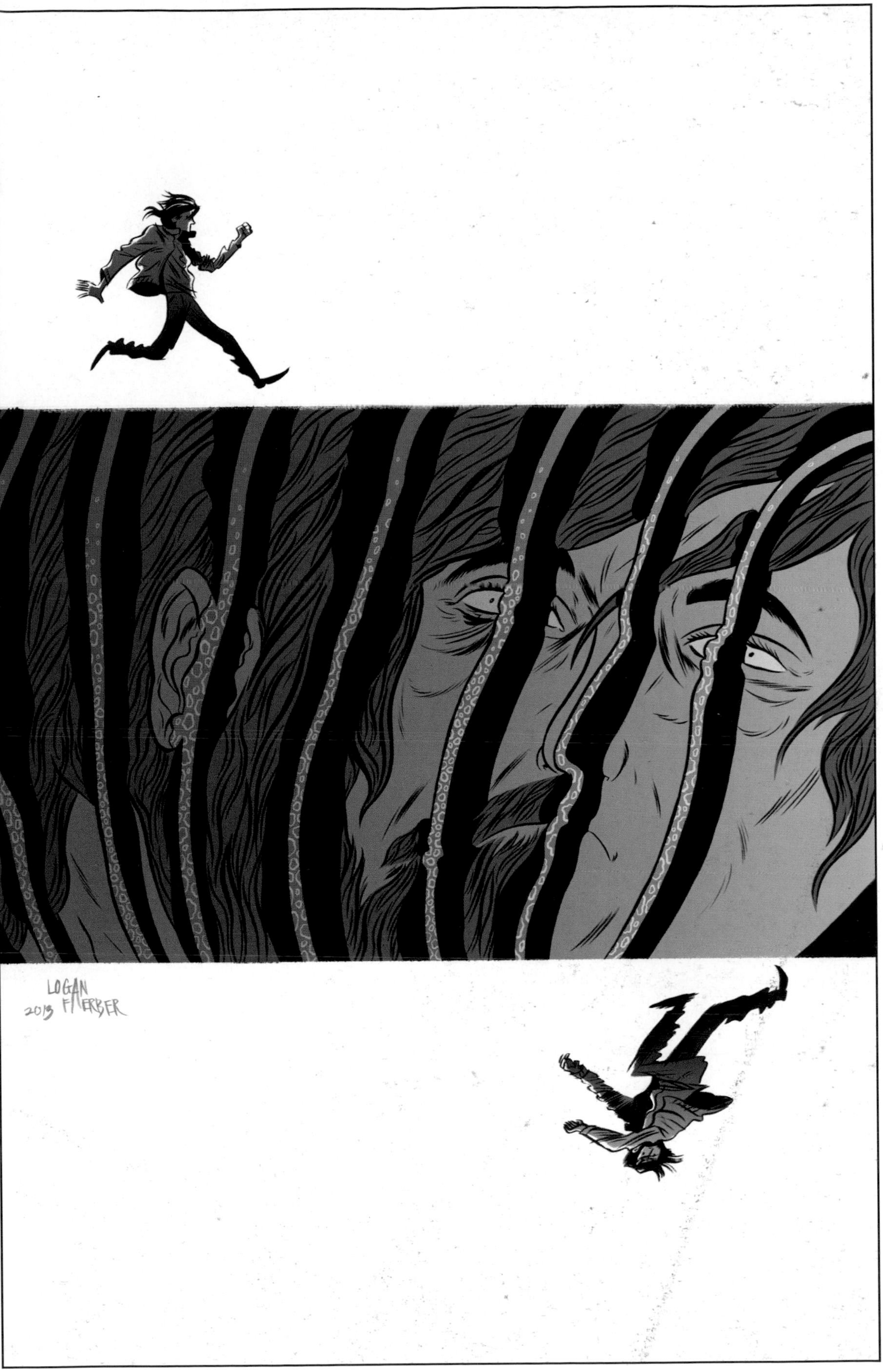
LOGAN FAERBER 2013

ISSUE FOUR
LOGAN FAERBER

"TRADEWAITER"

LET ME GIVE YOU A LITTLE TIP:
JUST BASE YOUR CHARACTER ON YOU
SO WHEN YOU PUT HIM THROUGH THE RINGER
WELL, AT LEAST IT'LL RING HALF-TRUE

SPARE NO DETAIL, DIVULGE IT ALL
THEY'LL EAT IT UP WITH WILLING HANDS
SO, NOW WE TELL MY LITTLE TALE
BECAUSE THE COLLECTORS DEMAND:

PUT IT ALL IN ONE
TIGHT LITTLE PACKAGE THAT YOU SELL
BECAUSE AS INDIVIDUAL STORIES
IT HURTS LIKE HELL
IT HURTS LIKE HELL

SO, WHEN YOU SEE ME ON YOUR SHELF
PLEASE REMEMBER ALL THE PAIN
THAT I WENT THROUGH TO WRITE THIS BOOK
AND SING THIS TYPICAL REFRAIN

IT WAS A TOTEM TO
UNWILLINGNESS TO JUST LET GO
AND JUST WAIT TILL YOU SEE WHAT COMES NEXT
YOU WON'T KNOW WHAT HIT YOU
NO

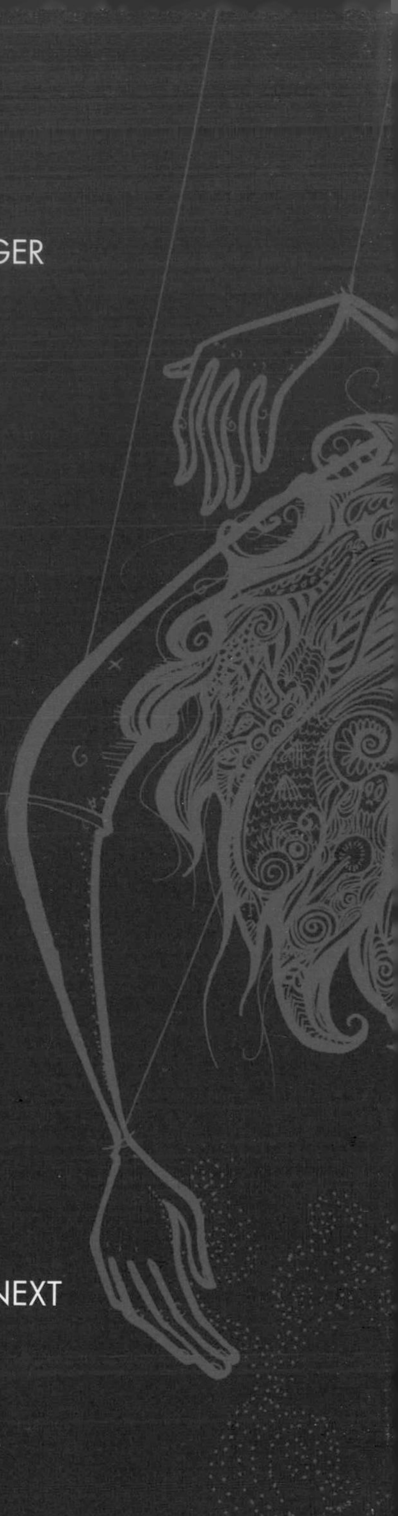

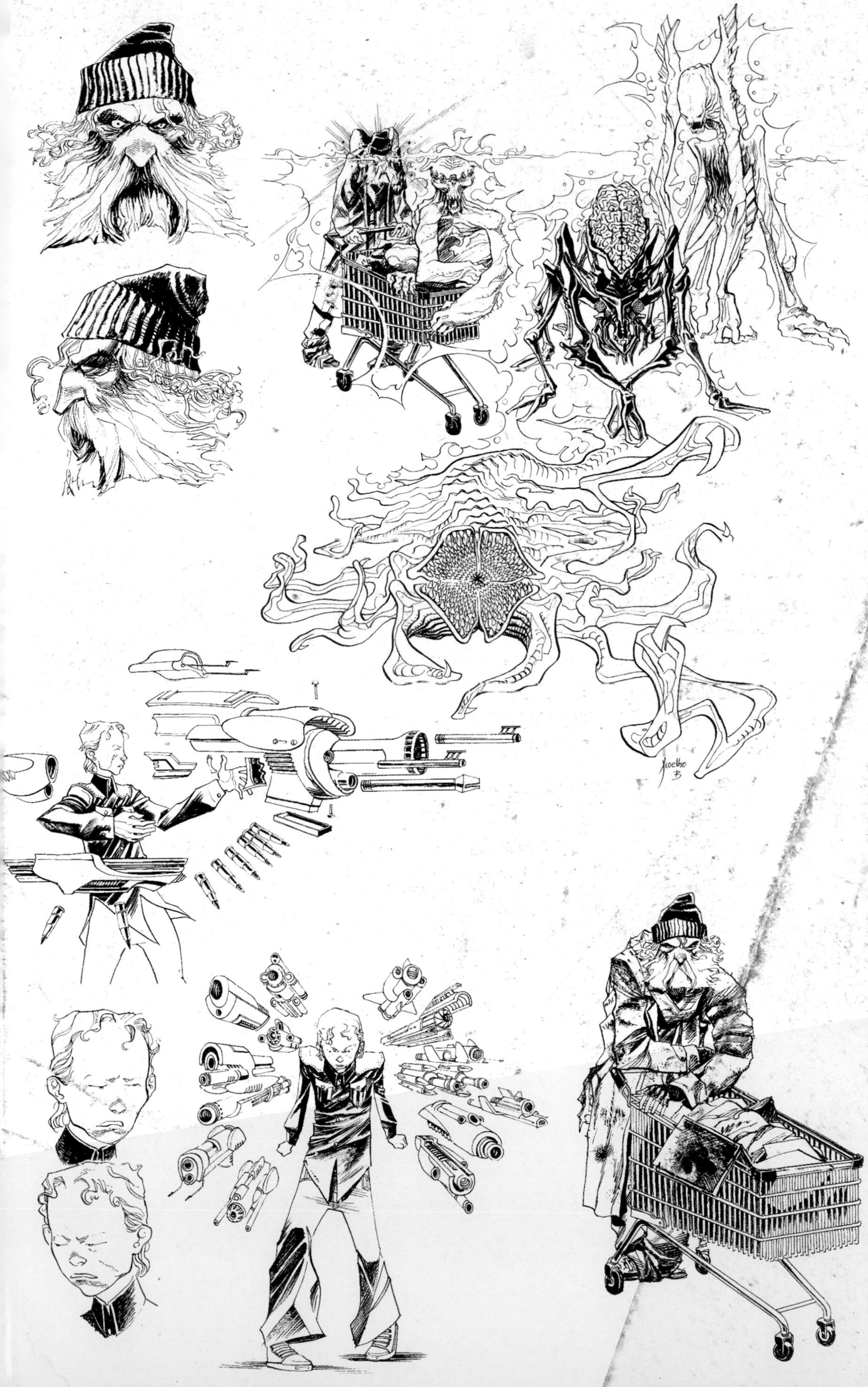

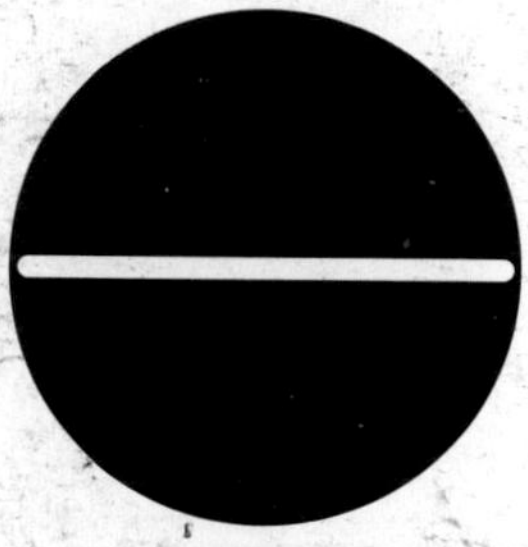